SAINTS ALIVE!

THE GOSPEL WITNESSED

SAINTS ALIVE!

THE GOSPEL WITNESSED

By Marie Paul Curley, FSP, and Mary Lea Hill, FSP

With a foreword by Celia Sirois

auline
BOOKS & MEDIA
Boston

Library of Congress Cataloging-in-Publication Data

Curley, Marie Paul.
  Saints alive! the gospel witnessed / Marie Paul Curley, FSP, and Mary Lea Hill, FSP ; with a preface by Celia Sirois.
    pages cm
  ISBN-13: 978-0-8198-7290-6
  ISBN-10: 0-8198-7290-3
  1. Christian saints–Biography. I. Title.
  BX4655.3.C872 2013
  270.092'2–dc23

                          2013011123

Scripture quotations contained herein are from the *New Revised Standard Version Bible: Catholic Edition*, copyright © 1989, 1993, Division of Christian Education of the National Council of the Churches of Christ in the United States of America. Used with permission. All rights reserved.

Excerpts from Pope Benedict XVI, *Post-Synodal Apostolic Exhortation Verbum Domini of The Holy Father Benedict XVI to The Bishops, Clergy, Consecrated Persons and The Lay Faithful on The Word of God in the Life and Mission of The Church*, copyright © 2010, Libreria Editrice Vaticana. Used with permission.

Excerpts from Nicholas Lash, *Theology on the Way to Emmaus*, copyright © 1986 Wipf & Stock. Used by permission of Wipf and Stock Publishers, www.wipfandstock.com.

Excerpts from *The Art of Reading Scripture,* ed. Ellen F. Davis and Richard B. Hays, copyright © 2003, William B. Eerdmans Publishing Company. All rights reserved. Used with permission.

Excerpts from Luke Timothy Johnson and William S. Kurz, SJ, *The Future of Catholic Biblical Scholarship: A Constructive Conversation*, copyright © 2002, William B. Eerdmans Publishing Company. All rights reserved. Used with permission.

Excerpts from Michael J. Himes, "Communicating the Faith," in *Handing on the Faith: The Church's Mission and Challenge*, ed. Robert P. Imbelli, copyright © 2006, The Crossroad Publishing Company. Used with permission.

Cover design by Rosana Usselmann

Published by Pauline Books & Media, 50 Saint Pauls Avenue, Boston, MA 02130-3491. www.pauline.org

Printed in the U.S.A.

Pauline Books & Media is the publishing house of the Daughters of St. Paul, an international congregation of women religious serving the Church with the communications media.

1 2 3 4 5 6 7 8 9   17 16 15 14 13

Dedicated to St. Paul, Blessed James Alberione,
Venerable Thecla Merlo,
Blessed Timothy Giaccardo,
and all the Pauline saints
who have inspired us
to put on the mind and heart of Christ

Contents

Give . . . in the name of a disciple . . .

. . . Only through prayer . . .

Occasions for stumbling are bound to come . . .

What is sown on good soil . . .

I am the gate for the sheep . . .

Whatsoever you do to the least . . .

The kingdom of God is like yeast . . .

He passed through the midst of them . . .

Blessed Miguel Agustín Pro

No one has greater love than this . . .

Saint Edith Stein

You give them something to eat . . .

Blessed Manuel Lozano Garrido

Unless I see . . . I will not believe . . .

Blessed Mary Elizabeth Hesselblad

Proclaim the Good News to all . . .

Saint Mark the Evangelist

Foreword

The British theologian Nicholas Lash has observed, "We talk of 'holy' scripture, and for good reason. And yet it is not, in fact, the *script* that is 'holy,' but the people: the company who perform the script."[1] To think of Sacred Scripture as a "script" is to recognize that it is just words on a page until it is embodied in the life of the believing community The thirty holy men and women whose stories are told in this book are people who have "performed the script" and who can therefore serve as models and mentors for the Church today.

Writing about Saint Francis of Assisi, James Howell notes, "The narrative of Christ was not merely something in which [Francis] believed; that narrative was the script for his life." Later, in the same article, Howell remarks that "Mother Teresa's entire life was a profound exegesis of Matthew 25:31–46."[2] The writings of Lash and Howell present a metaphor to help us better understand and appreciate the communion of saints, the subject of this book. As a glance at

---

1. Nicholas Lash, "Performing the Scriptures," in *Theology on the Way to Emmaus* (Eugene: Wipf & Stock, 1986), 42.

2. James C. Howell, "Christ Was Like St. Francis," in *The Art of Reading Scripture*, ed. Ellen F. Davis and Richard B. Hays (Grand Rapids: William B. Eerdmans Publishing Company, 2003), 92, 105.

the table of contents will show, each saint is introduced by a line or two from Sacred Scripture. The implication is that the life of each saint serves as an interpretation, or "exegesis," of the sacred text. Pope Benedict XVI seems to endorse this idea when he writes in his post-synodal apostolic exhortation, *Verbum Domini*, "The most profound interpretation of Scripture comes precisely from those who let themselves be shaped by the word of God through listening, reading, and assiduous meditation." He goes on to list some twenty saints, noting that "The Holy Spirit who inspired the sacred authors is the same Spirit who impels the saints to offer their lives for the Gospel. In striving to learn from their example," he says, "we set out on the sure way toward a living and effective hermeneutic [interpretation] of the word of God."[3]

This volume will be welcome news as well for all those Catholics who have until now labored under the assumption that faithful, fruitful engagement with God's word was the purview of a privileged minority. How liberating to learn that Augustine never mastered biblical Hebrew or Greek (his story is in the companion volume, *Saints Alive: The Faith Proclaimed*), and that many saints could not read the sacred text at all. Yet they embodied the word of God in lives of sanctity and service. On this point, Howell goes so far as to claim that "there appear from time to time singular or striking lives of persons who embody what *texts* are about, who answer the riddles in ways that not only illustrate but even correct our enshrined interpretations, who even rouse our wills to 'go and do likewise.' "[4] Many of these "singular or striking lives" will be found in these pages.

---

3. Pope Benedict XVI, *The Word of the Lord* (Verbum Domini) (Boston: Pauline Books & Media, 2010), 75, 77.

4. Howell, 102.

So what is to be learned about saints and about Sacred Scripture in this book? Three things come immediately to mind.

First, one of the great contributions of the Second Vatican Council was to recognize the centrality of Sacred Scripture in the celebration of the liturgy. The Holy Father's exhortation *Verbum Domini*, cited above, concurs and tells us that the Church is "*the home of the word*" and that not the library but "the liturgy is the privileged setting in which God speaks to us in the midst of our lives . . . . Even more, it must be said that Christ himself 'is present in his word, since it is he who speaks when Scripture is read in Church.' Indeed, 'the liturgical celebration becomes the continuing, complete, and effective presentation of God's word.' "[5]

For believers, the interpretation of the biblical text is never primarily an academic undertaking although, as Lash himself cautions, "the performative interpretation of scripture, needs . . . the services of scholarship and critical reflection."[6] Still, the goal for the faithful reader is not mastery of the text, but ministry of the word, not specialization but service. As Ellen Davis puts it, "Faithful interpretation of Scripture requires its faithful performance."[7]

Second, every serious hearer or reader of Sacred Scripture has at one time or other been troubled by the literal sense of a biblical text. The interpreter, however, is required to deal with such a text *charitably*. This is the principle "based on the understanding that all Scripture, when correctly interpreted,

---

5. Pope Benedict XVI, 85–86.

6. Lash, 43.

7. "Nine Theses on the Interpretation of Scripture: *The Scripture Project*," in *The Art of Reading Scripture*, ed. Ellen F. Davis and Richard B. Hays (Grand Rapids: William B. Eerdmans Publishing Company, 2003), 4.

conduces to love of God and neighbor," that Saint Augustine set forth in his book *On Christian Doctrine*. What this means, as Davis explains, is that "Whenever a literal interpretation does not serve that end [that is, love of God and neighbor], then another approach is necessary."[8]

In a chapter on "Augustine and the Demands of Charity," Luke Timothy Johnson notes that "Augustine sees the goal of biblical study to be the building up of the church in charity." He goes on, citing Augustine: "Whoever then appears in his own opinion to have comprehended the Sacred Scriptures, or even some part of them, yet does not build up with that knowledge the twofold love of God and his neighbor, 'has not yet known as he ought to know' (I, 26 [40])."[9] As unscientific or unscholarly as Augustine's principle may sound, it comes remarkably close to the words of Paul: "And if I have prophetic powers, and understand all mysteries and all knowledge, and if I have all faith, so as to remove mountains, but do not have love, I am nothing" (1 Cor 13:2).

Finally, in an interesting article on "Communicating the Faith," Michael Himes revisits the notion of the communion of saints with which we began. Having suggested "that to introduce people into the faith is to introduce them into a community that has a history," he goes on to say, "To be truly a participant in a historical community [that is the communion of saints] is to enter into conversation with persons who do not happen to be living at the same time as we are."

---

8. Davis, Ellen F. "Critical Traditioning: Seeking an Inner Biblical Hermeneutic," in *The Art of Reading Scripture*, ed. Ellen F. Davis and Richard B. Hays (Grand Rapids: William B. Eerdmans Publishing Company, 2003), 164.

9. Luke Timothy Johnson, "Augustine and the Demands of Charity," in *The Future of Catholic Biblical Scholarship: A Constructive Conversation,* Luke Timothy Johnson and William S. Kurz, SJ (Grand Rapids: William B. Eerdmans Publishing Company, 2002), 111.

"Being dead," he adds wryly, "in no way diminishes their value as members of the tradition."

Himes insists that "Believers have a right to enter into the ongoing conversation within the tradition that we sometimes call the commun[icat]ion of saints." He is not so much urging readers to study the lives of the saints, as he is encouraging them to "ask [the saints] questions and open themselves to be questioned by them, that they fight with them and agree with them on some things and disagree with them on others, in short that they do all the things people do when they talk with one another."[10] This book offers the reader a rare opportunity to do just that, to engage the communion of saints in conversation.

As Nicholas Lash concludes his essay on "Performing the Scriptures," he points to the celebration of the Eucharist as the best illustration of what the performance of the biblical text might mean. He finds, in the Eucharist, the "interpretive performance in which all our life consists."[11] In *Verbum Domini*, Pope Benedict comes to the same conclusion. He writes, "The relationship between word and sacramental gesture is the liturgical expression of God's activity in the history of salvation through the *performative character* of the word itself. In salvation history there is no separation between what God *says* and what he *does*." Reflecting on the "Eucharistic Discourse" in John 6 and Jesus's encounter with the disciples on the road to Emmaus in Luke 24, the Holy Father concludes, "From these accounts it is clear that Scripture itself

---

10. Michael J. Himes. "Communicating the Faith," in *Handing on the Faith: The Church's Mission and Challenge*, ed. Robert P. Imbelli (New York: The Crossroad Publishing Company, 2006), 127.

11. Lash, 45–46.

points us toward an appreciation of its own unbreakable bond with the Eucharist . . . . Word and Eucharist are so deeply bound together that we cannot understand one without the other."[12]

"I pray [with Paul] that you may have the power to comprehend, with all the saints, what is the breadth and length and height and depth, and to know the love of Christ that surpasses knowledge, so that you may be filled with all the fullness of God" (Eph 3:18–19).

CELIA SIROIS

---

12. Pope Bendict XVI, 88, 90–91.

Saint Marguerite Bourgeoys

Woman of Compassion

In those days Mary set out and went with haste to a Judean town in the hill country, where she entered the house of Zechariah and greeted Elizabeth. . . . And [Elizabeth asked] why has this happened to me, that the mother of my Lord comes to me? (Lk 1:39 40, 43).

The attractive, simply dressed young woman stared at the governor of Ville-Marie, New France. Her usual calm reserve deserted her.

"You want me to go with you to New France to start a school? As an associate of the Sisters of Notre Dame of Troyes, I told the sisters that if they went to New France, I would consider going *with* them. But not as a laywoman, alone!" Marguerite Bourgeoys looked around the parlor in an effort to gather herself, then turned back to the governor sitting quietly across the room. "I am not sure how to answer you," she finally got out. "I will pray over it."

The governor, Paul de Chomedey, sieur de Maisonneuve, nodded at her. "I do not know what the Lord's will is for you. Life in New France is full of dangers and challenges. But I can tell you that we have great need for a teacher, and the colony cannot yet support a convent. I will wait to hear from you." As the governor rose to his feet, he added, "My sister speaks very highly of you. We need women like you to shape the future."

"Your sister has told me much about the mission of Ville-Marie, and I desire to serve wherever the Lord calls me," Marguerite said. "I really will pray over it."

The governor nodded and left.

Marguerite went distractedly through the day's duties. She had heard all about the colony Ville-Marie, founded in 1642—just ten years ago—by Paul de Maisonneuve and the nurse Jeanne Mance with the intention of evangelizing the Native Americans. Marguerite knew the governor to be well-respected for his integrity, piety, and leadership. She also knew that to go to the missions required a deep spirit of service—and wasn't that her desire, to serve?

But she had been hoping for years to join or form a new kind of religious community of women who lived in imitation of Mary, the Blessed Mother. She wanted to commit herself to the same vows as other sisters, but her way of life would be different—not barred from serving the world by cloistered doors. Her community would live side by side with the people whom they served. If she left France to go to Canada as a lay missionary, she might never become a sister!

Not that I've always wanted to be a sister, she mused. Twelve years ago, Marguerite had been a frivolous, chic young woman who loved stylish dresses and thought mostly of making herself attractive. During a procession on Rosary

Sunday in her home of Troyes, Marguerite had looked up at a stone statue of the Blessed Mother that was placed over the door of the convent. And in a moment, everything had changed.

Even now, Marguerite felt her tears rise at the memory of the interior light she had received as she gazed at the statue, and of her startled realization of the beauty of Mary's life of love. From that day, Marguerite's life had been inspired by that new understanding of the Blessed Mother's self-giving love, strength, and closeness to Jesus. She understood her own call to be one of loving service like Mary's, a call so compelling that Marguerite had immediately given up her fancy clothes and sought a life of prayer and service. Her family and friends quickly noticed the change in her.

God made his desire and presence unmistakable at that moment. Since the gift of her "great conversion," Marguerite had dedicated herself to prayer and service. She had applied to enter the Carmelites, but was refused. She had become an associate of the Congregation of Notre Dame of Troyes, assisting the cloistered sisters in their mission of helping poor young women. She had also taken private vows of chastity and poverty. With the guidance of her spiritual director, Father Gendret, Marguerite had even tried to form a new community, but it had failed quickly: one member died and the other left, leaving Marguerite alone.

What if this mission to New France was another failure? The governor had been clear that it faced many risks: only fifty settlers were left, and the Iroquois continued to attack the settlement. Would Marguerite even be able to teach when she arrived?

That evening as she knelt to end her day in the presence of her beloved Lord, Marguerite prayed from her heart. *My*

Good God, help me to know how you are calling me. If I go to New France, would I have to give up my dream of becoming a religious sister? What is your dream for me? Something stirred in my heart when the governor spoke about the needs of the colonists, their purpose in settling there to bring the Gospel to the new world. The governor said that they desperately needed women who faithfully live the Gospel, even in poverty and danger of death.

As her confusion didn't abate over the next few days, Marguerite went to see her spiritual director. Father Gendret listened as Marguerite poured out her heart, her doubts, and the fruit of her prayer. A long silence followed. Finally, Father Gendret spoke. "Perhaps your efforts here in Troyes were not meant to succeed, but to teach you something. Perhaps in New France, you will have the freedom to begin the new kind of congregation that will truly imitate the life of the Blessed Mother."

"But I will be going alone, Father! I am not a community," Marguerite protested.

"With your guardian angel and mine, you will be three," Father Gendret smiled.

"And what about an unmarried woman traveling alone, with the governor? It's . . . unusual," Marguerite raised her last objection.

"De Maisonneuve is an upright man," Father Gendret said. "Anyone who knows you and him will realize that you are bound together for a higher purpose—for the sake of bringing the Gospel to this new land and its people. I encourage you to keep praying and consulting others. This could very well be God's will for you."

As the days passed and Marguerite consulted with the rector of the cathedral and others whom she respected, they encouraged her. Despite the hardships, the danger, and the sadness of leaving her family behind, she decided to go. As she traveled to meet de Maisonneuve in Nantes, she continued to look for confirmation that this was God's will. Stopping in Paris, she received an unexpected and longed-for invitation. The Carmelite superior in Paris, with whose sister she was staying, sent her word that if she still wished it, she could now enter Carmel.

Was *this* the call from God that she had been looking for? Marguerite delayed the next stage of her journey to Nantes, losing her deposit on the carriage reservation. Torn with doubts, she next visited the Jesuits. The Jesuit priest who spoke to her had been to New France and shared his own experiences there. Reassured, Marguerite decided to go on. But she struggled with her last big doubt: what if, by going to New France, she never became a religious? Why would the Carmelites accept her now, of all times?

While waiting in Nantes for de Maisonneuve, Marguerite consulted with one more person, a Carmelite, who reproached her for not entering Carmel. The conversation brought all of Marguerite's doubts to a crisis. Overwhelmed, she sought a nearby chapel where the Blessed Sacrament was exposed for adoration. Praying before Jesus in the Blessed Sacrament, Marguerite received not just comfort and strength, but the inner clarity she sought. She left the chapel, fully convinced that God was calling her to serve in Canada. Shortly afterward, Marguerite had a vision of a tall woman, dressed in white serge, who told her, "Go! I will never forsake you." This vision of Mary, along with the conviction she received at the foot of the Blessed Sacrament, convinced Marguerite that she should go forward through all the dangers that lay ahead.

The perilous ocean voyage to New France was so frightening that most of the passengers wanted to abandon ship and return home. Then a serious sickness swept through the ship. Before the vessel arrived at Quebec, eight people had died. Marguerite was deeply disturbed at the spiritual state of many of the men who had come so close to the point of death, and sought to do whatever she could for them. She tirelessly nursed the sick and spiritually prepared the dying to enter eternity. By the end of the three-month voyage, the men who had been so vulgar and eager to disparage her relationship with de Maisonneuve had come to respect and cherish the goodness of this lone thirty-three-year-old woman who, in the midst of peril and danger, offered a courageous and gentle charity.

Marguerite arrived in Ville-Marie in mid-November 1653. Besides the men, only fourteen women and fifteen children lived there. It would be five years before she started a formal school. But she began by caring for an orphan immediately entrusted to her care, teaching others one by one, and serving anyone in need. As she got to know all the inhabitants well, Marguerite became someone they confided in and turned to for help. During her first winter, Marguerite gave away her bed, mattress, and two blankets to the men who came to her about the cold. (Marguerite and her roommate were left with only a pillow and their aprons to sleep with!) A new bride came to her in distress after one day of marriage, and Marguerite helped to reconcile the bride and bridegroom. Marguerite's tact, her gifts for organizing and involving others, and her kind efficiency meant that she was soon considered the "compassionate mother" of Ville-Marie.

Because Ville-Marie was still in danger from Iroquois attacks, most of the villagers remained inside the fort. But de Maisonneuve assigned thirty men to go on pilgrimage with Marguerite to a famous cross that he had erected after their village had been saved from a flood. The cross had been knocked down, and the group spent three days putting up a new cross and reinforcing it so it would remain upright. Marguerite found the remnants of a banner given to de Maisonneuve by the Congregation of Notre Dame of Troyes, with the message: "Holy Mother of God, pure Virgin with a royal heart, save a place for us in your Montreal." Marguerite had already realized that her great conversion and the foundation of Montreal, including the original fort at Ville-Marie, had happened during the same year. Now, finding the prayer on the banner, Marguerite felt confirmed that the will of God had led her here: the "place" reserved for the Blessed Mother in Montreal was for her and the new congregation that she would begin. Great joy filled Marguerite's heart at this sign of God's special and loving call.

With that same joy, Marguerite Bourgeoys served the people of Montreal for forty-seven years. She energized the entire village to help build Our Lady of Bon Secours Chapel. In 1658, she opened Montreal's first school, in a stone stable. That same year, Marguerite returned to France and brought back the first young women who would help her form her new congregation, the Congregation of Notre Dame of Montreal. She would serve as superior for most of her life, guiding the sisters in initiatives, in spirituality, and in fidelity to their apostolic spirit of service. She founded multiple schools throughout Quebec, thus establishing the future school system. Finally, in 1698, when Marguerite was seventy-eight years old, her congregation—with its new apostolic way of life—received formal approval from the Church. With this official recognition, Marguerite and her sisters, who had only been permitted to make private vows up to this point, were finally able to make public vows of chastity, poverty, and obedience.

Marguerite died on January 12, 1700. The inhabitants of Montreal immediately recognized her—their mother, a woman of great compassion—as a saint.

Prayer

Saint Marguerite Bourgeoys,
inspired by the example of the Blessed Mother,
you dedicated yourself to the service of God's people,
regardless of class or status.
You found the strength to give so fully of yourself
in Jesus in the Blessed Sacrament.
Help me to be open
to God's invitation to serve,
no matter where it leads me.
You nurtured the young families of Montreal,
offering them motherly advice and help
so that they could grow in their vocations to love.
Guide and protect my family;
help us to grow in love for one another,
and to reach out to those in need,
as Mary did when she visited Elizabeth. Amen.

About Saint Marguerite Bourgeoys

Born: April 17, 1620, in Troyes, France

Died: January 12, 1700, in Montreal

Feast Day: January 12

Canonized: October 31, 1982, by Pope John Paul II

Patron: people who are poor, orphans, those refused
    entrance into religious life

Notes on Her Life

- The seventh of thirteen children, Marguerite grew up in France's Champagne province, famous for its merchants and poets.

- Marguerite experienced her great "conversion," which she also considered her great gift, when she was twenty years old.

- She tried to found an active, noncloistered community of women religious in France, but failed; one companion died and the other left.

- Marguerite prayerfully discerned a call to serve as a teacher in New France after she was invited by the governor of Montreal when she was thirty two.

- She started the first schools in Quebec, thus establishing the province's first school system.

- She founded the Congregation of the Sisters of Notre Dame of Montreal, one of the first noncloistered communities of women religious—although it took almost her entire lifetime for it to receive full approval in the Church.

- Marguerite had to constantly insist that the sisters' way of life remain noncloistered to better serve the needs of the people.

- She wanted always to be "with the people," by their side, and she rejected offers for herself or her sisters that would give them special treatment or remove them from the people they served.

- She was called "Mother of the colony" and is considered by many to be one of the founders of Montreal.

Lesser-Known Facts

🙦 Marguerite's devotion to the Blessed Mother as a woman of service, focusing on Mary of the Visitation, was unusual for her time.

🙦 Marguerite considered the Blessed Mother the true founder of the congregation.

🙦 When she was seventy-nine, Marguerite offered her life for another sister who had fallen ill. The sister immediately recovered; Marguerite died a few days later.

🙦 Marguerite was so reserved about her interior life that we know little about her prayer, with the exception of the advice she left for her sisters and her letters.

🙦 She used the most advanced pedagogy of her time for teaching. At a time when corporal punishment was used routinely in schools, Marguerite believed it should be used very sparingly. Her goal was always to help to build *understanding*.

🙦 Marguerite taught not just reading and writing, but also working skills for those who would need to earn their living.

🙦 When her congregation was approved and Marguerite and her sisters able to make their solemn vows, Marguerite chose the name Sister Marguerite of the Blessed Sacrament.

In Her Own Words

"All that I have ever desired most deeply and what I still most ardently wish is that the great precept of the love of God above all things and of the neighbor as oneself be written in every heart."

Servant of God
Satoko Kitahara

Mary of Ant Town

And she gave birth to her firstborn son and wrapped him in bands of cloth, and laid him in a manger, because there was no place for them in the inn (Lk 2:7).

*H*ere is the man I must contact, Satoko thought as she stared at the front-page picture of Brother Zeno. The accompanying story praised the Polish Franciscan as the mysterious man of charity who appeared throughout Japan begging money for the poor and generously filling the hands of anyone who approached him. *He sounds like Koya, the Buddhist pilgrim to the poor,* she thought, and then proclaimed aloud, "If the brother is still in Tokyo, I will find him."

The next afternoon Satoko spotted the black robes of Brother Zeno as he hurried through the streets toward the Sumida River. *Where can he be going?* Satoko thought. *Certainly nothing is down there but garbage. He was moving quickly, his steps firm and sure. Satoko strained not to lose sight of him. And as she struggled along, she brushed against dirty walls and tripped over discarded junk. Mother wouldn't be pleased to see me in this soiled kimono. Neither she nor Father will. . . .* She stopped short. What was this place? Satoko was stunned as she stood staring at what looked like shacks among heaps of refuse. Shaking off her dismay, Satoko hurried past a makeshift gate and nearly collided with Brother Zeno.

"Pardon me, Mother," he said to the woman with whom he had been speaking. Turning to Satoko, he asked, "And who might this be? Are you lost, or have you followed me here to Ant Town?" He was a big man. Satoko looked up at him in wonder, but his smile was disarming.

"Oh, yes . . . I am Satoko Kitahara from Asakusa and I did follow you here."

"Well then, follow me a little farther. I must talk to the Boss and the Professor," he said. In a moment they were face to face with a tall thin man with a natural air of elegance and a short, fierce-looking man who appeared to be in charge. Satoko was introduced, and then ignored, as the three men engaged in an animated discussion. Then suddenly, Brother Zeno took Satoko by the elbow and turned with her to leave.

"But, Brother," she said with some irritation, "I just got here. There must be something I can do."

"No, no, miss. Come with me. I will accompany you to your door. It is getting dark." Once they were outside the gate, Brother Zeno told her the two men were unimpressed and pegged her as a mere do-gooder. "They are proud people, Satoko. They are used to taking care of one another without any outside help. 'No help, no hindrance!' That is their motto. They are even leery of me. But, come with me and I will show you the Tokyo I know."

With this they set out in the direction of Satoko's apartment. Along the way, Brother Zeno pointed out an endless crowd of people: the homeless, prostitutes, orphans, the mentally ill, casualties of war, the destitute. These poor souls huddled in doorways, under bridges, in parks, at bus or train stops—it seemed to Satoko that they were everywhere, but she had never seen them before. Where had they been, she wondered? At last, she and the friar arrived at her door.

"Here, Brother Zeno. Please come in for some tea. I have much more to say." As she served the hot tea and sandwiches, Satoko began sharing her story with the good Franciscan. She related how she had followed two nuns into a Catholic church one day purely out of curiosity, but once inside became mesmerized by a statue of Our Lady of Lourdes. "It was a statue, but I felt a real presence. I went for instruction and received Baptism. That was some months ago. Now I want to do something to show my commitment. That is why I followed you. The newspaper story inspired me, and now there is Ant Town. I can surely help with the children, Brother Zeno."

"Ah, yes, the newspaper!" Zeno sighed. "You know, I don't care for all the fanfare, but the publicity is good for my poor people. People read the stories and money comes in." He abruptly rose and announced, "I must be off now. Perhaps I will see you again in Ant Town." Out he went into the misty darkness to serve the city's invisible poor.

Unable to sleep that night, Satoko Kitahara reviewed her life. *I am twenty-one years old,* she thought. *My parents are respected members of the community. I am well-educated with my degree in pharmacology. In fact, I should be seriously preparing to settle down, as my parents hope, with a nice young man. Ah, yes,* she smiled to herself, *my parents don't realize that my heart is set on something else. So far the only thing that has kept me from entering the convent has been my health. As soon as my lungs are strong I will try again. . . . I will try again, yes . . . , but tomorrow I will try Ant Town again.*

"Gentlemen, I am Satoko Kitahara and I place myself at your service. How can I help?" The two men, Ozawa San and Matsui Sensei—the Boss and the Professor—looked at each other and then at Satoko.

"All right," Osawa said. "You can help us decorate for Christmas."

"You celebrate Christmas here?" she asked.

"Is that so surprising?" a voice boomed from behind her. It was Brother Zeno, who immediately took over the situation. "Yes, Satoko, and I am very pleased to see you because we need someone to organize the children to do a Christmas pageant."

"Oh, come now, Brother Zeno," the Professor sneered. "These children know nothing about Christ. All they know is Santa Claus and decorations."

"Dear Professor, remember the television crew will be here," Brother Zeno said, "and we want to show how we celebrate Christmas in Ant Town. It has to be good, really good!"

And it was. Satoko taught the children the story of the first Christmas and in place of carols practiced some traditional songs with them. The high point was the grand finale with everyone kneeling before the crèche saying the Rosary. When the television crew left, the Boss, knowing how much the good publicity would help his people, thanked Brother Zeno for such a great celebration.

"Oh, but thanks belong to Satoko. She is the one who organized the children and got the costumes and music ready."

"Will we see you again without the lights and cameras, Satoko?" the Professor asked tersely.

"You will," she replied with a smile. "I'll be here as often as I can."

True to her word, Satoko came almost every day to help the children with schoolwork, to make sure they were clean and fed. She played games with them and even took them out of Ant Town on excursions. One day she proposed that the children come with her for a few days to a friend's house in the mountains. The fresh air would be a blessing for them. The Boss was suspicious. He demanded to know where the money for this would come from.

"Actually," she replied, "I'm not sure yet. But I know God will provide."

That evening as she was praying, her mother came with a message from her father. "He has a friend who wants to dispose of many large milk cans. Could they be recycled for Ant Town?" her mother asked.

"Oh, yes, Mother," Satoko said as she jumped to her feet. "I will go round up some of the men to haul them away."

The money brought in from the sale of the cans covered the exact expense of the children's vacation. Now Satoko was an established part of Ant Town. For some time she had been begging the Boss for permission to go out with the group of ragpickers.

"I'm sure I can do it. Let me try, please." Finally, he handed her a large wicker basket and sent her out. She came back with her basket full of twine and hay, which was sold for a good sum. The Boss was so pleased that he presented her with an "official" ragpickers cart. With this she went about the city collecting anything that could be sold. She even obtained a ragpickers' license, which gave her a bit of legitimacy in her new "profession."

The news media began referring to her as "the Mary of Ant Town." However, people whispered about the poor young woman, obviously well-bred, who must be one of the tragedies of the war. For her part, Satoko went about smiling and content. She was a ragpicker by day and a big sister to the children of Ant Town by night. This bustle of activity, however, was wearing on her fragile health. Her wartime work in an aircraft factory had seriously damaged her lungs. Satoko had to admit that her goodwill was not enough. She had to relax her efforts. When she brought this news to the Boss and the Professor, they told her to take a year off, go to the mountains and get well. Satoko did go away for a year.

When she returned, however, a couple had been put in charge of the children. She was no longer needed. Satoko took this as a sign that she should apply again to the Mercedarian Sisters of the Blessed Sacrament. They were pleased and set a date for her entrance. However, her illness returned and those plans had to be canceled.

In the hospital her condition worsened. Her parents met their daughter's friends from Ant Town and agreed with them that she would only recover if she was brought to the town. With the doctor's permission, Satoko was settled in a small room off the central building. Brother Zeno arrived with a large statue of Our Lady of Lourdes, which was set in the room where Satoko could see it.

During this crisis the city laid another burden on Ant Town—officials wanted to relocate the whole settlement. A new site was designated for the refuse dump and a number of acres were to be made available to the new Ant Town. The catch was that the city supervisors were charging an enormous amount of money for the new site—twenty-five million yen, to be paid in cash.

"That's outrageous!" the patrons of Ant Town agreed.

Satoko spoke up, "I promised you once that I would lay down my life for Ant Town. Now seems to be the time."

The Professor was chosen to go to talk to the city officials. Satoko armed him with her most precious possession, a rosary blessed by the pope.

"This will give you courage and confidence," she promised. "I will be praying for you here."

The Professor arrived for the meeting, rosary in hand, carrying a copy of *The Children of Ant Town*, a book Satoko had written. The Professor explained the simple desire of the inhabitants of Ant Town: to have a place to live where they had some degree of safety and could be self-reliant. The official thanked him and said the council would send an answer soon. During the wait Satoko's strength diminished. When the Professor was called back for the decision, Satoko could no longer speak, but she signaled that her prayers would accompany him. At the city office, the Professor noticed Satoko's book on the desk of the man in charge. The official began by saying that the council had conferred and it was clear that Ant Town was an important part of the city of Tokyo. So, although the move was still necessary, the city would only ask for fifteen million yen, payable over five years.

Everyone was thrilled, but none more so than Satoko, whose sole response was a radiant smile. Ant Town was relocated on January 20, 1958. Three days later God called Satoko Kitahara, the Mary of Ant Town, to her eternal reward.

Prayer

Dear God, thank you for blessing the Church in Japan
with the presence of Satoko Kitahara. This young Shinto
  Buddhist
was drawn to you by an attraction to your
  Virgin Mother.
Satoko became a motherly figure in Ant Town in Tokyo,
imitating Mary by offering her love and attention to the
  poor, neglected children.
Like your Son, Satoko wanted to become one with the
  people with whom she lived.
In the end, with Christ she offered her life for the salvation of Ant Town.
Teach us by her attractive example to make ourselves
  totally available
for the needs of others, and above all to make ourselves
humble imitators of your Son. Amen.

About the Servant of God Satoko Kitahara

Born: August 22, 1929, in Suginami (Tokyo), Japan
Died: January 23, 1958, in Arinomachi, "Ant Town"
  (Tokyo)
Declared Servant of God
Patron: those who work with the poor

Notes on Her Life

☙ Daughter of privilege.

☙ In 1944 she went to work in an aircraft factory.

☙ In 1945 she suffered a bout of tuberculosis.

In 1946 she enrolled in pharmaceutical college.

A visit to a Catholic church piqued her interest.

In 1949 she was baptized as Elisabeth, and confirmed as Maria.

She accepted and lived out the Mercedarian spirituality of self-offering.

In 1950 Brother Zeno Zebrowski, OFM Conv., introduced her to Tokyo's poor.

She began volunteer work in Ant Town.

Around 1953 she faced another health crisis and took a year of rest.

After recovering she decided to enter the Mercedarian Sisters, but illness intervened.

In 1957 she offered her life for the security of Ant Town.

Satoko died three days after Ant Town received a reprieve and a new location.

She was buried at Tama Reien Cemetery in Fuchu City, Tokyo.

Lesser-Known Facts

She wrote *The Children of Ant Town* in 1953.

Due to her example Ozawa San and Matsui Sensei became Catholic.

She was a licensed ragpicker.

She was also an accomplished pianist.

She nearly died in an Allied bombing of the aircraft factory where she worked.

Ant Town is so named because the inhabitants resemble industrious ants.

In Her Own Words

"I suddenly realized what I had been doing. I was too proud and insensitive to understand what God was trying to show me. I was giving my free time to assist the Ant Town children with their studies. God, in order to save us, had sent his Son as one of us. He really became one of us! There it was: the only way I could really help these poor children was to become a ragpicker like them."

Saint Patrick

The Impossible Dream

"Follow me, and I will make you fish for people" (Mt 4:19).

Patrick flung off his bedcovers. It was impossible to stay still any longer after what he had just seen and heard. The troubled young man got up and slipped outside.

In the chill night air, Patrick paced outside his family's home. After six years of slavery and the harsh outdoor life of a shepherd, Patrick had rejoiced in freedom and the safety of his home. During the day, his mother's tearful, joyful glances made him thank God for his safe return. But at night, his past still haunted him.

Patrick thought back to that first night of terror. He'd been only sixteen when raiders had kidnapped him from his wealthy home in Britain. He hadn't known who in his family had been left alive or dead in the raid. Bound and bruised, he'd

21

huddled in the bottom of the boat against the sickening surges of the sea.

He had soon found himself on the feared and wild Irish shore, to be sold as a slave. Patrick's new owner, an Irish chief named Milchu, dragged him far away to his lands and forced him into heavy labor. Escape was too arduous and dangerous to attempt. But the physical hardships of Patrick's enslavement had not been his worst sufferings. At first, his terror forced him to think only of survival—from the harsh environment and from wolves. Then his terror had turned to rage, and his rage to despair. Having never taken his faith seriously, Patrick didn't even have the comfort of the faith he'd been raised in. Humbled by his daily hunger, nakedness, and hopelessness, Patrick began to pray.

Patrick's status as a slave exiled him to the isolated life of a shepherd. He lived completely alone and unprotected in the rugged, sometimes savage, hills and forests. His only companions were the sheep, wind, frost, and rain. Gradually, Patrick started to sense a Presence with him. His isolation was transformed into solitude as he began to pray to God in earnest. Patrick's long-neglected faith finally took root and grew. Later, in his *Confession*, Patrick would write of those years:

> Now after I came to Ireland I herded flocks; and often during the day I prayed. The love of God and the fear of him increased more and more, and my faith grew, and my spirit was aroused, so that in a single day I said as many as a hundred prayers, and at night nearly as many, even when I was out in the woods and on the mountains. Before the dawn I used to arouse myself to prayer in snow and frost and rain; and I minded no pain, nor was there any sluggishness in me . . . because the spirit was fervent within me.

For six long years, Patrick suffered the hunger, anguish, and physical hardships of slavery. He grew to respect the Irish people, began to speak their language, and learned about their religion. But, despite his gratitude in finding God in his captivity, Patrick longed for escape.

One night, God spoke to him in a dream, saying, "Your ship is ready." Guided by his faith, Patrick decided to attempt what before had seemed impossible. He walked the dangerous 200 miles to the coast. When he arrived, Patrick saw a ship in the harbor. He asked the steersman if he could be taken on as a crew member. "No way!" retorted the steersman. Perhaps he suspected Patrick was a runaway slave. Sadly, Patrick walked away, praying. If he couldn't board the ship, he had no idea what to do next. Suddenly, one of the sailors shouted, "Come quickly! The men are calling you." God had touched the hearts of the crew, who welcomed Patrick aboard.

After a difficult and long trip home, Patrick finally rejoined the remaining members of his family. They had a happy reunion, and they had begged him not to leave ever again. Patrick had rejoiced in a sense of safety, security, and belonging. Until tonight.

God spoke to him, and it deeply troubled Patrick.

At first, the vision seemed just an ordinary dream. A man from Ireland came to him, holding many letters, and gave one to Patrick. He began to read the letter aloud, beginning with its title, "The Voice of the Irish." But as Patrick continued to read, he heard voices crying out—voices he somehow knew came from the forest of Foclut in Ireland. "We beg you, holy youth, come and walk once more among us."

The intensity, pain, and longing of these voices pierced Patrick's heart. Suddenly, the vision was over, and he was left alone in confusion. Alone except for the ache in his heart and his own terrible fears.

It is a vision from God, his heart told him. *God is calling me to preach the Gospel to the Irish people.*

No! Patrick's head shouted. *I can't go back. To them, I am just a runaway slave—naked, humiliated, powerless. I suffered so much there. How can I go back?*

His heart countered, *I discovered God in the Irish wilderness. The Irish live in their pagan wilderness, waiting to discover God. Can I abandon them if God is telling me they are his beloved people?*

Putting his head down, Patrick wept. The call to be a missionary to the Irish seemed impossible. Patrick wasn't even a priest. Yet, he knew that he couldn't ignore the call of the God who had loved him and saved him, and who now wanted Patrick to be a messenger of God's loving salvation to others. Patrick sighed and lifted his head. In his heart he prayed, "Lord, faithful God, you who chose me for this service, I commend my soul to you. I am ready—grant me to drink of your chalice."

His fears remained, but a deep and steady joy filled his heart—the joy of doing Christ's will.

From then on, Patrick focused all his efforts to prepare himself to become a missionary to Ireland. He studied for the priesthood and was ordained. Eventually, despite a painful betrayal of confidence from a friend that almost destroyed Patrick's reputation, he was ordained a bishop.

Patrick left for Ireland, never to return to his beloved homeland. As he stepped off the boat onto the Irish shore, Patrick confronted his deepest fears. But his old fears of rejection and humiliation at the hands of his former enslavers were transformed into a deep love for the Irish people. Patrick became an unstoppable whirlwind of the Holy Spirit, sweeping through Ireland, rapidly gaining converts to Christianity though his bold witness. Many of his converts were women and slaves, but he also approached the chieftains with the Gospel. This dangerous tactic allowed Patrick to reach many of the Irish people, but it also put him in danger of imprisonment and assassination. Patrick spent the rest of his life as a missionary to the Irish people, facing persecution, imprisonment, ridicule, poverty, itinerancy, and death threats.

Despite the unending challenges Patrick's enthusiasm and gratitude to God buoyed his spirit:

> . . . Guided by God, I neither agreed with them nor deferred to them, not by my own grace but by God who is victorious in me and withstands them all, so that I might come to the Irish people to preach the Gospel and endure insults from unbelievers; that I might hear scandal of my travels, and endure many persecutions to the extent of prison; and so that I might give up my free birthright for the advantage of others, and if I should be worthy, I am ready [to give] even my life without hesitation; and most willingly for his name. And I choose to devote it to him even unto death, if God grant it to me.
>
> I am greatly God's debtor, because he granted me so much grace that through me many people would be reborn in God.

Patrick's love for Christ lit such a fire that numerous convents and monasteries sprang up during his lifetime and immediately after his death. Patrick had come to a pagan Ireland, and died leaving almost all of Ireland profoundly Christian.

The very popular and ancient prayer "Saint Patrick's Breastplate" was probably not written by Saint Patrick, but like many of the stories about him, expresses his spirit:

Christ be with me,
Christ within me,
Christ behind me,
Christ before me,
Christ beside me,
Christ to win me,
Christ to comfort and restore me.
Christ beneath me,
Christ above me,
Christ in quiet,
Christ in danger,
Christ in hearts of all that love me,
Christ in mouth of friend and stranger.

Prayer

Saint Patrick,
you suffered greatly in your life:
kidnapping, loss of family, slavery, isolation,
    and betrayal.
Your sufferings did not embitter you
but brought you to a deeper relationship with Christ
and gave you a great desire to share the Gospel
with those who suffer.
Have pity on those who suffer violence and slavery
    in our own day.
Set us afire to spread the Gospel,
to live the spirit of forgiveness,
and to love with the heart of Christ. Amen.

About Saint Patrick

Born: ca. 387 in Britain (England or Scotland)

Died: ca. 460 in Ireland

Canonized: universal acclaim

Feast Day: March 17

Patron: engineers, "outsiders" such as slaves or immigrants, Ireland, protection against snakes

Facts and Legends: Discovering the True Patrick

Two documents are regarded as authentically written by Patrick: his *Confession* and his *Letter to the Soldiers of Coroticus*, protesting the murder and enslaving of Christian converts. These documents confirm the basic facts about Patrick's life:

- Patrick was born a Roman citizen, son of the deacon Calpornius.

- He was kidnapped and enslaved at age sixteen, and remained a slave for six years, after which God inspired him to escape.

- Patrick was not well educated; in his *Confession* he quotes the Bible, but does not refer to the Fathers of the Church or his contemporary, Saint Augustine.

- As missionary to Ireland, Patrick baptized thousands of people. Yet despite this huge success, Patrick remained very humble. He considered his mission entirely the work of God.

- Before being ordained a deacon, Patrick confided to a close friend about a serious fault he committed during his youth at age fifteen. At some later point—perhaps while Patrick was being considered for bishop, or after his initial success in Ireland, his friend betrayed his confidence and made the fault public, thus damaging Patrick's reputation. Patrick was deeply wounded by his friend's betrayal, and it prompted him to write his *Confession*.

 Patrick's vision of his mission to Ireland was confirmed most likely by the bishops of Britain, perhaps by the pope in Rome.

Many legends grew up around Patrick after his death; some of the most famous stories cannot be confirmed historically, such as his miraculous confrontations with the druids, the story about using the shamrock to explain the Trinity, and his expelling the snakes from Ireland. If not historically accurate, these stories reveal how Saint Patrick's influence shaped the faith of the Irish. The legend of Patrick banishing the snakes may symbolize how he expelled the religion of the druids from Ireland. While he does not mention the shamrock in his *Confession*, Patrick does make numerous references to the Most Holy Trinity.

Some suggest that Patrick's great humility may have been partially shaped by the trauma of being enslaved, and that he is the first Christian to publicly denounce slavery, not just the poor treatment of slaves.

In His Own Words

"I am a servant in Christ to a foreign people, for the inexpressible glory of eternal life, which is in Christ Jesus my Lord."

Saint Clare of Assisi

Hidden Light

"Is a lamp brought in to be put under the bushel basket, or under the bed, and not on the lampstand?"
(Mk 4:21)

L ate in the evening of Palm Sunday in the year 1212, the little city of Assisi peacefully slept, with doors barred and windows dark. But behind one barred door, the bright flame of hope burned in the heart of a young woman.

Clare, the oldest daughter of the house of the noble Offreduccio family, worked quickly and quietly to clear away the rubble blocking the forgotten door. Every time she inadvertently put a stone down too heavily or made a noise, she froze, listening for the steps of a wakened family member. But no one came.

As Clare worked, she thought about her last conversation with her mother. Devout as she was, even her mother thought that Clare should get married and serve Christ as a noblewoman who enjoyed the luxuries of her status. *If Mamma could only understand why,* Clare mused to herself. *The poverty that Francis lives is true freedom. All the wealth that I possess is like this rubble I have to clear away, in order to walk through it. This inner doorway that will lead me closer to Christ has to be clear of obstacles, of anything extraneous. What an exchange: the things of this world for those of heaven!* Clare felt a stab of hope: how she longed to finally be free to live just like Jesus, the poor and gentle Master.

Finally, she finished clearing the rubble away. Heart pounding, Clare slid back the heavy bolt, pulled open the door, and stepped outside. As she closed the door behind her, a figure stepped out of the shadows. In sudden panic Clare caught her breath, then she recognized her friend's familiar figure and breathed a sigh of relief.

Her friend gave Clare a quick hug, then stepped back and looked into her eyes. "Are you sure you want to do this?" Clare's bright, smiling nod erased all doubts. The two women walked quickly through the city, and then beyond its walls.

Together, they walked softly past silent olive groves. Clare's heart was still pounding—with excitement? fear? joy? *Perhaps a little of all three.* The night was so vivid! Clare drank in every detail around her—the blue leaves glistening silver in the moonlight, the freshness of the cool night air, the pinpricks of torchlights up ahead. Clare felt giddy with joy. Her dream of following in the footsteps of the Master, of belonging *entirely* to Jesus, was finally going to happen!

In the torchlight, Clare could see the brown cowls of two men waiting outside the Portiuncula. Francis, the Poverello of Assisi, the one whom everyone called crazy, smiled his welcome. As Clare's eyes met his, she thought back to the first moment she had seen that glow of Christ in Francis's eyes. She had not paid attention to the rumors about the popular, rich, and carefree young nobleman who had crazily thrown away his wealth, his inheritance, and the respect of the townspeople. But when she had witnessed the way Francis served the poor, she had sent gifts of food to the friars. Over the past few months, she had been struck to the very core of her being by the depth of his commitment to imitating Jesus in his poverty, his sharing in the life of those who were poor, and above all, by his unquenchable joy.

Francis's lifestyle inspired Clare to search for the *something more* she had always secretly longed for. She met with Francis several times, and his words lit a fire in her soul. She soon felt Jesus calling her to live the same radical poverty. Clare wished she could live by the side of the friars and Francis himself, sharing in their radical poverty and dependence on God. But she and Francis both knew that this wasn't practical or safe. So Clare and her companions would live in a cloistered convent, in Francis's own spirit of radical poverty and joy.

Clare felt the joy in her heart explode as Francis took her hand and led her inside, to the foot of the altar.

"What do you seek here?" Francis asked the beautiful young woman.

"The Lord's mercy and yours," she replied.

Then, in a short but meaningful ceremony, Clare exchanged her satin and pearls for a rough sackcloth tunic. She tied the tunic around her waist with a cord. Francis himself cut her long hair, and Clare covered her shorn head with a veil. From now on, Clare would be consecrated to God forever.

Francis had already arranged for Clare to begin her life of consecration in a Benedictine convent. It did not take long for the Offreduccio family to follow her there. The very next day they arrived at the convent and demanded that she return home immediately. Despite their pleas and threats, the only answer they received was Clare's stubborn silence as she knelt at the foot of the altar, eyes fixed on the crucifix. Finally, when they tried to violently force her to her feet, Clare pulled off her veil, revealing her shorn hair—a sign of her consecration to God. In frustration her family finally left, assuming that soon enough Clare would tire of hardship and give up her foolish ideas. Clare knew better.

Instead, Clare's valiant determination inspired others—including her younger sister Catherine. Two weeks later, fourteen-year-old Catherine (who later took the name Agnes) also fled the family estate to join Clare in her life of poverty and prayer.

Infuriated, the girls' uncle rode out to the convent with a band of soldiers. Bursting in, the soldiers went from room to room until they found Catherine. Her uncle seized her and struck her repeatedly, and several of the soldiers started dragging her away by her hair. Clare fell to her knees before the crucifix and began to pray. Suddenly, Catherine's frail body became so heavy the soldiers couldn't move her. As her uncle continued to strike her with his armored fist, he suddenly felt a piercing pain through his arm. Terrified at these signs of God's protection, the uncle and his soldiers fled.

Francis and his friars prepared a simple dwelling for Clare and her sisters next to the Church of San Damiano. Initially, Francis directed and guided the new community, but soon Clare was asked to become abbess. Reluctantly, Clare agreed. As abbess, Clare had the authority to guide the new community of sisters, though she sought advice from Francis and other wise spiritual leaders.

The life that the "Poor Ladies" lived was unheard-of for women of that time. Dedicating their days to prayer and manual labor, they lived simply and austerely. They had nothing, individually or collectively, except the absolute necessities. They received some support from the friars who begged for them, but the lack of a steady income meant that the sisters were completely dependent on God.

At first, they based their lifestyle on the notes that Francis gave them. Then, Clare wrote their rule of life. Clare is the first woman to write a rule of life for a monastic community. Her intelligence and holiness won her the respect of all, but throughout her life, she continually faced opposition from the bishops and the pope himself, who felt that the radical poverty that both Francis and Clare wanted for their communities was too strict. Several bishops tried to impose the Benedictine Rule on the Poor Ladies. All her life, Clare fought for her sisters to be allowed to live the Franciscan life and the ideal of radical poverty. She would only receive this grace on her deathbed.

The Poor Ladies were a spiritual powerhouse for the active Order of Friars Minor. Clare stayed close to Francis throughout the rest of his life, encouraging him, caring for him in his later illness after he had received the stigmata, and treasuring his advice. After his death, she was considered his closest, most faithful follower, who loved poverty and lived in his spirit of radical joy.

Clare spent forty silent, prayerful years serving as abbess within the cloister of San Damiano. When she was only thirty years old, she started to suffer from serious illness. Despite her frail health, which often forced her to remain in bed, she guided her community and the rapidly growing order. In addition to her sister Agnes, Clare had the joy of welcoming her youngest sister, her aunt, and her mother into the community. Within Clare's lifetime the Poor Ladies spread throughout Europe—more than 150 monasteries were associated with Saint Clare and her Poor Ladies by her death in 1253. Clare urged them to hold fast to the spirit of poverty and the rule she had given them.

Clare's deep spirit of faith, contemplation, and charity enabled her to live the daily renunciations of the rule of life she had written: to live the Gospel in its entirety. Twice her faith shone out dramatically when the monastery at San Damiano was attacked. The first time, soldiers planning to invade Assisi approached the monastery and starting climbing its walls at night. Clare arose from her bed and, ill though she was, brought the Blessed Sacrament to an open window. With great faith, she lifted the Blessed Sacrament high. The attacking soldiers retreated under the dazzling presence of Christ. During the second, larger attack, the sisters gathered around Clare in prayer. A fierce storm arose, scattering the soldiers—once again saving the monastery and Assisi from attack.

Clare, worn out by her illness and life of austerity, died on August 11, 1253. She was not yet sixty. Her sister Agnes (who was superior in Florence) returned to San Damiano to be with her, as did three of Francis's earliest companions, as well as Pope Innocent IV, who finally confirmed Clare's rule of life—something Clare had worked for her entire life. Clare remained peaceful and joyful to her last breath, serenely abandoning herself for the last time into the hands of the Poor Crucified, upon whom she had focused her gaze and her heart for her entire life.

Though she was a contemplative sister who never passed beyond her monastery walls, the light of Clare's influence reached all over Europe in her own day. Now from heaven, her brilliant light shines even more brightly, inspiring women all over the world who seek to live the same evangelical poverty and joy, and who, since Clare's death, have been known as the Poor Clares.

Prayer

Saint Clare,
you received a special gift:
the call to live the joy of the Gospel.
Your hidden life
did not prevent you from being a light to the world
because you were faithful to your call
to imitate Jesus in a life of radical poverty.
Today, in a culture obsessed with material wealth,
your example can shine a light on my life.
Help me to discover what I need to leave behind
to follow Jesus more closely
and live the Gospel. Amen.

About Saint Clare of Assisi

Born: ca. 1194 in Assisi
Died: August 11, 1253, in Assisi
Feast Day: August 11
Canonized: September 26, 1255, by Pope Alexander IV
Patron: television, sore eyes

Notes on Her Life

- Born Chiara Offreduccio of noble parents.

- A devout child, Clare was inspired by her mother's life of prayer.

- Clare fled to enter the convent at night because her family was trying to force her to marry.

- The community of women that Clare started with Francis was called the Poor Ladies. After Clare's death, they become known as the Poor Clares.

- Clare's fidelity to the Gospel and to following the inspiration of Saint Francis led people to call her "another Francis."

- Clare is the patron of television because one Christmas Eve, she was too ill to go to chapel. After remonstrating with Jesus that she would miss the Christmas Mass, Jesus gave her a vision in which she could see and hear everything that happened in the chapel that night—and afterward she was able to tell the sisters details of what she had mystically witnessed.

Lesser-Known Facts

- Besides her sister Agnes, who joined Clare only a few weeks after she left home, eventually their younger sister, Beatrix, their aunt Bianca, and their mother, Ortolana, also entered the cloister.

- Francis guided the community only in its early days. After Clare was declared abbess of San Damiano in 1216, she formed the order, with the assistance of others.

- Clare and the Poor Ladies were trying to live a new form of religious life for women. Clare's insistence that the Ladies live in strict poverty was so radical that several bishops and popes tried to force her to change the rule.

- Clare's sister Agnes is also a canonized saint.
- In addition to the rule of life, we have four letters that Clare wrote to Saint Agnes of Prague—not her sister Agnes, but another woman who was seeking Clare's guidance in living the Franciscan life.

In Her Own Words

"Embrace the poor Christ."

— Second letter of Saint Clare to Saint Agnes of Prague

Saint Benedict of Nursia

Man of Prayer and Work

"You are the salt of the earth. . . . You are the light of the world. A city built on a hill cannot be hid" (Mt 5:13-14).

School had been very difficult today. Young Benedict sighed as he strode the streets of Rome, headed for home. "I really don't belong here," he thought. "There is no morality or sense of decency. Even my friends are living too freely for me. It's as if they never heard of Christ and his law of love." Benedict felt disgusted, and his face must have shown it as he threw open the front door.

Cyrilla shook her graying head as soon as she saw Benedict. She was his governess, a grandmotherly woman who had been his nurse from childhood. When his parents decided to send him to Rome to study—as befitted the son of a noble— they sent Cyrilla to care for him.

"You've been fretting again, Master Benedict." She smiled wisely as she stirred the soup kettle on the fire. "Are you still thinking about that hermit notion of yours?"

There was no doubt about the way Cyrilla felt. Benedict looked at her uneasily. He didn't want to hurt anyone. Yet what could he do? Rome, the great city where so many people spent their days trying to be rich and powerful, was not to his liking. He himself longed for the quiet of the countryside, for some small cave where he could spend his days in prayer.

"Don't worry," he said kindly. "I've heard that a hermit's life is really very healthy. Lots of fresh air, sunshine, simple food. . . ."

"And cold winds, rain, and snow! Master Benedict, you know you're not used to such things. Why, you'd die of hardship within a month!"

"Not unless it was the will of God, Cyrilla. Remember how God looks after everyone on this earth, even the birds and the flowers in the fields?"

Cyrilla scowled. "If you're going off to be a hermit, it won't be by yourself. I'll go with you and see that you don't starve to death."

A few days later Benedict and Cyrilla left Rome and headed eastward into the hill country

But even after just a day of walking, Benedict could see that Cyrilla was having difficulty. He knew she could not go on. In spite of Cyrilla's fierce loyalty to his family and her motherly concern for him, Benedict would have to leave her as soon as they found a friendly village where she could stay. He knew she would understand. The burning call in his heart could not be stilled or put off any longer.

Enfide was that village. Within a very short time, Cyrilla was well established—she found it easy to make friends. Benedict felt that now he was free in conscience to follow the urging of his heart. One night he left a note for his governess and slipped off into the rugged countryside.

He walked on and on. As day broke the going became rougher—just the sort of country he was looking for. Benedict's smile broadened as he trudged up into the mountains.

Suddenly a deep, silent valley opened up before him. No one would be here; no one would want to live in such desolation except someone like Benedict, who sought only God.

"That cave looks perfect," Benedict breathed. "Could it be that God is guiding my steps to it?" He approached the cavern with a singing heart. "May you be praised, my Lord!" he exclaimed.

"Now and forever!" a voice replied.

Startled, Benedict spun around to try to locate the speaker. A few feet away stood an old monk with a very kind face!

"I wanted solitude," Benedict murmured.

"You will find it here," replied the monk. "But tell me, who are you?"

In a few words the young man told the story of his life and his great desire to leave the world and draw close to God. As the monk listened, he thought of his own call. He provided Benedict with the rough leather garments of a hermit and promised to bring him food from time to time. Nothing could have suited Benedict better. Poverty and privation, cold and discomfort were to be Benedict's life. Through them he planned to conquer himself and seek God.

One would think that, being tucked away from nearly all human contact, Benedict would find it easy to be absorbed in God alone. Of course, he enjoyed some times of intimacy with his creator, but Benedict was far from having constant blissful tranquility. "Lord, how I long for heaven," he often thought. Violent temptations often assailed him. Satan attacked Benedict's imagination, placing before his mind's eye the most attractive distractions, insinuating that the young man deserved them.

"After all," the Evil One whispered on one occasion, "you deprive yourself of so much. A few minutes of enjoyment won't hurt."

Instead, Benedict plunged headlong into a thicket of briars and nettles. He tossed himself about until he was covered with scratches and free of the tempting thoughts.

Prayer and penance—he thrived on this daily fare. Slowly, one by one, Benedict dominated his weak points and drew even closer to his God.

Though he did not know it, the years of Benedict's solitary life were drawing to a close. God had plans for his servant—plans that would echo down through the centuries.

This new phase began with an unpromising event. Early one morning, as the mists began to lift from the valley and slopes of Subiaco, a motley group of men struggled up the rugged incline toward Benedict's cave. Obviously they were not used to this exhausting sort of physical exertion, even though, being dressed as monks, they should have been familiar with bodily discipline. They came from Vicovaro, a hilltop between Tivoli and Subiaco, where they had built a rudimentary sort of monastery. They had no real rule in the modern sense of the word. As yet none had been formulated in Christendom save that of Saint Basil in the distant East. The tenor of life of a community often depended on the leader of the moment, or the whim of the group—an unstable foundation on which to base an entire lifetime. So it was that sometimes these would-be groups lost the initial enthusiasm and conviction of a life dedicated to God. These men of Vicovaro were an example of this.

As Benedict watched the men approaching the mouth of his cave, a sense of misgiving came over him. When they arrived, the spokesman of the group stepped forward to plead their cause.

"Recently we have been stricken by the death our abbot," one man wheezed. "We have heard of your growing fame, holy Benedict. We have come to beseech you to be abbot of our humble community."

At first Benedict refused—he could see so plainly through their mask of pretended piety. "My ways are not yours," he warned. "Prayer and work is my rule of life. I do not think that we would agree."

But they persisted and finally persuaded him to return with them. It was soon evident that the severe monastic discipline that Benedict instituted did not suit them, and in order to get rid of him the monks decided to poison his wine. When, as was his habit, he made the sign of the cross over the cup, it broke as if a stone had fallen on it.

"God forgive you, brothers," Benedict said serenely. "Why have you plotted this wicked thing against me? Didn't I tell you beforehand that my ways would not agree with yours? Go and find an abbot to suit your taste. After what you have done to me I can no longer stay here. I am returning to Subiaco."

Benedict was not left alone for long. Sanctity is like a magnet. Others who were eager to dedicate themselves entirely to the service of God came to the young hermit and asked him to tell them his rule of life so that they could follow it, too. Benedict accepted them as brothers and formed them into communities of monks.

By the year 520, twelve monasteries dotted the countryside around Subiaco. Benedict felt it was time to begin a new foundation, so he set out for the little town of Cassino. Here, with prayer and work—large amounts of both—Benedict and his monks began building the great church and monastery that would later be known the world over as Monte Cassino.

It is thought that it was here, at Monte Cassino, that Benedict first set down in writing his way of life. This *Rule of Saint Benedict* was to form and nurture thousands of spiritual sons and daughters and to give to its author the undying title of Father of Western Monasticism. "Prayer and work" is the summary of his rule and the motto of Benedictines.

Women were also attracted by his balanced plan of life. It is believed that his twin sister, Scholastica, came to live near the base of Monte Cassino following the death of their father. She had consecrated her life to God from a very early age and mirrored her brother's strong spirit of prayer. For centuries she has been the model of feminine Benedictine spirituality.

Monte Cassino! Here Benedict had lit a fire that would never be put out. In the Dark Ages soon to come, Benedictine monasteries would preserve the elements of Christian civilization in the midst of chaos. And those same monasteries would rebuild and recivilize the world in the aftermath of so much death and destruction.

Perhaps God let Benedict glimpse some of this as he lay dying early in the year 543. "Brothers, God is calling me!" He whispered softly. "Please help me into chapel."

The monks attending him lifted Benedict and carried him into chapel, where he fervently received Holy Communion. With the strength of the sacrament, Benedict rose from his place, raised his arms toward the heavens and breathed his last.

He had foretold the day of his death, and good father that he was, even those brothers not present at Monte Cassino received a sign of his passing. These brothers received a vision of a wide, well-carpeted road that stretched into the distance, disappearing into the heavens.

When an angel appeared, he told the brothers that the road was "the pathway which Benedict, God's beloved, took to reach heaven." The longing in his heart for God finally could no longer be contained in a body made of flesh and blood, and his soul flew to its Creator.

This holy patriarch was buried in the Chapel of Saint John the Baptist, which Benedict built on a site formerly dedicated to Apollo. A ceaseless stream of miracles has been recorded through his intercession, the greatest of which is the flourishing spiritual family he founded.

෬෬

Prayer

Saint Benedict, Father of Western Monasticism,
    patron of Europe,
you were truly a man of blessing. You generously
    followed God,
forsaking a life of privilege and embracing a life of prayer
when you left Rome to settle in a cave near Subiaco.
There you mortified your own desires and listened at-
    tentively to God,
who eventually called you to establish the great
    monastery at Monte Cassino.
From there you gave the Church a balanced rule of life,
of true blessing against the power of evil and the poison
    of vice.
Hold the cross of Christ high over the whole Church
so that we will remain attentive to the Gospel
and live our vocation to be salt and light for the world.
    Amen.

About Saint Benedict of Nursia

Born: 480 in Nursia, near Rome

Died: March 21, 547, at Monte Cassino

Feast Day: July 11

Canonized: 1220, by Pope Honorius III

Patron: monks, especially Benedictines; Europe; against poison; the tempted; students

Notes on His Life

- Benedict was the son of a Roman noble.

- His twin sister, Scholastica, was a consecrated virgin and also became a saint.

- He fled Roman studies for solitude at Subiaco.

- A local monk, Romanus, gave Benedict the habit.

- His attempt to lead the monks of Vicovaro failed.

- He started twelve monasteries around Subiaco.

- He went to Monte Cassino for a new foundation.

- He wrote the *Rule of Saint Benedict.*

- He died while standing at prayer.

- His relics were moved to the monastery of Saint Benoit-sur-Loire, near Orleans, France.

- Pope Paul VI named him patron of Europe in 1964.

- In 1980 Pope John Paul II named him co-patron of Europe with Saint Cyril and Saint Methodius. There are also three female patron saints of Europe: Bridget of Sweden, Catherine of Siena, and Edith Stein.

Lesser-Known Facts

❦ Benedict was never ordained a priest.

❦ He based his rule on one written by Saint John Cassian.

❦ The popularity of his rule among religious led to Benedict's title as Father of Western Monasticism.

❦ At Monte Cassino he destroyed the temple of Apollo and built a monastery.

❦ His earliest biography is found in book II of *Dialogues* by Saint Gregory the Great, written in the late sixth century.

❦ Some monks of Vicovaro tried to poison Benedict, but his blessing broke the cup.

❦ Another time, a raven snatched poisoned bread from his hand.

❦ Common symbols of Benedict are the crosier, book, and raven.

❦ Anglican, Lutheran, and Eastern Orthodox communities also commemorate him.

❦ The Saint Benedict medal is popularly worn for protection against evil.

In His Own Words

"Therefore, whoever you are who hurry to your heavenly home, fulfill with the help of Christ this smallest of rules which we have written for beginners; and then, under God's protection, you will arrive at the heights of doctrine and virtue of which we have spoken."

— Rule of Saint Benedict, chapter 73

Venerable Pierre Toussaint

God's Provident Hand

"Beware of practicing your piety before others in order to be seen by them; for then you have no reward from your Father in heaven" (Mt 6:1).

Role reversal can be a very revealing game. It is an occasion to learn interesting things about oneself, things often hidden by daily circumstances. This proved true in the life of Pierre Toussaint. His role reversal, however, was not make-believe.

Although a slave, young Pierre Toussaint was able to live a comfortable life within his master's household. His mother, Ursule, was chambermaid for Mistress Bérard. He had free rein of the home and delighted his master's family with his games and dancing. Recognizing the child's intelligence and eagerness to learn, the Bérards saw to it that he was well educated and allowed to frequent the family library. In this way, Pierre grew up more of a servant than a slave, a member of the Bérard household.

One evening as he served at table, Pierre noticed a grave expression on Monsieur Bérard's face. This master was the younger Monsieur Bérard, who had very recently taken over the family's properties, and married a kind, aristocratic young woman. Unable to hold in his concern, Pierre moved close to his master and whispered to him.

"No, Pierre, I am not disturbed that you should ask me. Actually, there is bad news coming to us from the city."

Now everyone at table had ceased conversations to stare at Monsieur Bérard. What could this news be? True, the island of Hispaniola had felt the ripples from the French Revolution. Many plantation owners welcomed the revolution at first, seeing it as a chance to be free of French rule. But on Saint-Domingue, tensions rose between the ruling class and the free men who kept shops in town, who naturally wanted some of the rights and benefits gained by their equals in France.

"Tension is rising between the classes here," Monsieur continued. "I have heard reports of some violent incidents."

Madame Bérard stopped eating to ask, "Jean, what can this mean? What if it reaches us here?"

"Now, no need to be concerned," he said. "I have a plan." He turned to look at Pierre. "I have arranged for the immediate family to sail to New York. We have friends there." Then turning to his wife and seeing the questioning look on her face, he continued, "And they have offered to rent us their home, fully furnished. I was going to explain all this to you after dinner, my dear, but as the opportunity just arose, here we are in the middle of it unexpectedly. I fear this is a bit of a shock for you. Forgive me."

Quickly composing herself, his wife replied, "Oh, Jean, there is nothing to forgive. Thank you for preparing things so quickly. When are we leaving? We will have so much to do."

"I want us to depart on the next ship, my dear. You only need help to prepare your personal things. We will stay away for as long as the danger lasts here, but I am certain it will only be a few months, perhaps a year. It is a matter of prudence."

Unable to hold back his thoughts any longer, Pierre anxiously asked, "Master, we could be of assistance, especially to Madame. . . ."

"Oh, yes, Pierre. I am forgetting. I want you and your sister and aunt to come with us. It will be a comfort to Madame Bérard." Turning in his wife's direction, he added, "Isn't that right, my dear?"

"Yes, yes, Jean. We will start our preparations tomorrow morning."

Once the family was settled in New York among other prominent French families, life fell into a comfortable routine. This appearance of normality, however, came to an unexpected end when a courier brought news of Monsieur Bérard's sudden death. He had returned to Saint-Domingue to check on his estate. The difficult conditions and the tension brought on by the violence still raging there caused him to fall ill with pleurisy. He could not obtain proper care on the island, and the end had come quickly for him.

As Pierre closed the front door, he directed his sister, "Rosalie, help Madame be seated and then please bring her some scented tea."

"Oh, Pierre, he was to come back shortly," the young widow cried. "In his last letter Monsieur Bérard said the situation was very bad, but he was well and coming home. What will become of us now?" She buried her face in her hands and wept.

Toussaint knew a little of the family's situation and he could imagine the full weight now falling on his beloved mistress. "Madame," he assured her, "we are here to assist you however you wish. The master must surely be safe in God's kingdom. He was such a kind man."

Not long after this sad news, Madame Bérard approached Pierre carrying a small packet. She pressed it in his hand with these instructions, "My faithful Pierre, would you please bring these pieces to the jeweler. Be very discreet, but ask him for forty dollars. A certain bill has come due."

"But, Madame, are you sure? These are some of your favorite pieces and surely they are worth much more."

"Please, Pierre. We are in need. I am afraid the master was unable to secure any more money from his estate in Saint-Domingue. Tell the jeweler we need at least forty dollars."

"I am on my way, Madame," Pierre replied. However, he did not go to the jeweler's shop, but instead, to his own room. After some time, he returned carrying two small packets. When he handed the first to Madame Bérard she found exactly forty dollars. When Pierre handed over the second packet, his mistress was astonished to find it contained the pieces of jewelry she had entrusted to him earlier.

"Pierre," she began to reprimand him, "how did you?"

"Madame, please do not be upset that I did not exactly follow your instructions. Since the master arranged for me to learn hairdressing, I have been saving my tips. Let me contribute this small sum for the good you have always done for me and Rosalie."

"Thank you, my dear Pierre. This is all too much for me, you know." Suddenly she stood up and said to Pierre, "Could I entrust to you the household bookkeeping? You are so meticulous and I know you will be discreet."

The young man was taken aback, but he assured his mistress that he would be honored to serve in this way.

Madame Bérard had indeed done herself a favor by turning her accounts over to Pierre. Unknown to her, he filled in for all she lacked from his own funds. His reputation as a hairdresser and stylist had spread rapidly. The most fashionable ladies recommended him to friends. He kept up on all the latest trends, and become a creator of fashion in his own right.

In addition to his talent, Pierre was valued as a confidante by many of his clients. He would arrive almost on command, work miracles with coiffeurs, and entertain with lively conversation. Best of all, Pierre was as discreet as a confessor. He never indulged in even a hint of rumor or gossip. And from his payments he provided for the upkeep of Madame Bérard's household. He continued to do so even after she remarried years later.

Besides keeping up the appearance of stability for his mistress, Pierre would try to contrive ways to elevate her spirits when she became depressed. Some evenings he would return from his rounds of hairdressing and arrange for a small supper party for her friends. He would prepare all the things needed, deliver the invitations, and serve at table himself. Other days he would pick up a treat for Madame, something to surprise her and bring a smile to her troubled features, be it a little box of chocolates, a fragrant bouquet, or even a single rare flower that he would work into her hair.

The day came when Madame Bérard succumbed to illness. As she lay on her deathbed she called in her husband, Gabriel Nicolas, and her lawyer.

"I must do something that my first husband and I had discussed years ago. Before I die I want to have the legal papers written up that will grant freedom to my faithful Pierre," the dying woman declared. And so, in his grief following the death of his beloved Mistress, Pierre had the joy of knowing he was a free man.

One of the first things that Pierre did in this new state was to ask for the hand in marriage of the young woman, Juliette Noel, twenty years his junior, a woman whose freedom he had purchased earlier. They complemented each other perfectly and shared a life rich in charitable works. In the years ahead, Toussaint described Juliette as "the most beautiful woman in New York."

At the early death of his sister Rosalie, the Toussaints adopted her infant daughter, whom they named Euphemia. She was the delight of the couple. Unfortunately, she died of tuberculosis at fourteen.

Still, the life of Pierre and Juliette was happy, and although not blessed with children of their own, they found great satisfaction in taking in orphan boys for whom they provided a safe home and the opportunity for a successful life. The boys were taught manners, personal hygiene, and responsibility, as well as a trade. Pierre introduced many of these young men into the households of his clients, where they became valued servants.

One day Toussaint heard of a new project. Madame Larue, a woman he knew, intended to sponsor an orphanage for the growing number of homeless children walking the streets of New York.

"I believe I can help her," he told Juliette.

"But, my dear Pierre, we already have our own boys to care for. How can you even imagine taking on any more?"

"You are right, of course, Juliette. We do have the boys to think about. But, I have many wealthy clients and I already visit them regularly."

"You are a genius!" exclaimed Juliette. "You will ask your clients for donations. . . ."

"Yes," Pierre continued her thought. "I will then deliver their gifts to the sisters to whom Madame Larue will entrust the children."

Together with Juliette, Pierre carried out constant charitable works, including helping to fund the building of the
original Saint Patrick's Cathedral.

As his professional life proceeded, so did his religious
practice. As a black man, Pierre was unable to ride the public
transit system of New York; however, this provided him many
opportunities to do acts of charity. He could also pay visits to
the churches he passed in his travels. He had made it his
practice to attend daily Mass and to receive Communion
often, as well as pray the Rosary—a practice he kept up for
more than sixty years.

As Pierre Toussaint lay dying, a visitor asked if he wanted
anything. Smiling, he replied, "nothing on this earth."

Prayer

Dear God, we thank you for the luminous example of
   Venerable Pierre Toussaint.
He was a man of prayer and reflection who could easily
   have become embittered
by his fate as a slave, or even despondent at the burdens
   life placed on him.
Death robbed him of all those he had loved,
yet his heart remained joyful because he lived for you.
Give us eyes to see the needs of others, ears to hear
   their cries,
and hearts to comfort and console them.
Like Venerable Pierre, help us to be discreet and
   generous
friends toward all, especially the poor. Amen.

About Venerable Pierre Toussaint

Born: 1766 (or 1781) in Saint-Domingue (present-day Haiti)

Died: June 30, 1853, in New York

Feast Day: June 30

Declared venerable: in 1996, by John Paul II

Patron: hairdressers, Christian charity, philanthropists

Notes on His Life

✿ Born in 1766 (or 1781), Pierre was the son of Ursule, a slave of the Bérard family in Saint Marc, Saint-Domingue (present-day Haiti). Although 1766 has been a commonly accepted date of birth, more recent studies indicate 1781 is a more probable date; see *Pierre Toussaint* by Arthur Jones (New York: Doubleday, 2003).

✿ The Bérards taught him to read and write.

✿ In 1787 he accompanied Jean Bérard du Pithon, his master, to New York.

✿ There he was apprenticed to a famous hairdresser.

✿ Pierre supported Bérard's widow and her household when they were in need.

✿ He purchased the freedom of his sister, Rosalie, and his fiancée, Juliette Noel.

✿ On July 2, 1807, he was granted freedom.

✿ In 1811 he married Juliette.

✿ In 1815 his niece, Euphemia, was born to Rosalie.

✿ When Rosalie died, Pierre and his wife took in Euphemia, and cared for her until she died at the age of fourteen.

✿ In 1851 Juliette Toussaint died.

⟨❧⟩ He is buried in a crypt below the main altar in Saint Patrick's Cathedral in New York City.

Lesser-Known Facts

⟨❧⟩ For sixty years, Pierre went to daily Mass and prayed the Rosary at Saint Peter's on Barclay Street.

⟨❧⟩ He was a philanthropist and an accomplished violinist. He taught French, dancing, and manners to many children.

⟨❧⟩ He gave foster care to many boys, educating them and placing them in jobs.

⟨❧⟩ He personally attended the sick and dying throughout the city.

⟨❧⟩ As a black man, he was banned from public transportation and instead walked everywhere.

⟨❧⟩ In 1854, his first biography was published: Hannah Farnham Sawyer Lee's *Memoir of Pierre Toussaint, Born a Slave in St. Domingo.*

In His Own Words

"Madam, I have enough for myself, but if I stop work, I have not enough for others."

Saint Teresa of Avila

Human and Holy

"But when you fast, put oil on your head and wash your face, so that your fasting may be seen not by others but by your Father who is in secret; and your Father who sees in secret will reward you" (Mt 6:17–18).

On a warm, sunny day in the summer of 1530, the spacious home of Don Alphonso de Cepeda rocked with the laughter and merriment of his eleven children, eight nieces and nephews, and countless in-laws and friends. Maria de Cepeda, Don Alphonso's oldest daughter, had just been married. Everyone rejoiced with music, song, and dance. Gleeful little ones, always ready for a party, scampered up and down corridors, darting in and out of the ballroom and the dining hall, while the elegantly dressed men and women speculated on love, politics, and fortunes. Blushing couples swirled to the rhythmic swells of lutes, harps, and harpsichords.

Don Alphonso smiled as he surveyed the grand scene. It had been very hard to smile this past year and a half since he had lost his charming wife, Beatriz. She had been so good, so beautiful, so efficient, and so youthful. His consolation was that Beatriz lived on in her children!

A burst of laughter freed Don Alphonso from his sad thoughts. A twitter of excitement rushed through the room as another of his daughters entered it. Teresa's jet-black hair fell to her shoulders in soft curls, accenting her fair complexion and flushed cheeks. Her luminous eyes danced with laughter and lit up her full, oval face. She wore a modest gown of bright orange, bordered with black velvet bands. With all the grace of her fifteen years, she glided across the floor, curtsied, and kissed her father's hand. A group her own age then rushed her off to a corner of the ballroom to enjoy her wit and bubbly personality. Though also gentle and gracious, the young girl thrilled everyone with her vivacity, warmth, and generous efforts to please.

Don Alphonso watched Teresa for a few moments. His eye narrowed and his face clouded when another young woman joined Teresa's group. At that moment Maria, standing by her father, said, "I wish our cousin was not such a frequent visitor. She is lightheaded because of all the novels she is so fond of reading. I suspect she is passing them on to Teresa."

Sadly, Don Alphonso had to agree. That silly girl was exerting a bad influence on his fifteen-year-old daughter. "Yes, Teresa has changed considerably in these past months. She's becoming vain and frivolous, spending hours in empty talk."

Maria wished her younger sister would remember better the example of her lovely mother. "I don't think Teresa even realizes how often she compliments herself on her good qualities and talents. That is not an attitude she learned here at home, Father.'"

Don Alphonso pondered the matter for several days and reached a decision. Teresa would attend a boarding school.

Although at first hostile to the idea of being so restricted, the high-spirited girl eventually calmed down. She spent a year and a half with the Augustinian sisters and profited so much from their wise guidance that she began to pray to know God's will for her. How would she safely reach salvation?

"Just not a monastery, dear Lord," she prayed. "Anything, but that . . . oh, but I don't want to get married, either."

Fear of a perpetual commitment paralyzed her in indecision for the next four and a half years. During that time she became the efficient mistress of the de Cepeda home. Indeed, she was not as dedicated to her faith as she was to her household. Finally, no longer able to stand the turmoil in her soul, Teresa decided the best thing was to enter the Carmelite convent.

"Antonio, you have to help me," Teresa whispered to her brother. "I really do want to enter the Carmelite monastery, but Papa said no."

"Yes, I overheard your conversation with him. 'Not while I'm still alive!' he said."

In her heart of hearts, Teresa felt no attraction to the Carmelite way of life, but she was convinced that it would be the safest and surest way for her to save her soul. By the time word reached her father, Teresa had already received the habit. At the sight of her clothed as a Carmelite, Don Alphonso gave his consent and settled the dowry.

Despite several bouts of illness, the life seemed to suit her. The mitigated rule of sixteenth-century Carmel allowed for a comfortable life with no great demands. Teresa found herself happily spending hours in the parlors, talking with an endless stream of visitors and relatives. These empty, secular conversations soon riddled her prayer life with distractions. She had come to desire prayer, yet did not feel worthy to pray because of her love for the things of the world. And instead of detaching herself from these things, she just stopped praying. This precarious situation lasted for some time.

One day, Teresa was called to the parlor. As she stepped in to greet her guests, her face blanched. She looked beyond her startled guests and stared into the eyes of Someone they couldn't see. The stern, reproachful gaze of Christ threw her soul into confusion. Teresa blinked hard and mumbled under her breath, "I certainly have a very strong imagination." And then she dove into her conversation.

After the visitors left, Teresa walked slowly down the corridor to her cell. The relentless chiding of her conscience cut her deeply. She realized God was trying to tell her something, and she knew exactly what he wanted. Still, she did not make the necessary break.

Although her interior life was far from perfect, Teresa did practice an admirable charity toward her sisters in religion. She never uttered an unkind word and would never permit anyone to speak ill of others in her presence. She hid her interior turmoil under a mantle of characteristic wit and cheerfulness. She wasn't a bad sister; she just didn't want to give herself completely. After all, it was hard to give up everything! "What about fun?" she moaned to herself. "What about the great conversations we have here? I can't stifle my personality, can I?"

Sometime later, as Teresa was again walking down the corridor she passed a painting. It was not a new one, nor was it strange in any way. It was in the hall temporarily, on its way to another room. Suddenly Teresa stopped, rooted to the spot. Tears welled up in her eyes as she stared at that picture of Christ covered with the wounds of his passion. Her heart crumbled with remorse as she thought of those wounds and of her ingratitude. She sunk to her knees and began to sob uncontrollably. "My Jesus," she begged, "Strengthen me once and for all. I never want to offend you again."

However, eighteen years of mediocrity could not be overcome in one day. Teresa knew that her Spouse desired that she give up once and for all her idle moments in the parlor in order to converse with him and communicate to others what he taught her. Finally, she had given in completely to her God!

In order to live what she preached, she chose the most humble tasks for herself. Cheerfully and with real energy, she cooked, sewed, swept the dirtiest places in the yard; performed small, unnoticed services for her sisters; and fulfilled many hidden penances and prayers. At first glance, she seemed almost the same Teresa, but there had been total renewal of the inner Teresa.

Holiness does not destroy nature, but perfects it. For twenty years, Teresa worked hard to elevate and supernaturalize that affectionate disposition she was known for in her youth, and to be always meek and amiable. Her personality was a delightful blend of firmness with tenderness, lively wit, and imagination, with uncommon maturity of judgment.

In the midst of her own spiritual renewal, Teresa realized that God was asking her to undertake a more universal task. How would the nuns be able to live solely for God in the Carmelite convents, as material as they had become? As these thoughts steeped within Teresa, she made the acquaintance of Peter of Alcantara, who was in the process of a Franciscan renewal. He had set up a small house where the brothers tried to live the original rule of Saint Francis. Listening to his experience fortified Teresa's resolve. *We must purify our intentions and simplify our way of living*, she thought, *so the spirit of Carmel may thrive.*

From among her closest friends and relatives, who were her companions in the Carmelite convent in Avila, Teresa gathered a small group for her foundation. It took a number of months to obtain the necessary permissions to break away from their convent, but at last, in 1561, an old building was purchased and fitted out for the new convent of Saint Joseph. Many objections and stern warnings were issued; not least of these concerned the support for the new foundation.

"There are already too many monasteries," it was said. "Where do you propose to get the funds you will need?"

The new founder answered, "Teresa and three gold pieces aren't very much. However, Teresa, three gold pieces, and God—now that is everything! Our concern is not about what we will live on, but on how we will pray. If the community is one of fervor, people will not hesitate to give alms."

The humble little community began with the singular purpose of living the primitive Rule of Carmel. They would impose upon themselves silence, strict enclosure, and poverty in order to seek deeper prayer and union with God.

Under all kinds of trials and inevitable sufferings, Teresa was a picture of constant joy, patience, courage, and indomitable strength. Graced with an uncanny sense of humor, as well as intimacy with God, she had all the natural qualities of a leader and yet was a delightful mother to her spiritual daughters. She felt the sufferings of others more than her own. Many times she advised one of the sisters to relax her efforts at prayer. "God will lead us where he will. Be natural in your relationship with the Lord. Do not try to force contemplation. Just be open and attentive to God's presence," she counseled.

Teresa had indeed come a long way from the spirit of ease and pleasure that had marked her earlier years. "How great is the good which God works in a soul when he gives it a disposition to pray in earnest though it may not be prepared as it should be," she once said. "If a person perseveres in spite of sins, temptations, and relapses . . . our Lord will bring it at last—I am certain of it—to salvation. But one must be courageous in accepting suffering. Trials are a measure of God's love. Merit lies, not in visions and ecstasies, but in doing, suffering, and loving."

How often did Teresa herself lean on this conviction? God was leading her deeper into experiences of prayer. Visions and ecstasies became common occurrences, intermingled with days of physical suffering and exhaustion. God bore her up on the wings of mystical prayer and contemplation. But she remained always a realist. It is related that one day, sick and feverish, she traveled between two monasteries, bouncing along in an open carriage, drenched by rain. Suddenly the carriage lurched forward, dumping its occupants unceremoniously into a mudhole. As she struggled to get up, Teresa exclaimed to our Lord, "After so much suffering, Lord, this too?"

"My daughter, this is how I treat my friends," Jesus replied.

"Well," Teresa quipped, "that is why you have so few, my Lord!"

Teresa's friendship with God grew to the point of heroism. He required many sacrifices of such a chosen soul. By finally opening herself completely to God, Teresa made way for a wonderful plan of grace. With the support and collaboration of another Carmelite, Saint John of the Cross, Teresa led the ancient Order of Mount Carmel into a great renewal. Her own example spurred many other religious, both men and women, to return to that simplicity of life that enthroned God as the Center. The Discalced Carmelite tradition grew in the Church from the heart of this great woman of God.

Prayer

> Saint Teresa of Avila, Mother of the Carmelites and
>   Doctor of the Church,
> come to our assistance as we struggle in prayer.
> We long to feel the presence of the Lord, yet we
>   fear him.
> We romanticize mystical experiences, yet we are often lax
>   in our everyday duties.
> We dream of heroic exploits, yet we cannot bear
>   our share of aches and pains.
> Teach us the simplicity of prayer; teach us openness
>   and availability,
> generosity and love, so that our prayer will please
>   the Lord
> and become the joy of our lives. Amen.

About Saint Teresa of Avila

> *Born:* March 28, 1515, in Gotarrendura (Avila), Spain
> *Died:* October 4, 1582, in Alba de Tormes, Salamanca,
>   Spain
> *Feast Day:* October 15
> *Canonized:* March 12, 1622, by Pope Gregory XV
> *Patron:* headaches, those in need of grace, religious,
>   Spain

Notes on Her Life

⊗ She was born Teresa de Cepeda y Ahumada, the second child of Alphonso and Beatriz.

⊗ In 1528 her mother died.

⊗ In 1531 Teresa began boarding at the Augustinian convent of Avila.

⊗ She returned home in 1532 when she became ill.

⊗ Unable to obtain her father's permission to enter Carmel, she secretly joined Incarnation Monastery in 1535.

⊗ In 1536 she became a Carmelite novice.

⊗ She made her profession of vows on November 3, 1537.

⊗ Due to illness, she had to leave Carmel in 1538 but later returned.

⊗ In 1545 she received her first vision, and in 1555 her first great ecstasy and locution.

⊗ In 1558 the Inquisition suspected her of having diabolical illusions.

⊗ She began to plan the reform of Carmel in 1560.

⊗ She wrote many important spiritual works, including the *Book of Her Life* (1561), *Way of Perfection* (1562), the *Constitutions* (1567), *Soliloquies* (1569), *The Foundations* (1573), and *The Interior Castle* (1577).

⊗ She started the foundation of Saint Joseph in Avila on August 24, 1562.

⊗ On August 22, 1563, Teresa transferred to Saint Joseph.

⊗ Between 1567 and 1581 she began fifteen more foundations.

⊗ From 1567 to 1568 she began the reform of the Carmelite friars with Saint John of the Cross.

❧ She was elected prioress of the Incarnation convent in Avila in 1571, and the prioress of Saint Joseph in Avila in 1581.

❧ Pope Paul VI declared Teresa a Doctor of the Church in 1970.

Lesser-Known Facts

❧ She had a half-brother and half-sister from her father's first marriage.

❧ Her paternal grandfather, Juan de Toledo, was a Jewish convert to Christianity.

❧ At the age of six, she ran away with her brother Rodrigo, seeking martyrdom.

❧ Saint Francis Borgia, SJ, was her confessor in her early years.

❧ On the day after her death, calendars changed from Julian to Gregorian—October 5–14 were lost that year, so her feast is October 15.

❧ The greatest artistic representation of her is "The Ecstasy of Saint Teresa," a sculpture by Bernini.

In Her Own Words

"Let nothing disturb you,
nothing frighten you.
Everything passes,
only God will not change.
Patience alone gains everything.
If you possess God, you want nothing,
for God is enough."

Saint Katharine Drexel

The Banker's Daughter

"Do not store up for yourselves treasures on earth, where moth and rust consume and where thieves break in and steal; but store up for yourselves treasures in heaven . . . For where your treasure is, there your heart will be also" (Mt 6:19–21).

Kate Drexel, the daughter of the Philadelphia banker Francis Drexel, stood in the bright sunlight, staring down at the letter she had just read. So many images and events were whirling around in her head. She was a wealthy young woman with a world of possibilities before her. Her life was full of social engagements, fashionable balls, gala trips to Europe, not to speak of her many charities. But, for years Kate had wanted to enter the convent! She had longed to get off the relentless merry-go-round of life in high society in the elegant 1880s. She had finally wrung the permission from Bishop James O'Connor, her former pastor and spiritual mentor, who was now the vicar apostolic of Nebraska. Until now he had asked her to remain active in the life of the Church in Philadelphia. Now, in this letter, the bishop had relented. Her dreams of being a simple, ordinary sister spending her life in quiet prayer and service could begin, but. . . .

Kate shook off her thoughts and forced herself to rescan the letter's close handwriting. She again skimmed the beginning with all its prayerful greetings and politeness and focused on that thunderbolt of a paragraph:

> The more I have thought of your case, the more convinced I become that God has called you to *establish an order* to help the Indian and Black people. The need for it is clear to everybody. . . . You have the means to make such an establishment. God has put in your heart a great love for the Indian and the Negro. He has given you a taste and a capacity for the sort of business which such a foundation would bring with it. All these things point to your duty more clearly than an inspiration or revelation could. . .
>
> I was never so sure of any vocation, not even of my own, as I am about yours. If you do not establish the order in question, you will allow to pass an opportunity of doing immense service to the Church, which may not occur again. . . .

"I can't! I just can't!" Kate's heart pounded. Everything in her recoiled at the idea of founding an order. What about religious formation? Why, she didn't have the faintest idea of how a postulant should act, never mind how to establish an entirely new religious community! Besides, the whole thing might be one huge disaster; she might even do more harm than good. . . . The objections seemed to jostle one another into the foreground of her thoughts.

But there it was—the will of God—in Bishop O'Connor's own handwriting.

Really, it was her own fault. To say that Kate Drexel had long considered full-time dedication to the Native American and black population her mission in life was an understatement. In 1885, her father took his three daughters on a train tour of the Northwest. Kate was particularly impressed by the conditions of the Indian tribes. Because even government-sponsored programs had been cut, the people needed everything. The Bureau of Catholic Indian Missions became her favorite charity. She did all in her power to encourage others of means to make it theirs as well. Money from her family had already built missions and schools, obtained better housing, and raised educational levels. When on a pilgrimage to Rome, she had presented further desires and plans to the pope, begging him for missionaries for the black and Native American apostolate. And with his piercing yet fatherly gaze, Leo XXIII had leaned forward bearing a confidential, knowing smile.

"Why not become a missionary yourself, my child?" the Holy Father asked.

And here was Bishop O'Connor's letter saying the same thing. Suddenly the whole weight of her approaching responsibilities pressed on Kate's very being like a leaden yoke. Yet, this was what God wanted.

"Your will, not mine, be done."

With the guidance of Bishop O'Connor, Kate Drexel entered the Sisters of Mercy to prepare herself for what was obviously God's will, the founding of a new congregation.

Just a year later, in 1890, her dream seemed to be crumbling. Death snatched away her trusted spiritual father and friend, Bishop O'Connor. He had "gone to God," but that was little consolation to her. Still a novice, Kate, who had taken the name Mary Katharine, felt alone, completely alone. The bishop was gone. The work, the new community, the rule, the whole plan had been under his direction. She had counted on him, and bitter feelings of her own uselessness and helplessness flooded Sister Katharine's soul. The temptation came strongly, and it would keep coming back: "Give up, give up. Forget the whole idea."

She could enter the community where she was making her novitiate—an older, secure order. She could settle down to a normal religious life, as she had wanted to do in the first place. She hungered for that security. The future seemed like one great, dark unknown. Surely God would understand.

But the bishop's words rang clear; hauntingly clear: "If you do not establish this order, you will allow to pass an opportunity of doing immense service to the Church, *which may never occur again*."

This was God's doing, not hers. She had to go ahead.

On February 12, 1891, Sister Katharine made her first profession within her newly founded community, the Sisters of the Blessed Sacrament for Indians and Colored People. To the three religious vows of chastity, poverty, and obedience, she added a fourth—the dedication of her entire life to the service of the Native American and black people of America.

Young women began to flock to the new foundation. The Drexel family country home in Pennsylvania became the first convent. Years passed. The young community grew and its work expanded. To the Southwest, the mid-South and the deep South, then east and north went Mother Katharine's spiritual daughters. Soon not only the sisters, but all those to whom she gave herself so generously knew that "Mother" was not merely a title for this remarkable woman. It was a way of life.

Indians of every tribe: Navajo, Pueblo, Osage, Cree, Choctaw, and Chickasaw . . . , African Americans across the country, from Philadelphia to the bayou settlements of Louisiana, from Georgia to the industrial cities of the North— all felt the warmth of her love.

For Mother Katharine, love was constructive. This woman of quiet dignity, whose former social life had introduced her to the whirlwind of city glamour, knew that what the elite of society and tourists see is one thing; what missionaries and the people they serve see is another.

When Mother Katharine sent her sisters to the great American cities, so rich in culture and traditions, she was keenly aware that the people who had created these masterpieces of cultural splendor came from varied backgrounds. She did not view America as a melting pot, but rather as a vivid mosaic, in which every color, every hue of tradition and race, brought out the beauty of the whole.

If fearfulness and hesitancy had marked the young socialite at the beginning of her work, a humble self-assurance and determination now characterized Mother Katharine as the founder of the order. When it came to accomplishing her community's mission, she was certain and strong.

Years matured her beautiful qualities—her gentleness, her compassion—and deepened the marvelous practicality and keen business sense the banker's daughter had inherited along with her father's fortune. Time had also deepened the overpowering love she felt for Christ in the person of his black and Native American brothers and sisters. It was this same love, fanned into flame year after year, day after day, that consumed itself in overcoming hatred, bigotry, prejudice and misunderstanding.

In the early years of the twentieth century, Mother Katharine purchased land in the South to establish a school for the education of black young people. The deed had already been signed and the papers processed when the former owner insisted on retracting the deal. He had been ignorant, he wrote vehemently, of the purpose the land was to be used for. He would give the money back, with the commission he had made, but he insisted that the land be returned to him.

In her simple dignity Mother Katharine wrote to him. She explained, clarified points, soothed. With the sharp insight of a banker's daughter and true businesswoman, she spelled out particulars, and she refused to back down. With the Christlike spiritual leadership that was distinctively hers, she pointed out that more than property was in question. "Temporal things, after all, are only to be valued inasmuch as they bring us and many others—as many as possible, to the same eternal joys for which we were all created," she said.

When the furor continued to rage, Mother Drexel held her ground with great kindness and humility, without rancor and with the firm determination that this was, after all, God's cause, not hers. God would have to provide. And he did. The matter was settled in her favor and the school opened, and with it the foundation was laid for Xavier University of Louisiana, dedicated to the education of African American students.

Kate Drexel would have smiled at the prospect of being considered a leader in the cause of civil rights. Yet almost single-handedly, without billboards or bumper stickers, without rallies or editorials, she waged a campaign for millions of emerging Americans. And noiselessly, steadily, she prevailed. Decades before they were spoken, she had made a life program of the words of Pope Paul VI: "Peace must be built: it must be built up, every day, by works of peace."

Sister Katharine was working for the cause of Christian brotherhood. And brotherhood is peace.

A remarkable American, a remarkable woman, Kate Drexel was equally remarkable as a religious. The vast chain of undertakings—the legal red tape,, mounds of paperwork, piles of statistics, and financial reports without end—never for a moment were those concerns allowed to obscure her vision of the goal: the glory of God and the good of his people. She was not always understood; her work frequently met public disapproval, even hostility. It didn't matter. As she wrote to her closest associates,

> . . . They can think of me however they wish. All that we are here to accomplish is the mission that God has entrusted to us. We want to fulfill his will quietly, without fanfare. Remember, Sisters, do not seek to be praised, because only God sees the heart. . . .
> We are here to do God's work.

For Mother Katharine Drexel, it was that simple.

Prayer

> Saint Katharine Drexel, in founding the Sisters of the
>   Blessed Sacrament
> for Native and African Americans, you not only gifted
>   the Church
> with a religious community dedicated to the education
> and betterment of the neglected and persecuted,
> but you also gave a living example of the preaching
>   of Christ.
> Jesus taught that his followers should not seek their
>   fortune in this life,
> and you, who were heiress to millions,
> sought ways to divest your wealth for the good of others.
> You surrendered your life to serve those in need as

Christ himself had done.
May we learn from the example of your long life
how to be detached from wealth and power, prestige and
   influence,
in order to place ourselves completely in God's hands,
willing to serve where there is need and to give freely
   when we are able.
Lead us also to a tender and confident devotion
to Jesus present in the Blessed Sacrament,
where we will find our true calling in love. Amen.

About Saint Katharine Drexel

Born: November 26, 1858, in Philadelphia as Catherine
   Marie "Kate" Drexel

Died: March 3, 1955, in Bensalem Township, Pennsylvania, of natural causes

Feast Day: March 3

Canonized: October 1, 2000, by Pope John Paul II

Patron: racial justice, philanthropists

Notes on Her Life

❀ She was the second daughter of Francis and Hannah
   (Langstroth) Drexel, millionaire philanthropists.

❀ Her mother died five weeks after Kate's birth.

❀ In 1859 Francis married Emma Bouvier.

❀ In October 1863 her sister Louise was born.

❀ Emma died early in 1882.

❀ Kate had a mystical encounter with Our Lady in November 1883.

- In September 1884 the family visited Indian Territory.

- Francis Drexel died in 1885, and his daughters inherited the family fortune, to be given to charity at their deaths.

- In 1887 Kate received an invitation from Leo XIII to become a missionary.

- In 1889 she entered the Sisters of Mercy with the intention of founding a new community for Native American missions.

- Sister Mary Katharine Drexel made her first profession on February 12, 1891, and was introduced as the Founder of Sisters of the Blessed Sacrament for Indians and Colored People.

- In 1902 she left to start the first foundation in Arizona.

- In 1913 the Rule of Sisters of the Blessed Sacrament was approved.

- In 1915 Xavier University was begun in New Orleans.

- Some sixty missions and schools were established and maintained by her order.

- In 1935 Mother Katharine had a heart attack and spent the next twenty years in retirement and prayer.

- She died at ninety-seven and was buried in the chapel at the motherhouse in Bensalem, Pennsylvania.

Lesser-Known Facts

- Kate and Elizabeth joined Kate's stepmother in teaching Sunday school to workers' children at the Drexels' summer home.

- The Drexel family often traveled extensively around the United States and Europe.

- After the death of her parents, the three Drexel sisters continued their parents' charitable works.

- Bigots threatened to blow up the motherhouse being constructed for the Sisters of the Blessed Sacrament.

- At her death there were five hunderd sisters in her order.

- Contemporary tabloids called her "the world's richest nun."

- In 2000 she became the second American-born saint.

In Her Own Words

"My sweetest joy is to be in the presence of Jesus in the holy Sacrament. I beg that when obliged to withdraw in body, I may leave my heart before the Blessed Sacrament. When after benediction the priest locks the sacred Host in the tabernacle, I beg Jesus to lock me in the tabernacle until morning."

Blessed Franz Jägerstätter

"I Will Not Serve!"

"No one can serve two masters; for a slave will either hate the one and love the other, or be devoted to the one and despise the other. You cannot serve God and wealth" (Mt 6:24).

As the mechanic watched, a motorcyclist roared over the bridge and into a big, powerful arch, screeching to a halt right next to him. The rider swung off the seat as he declared, "That was some ride. Thanks, Willie! It's been some time since I've taken a ride like that. You know how Franziska is about me and motorcycles."

"You're very welcome, Franz. Come by anytime and take a little 'test drive.' I won't tell your wife."

"She's all right, Will. It's just that she worries about me because of the girls. She doesn't want anything to happen to their papa," Franz said with a grin. "You know," he added, "that my father died when I was very young."

"Oh, no, I didn't know that, Franz."

"Yeah, the Great War. He was Franz, too. Franz Bachmeier. My mother says he was a nice man, but they never married."

"And you, my friend," Willie teased, "you are very married."

"Yes, I am. And very happily married," Franz replied. "I never realized how wonderful married life could be or I'd have done it sooner. It would have saved a lot of fretting by the folks here in town."

The two friends enjoyed this memory. As the bad boy of the little Austrian town of Saint Radegund, Franz had torn the place up on his motorcycle and with his partying and frequent fighting. But that was before he met Franziska, the love of his life. He often bragged that she made him who he was today. And it was all good: a devoted husband, doting dad, parish sacristan, and successful farmer.

"Say, Franz," Willie blurted out. "Did the German army call you up again?"

"No, Willie. Not a chance. I've got a deferment because of my farm. Everybody has to eat, you know," he joked.

"Just be aware, my friend," Willie said seriously. "They came back again for another friend of mine. They said the cause was more important than anything he was doing at home."

"Well, I'm not worried. And even if they came back, I'm not going to be a soldier. I refuse to even wear the uniform of the Third Reich," Franz declared. "And that's final!"

Franz reported for his mandatory military training in 1940, but was released to attend to his farm. Then he was called again, and released again. Finally, as his friend had feared, the call had come a third time. He was to report for induction on February 25, 1943, at Enns. The first person to know about this latest stroke of fate was his wife.

"My dear Franziska," he announced simply, languidly waving the envelope. "It has come."

Trying to keep her rising panic in check, Franziska embraced her husband. "No words, my love?" he whispered.

"Oh, Franz, I know what you will do. There is nothing I can say. I can only pray now."

"About what? Pray about what?" asked Franz's mother, Rosalia, who came in at that moment.

"Orders to report, Mother," replied her daughter-in-law. "Franz has been called up again."

"Let me see that paper, Franz," Rosalia demanded.

As he passed it to her, Franz pointed out that he couldn't get out of this. He would have to make the trip and face the ordeal he knew awaited him. "Mother, I can't just ignore it. Then they would come looking for me and I couldn't risk any harm coming to any of you on my account."

"Go to the church, then, and ask Father Fürthauer for help," the older woman urged.

As he headed toward the door, his two oldest daughters came rushing down from the second floor. "Papa, where are you going?" demanded six-year-old Rosalia.

"Yes, Papa, you just got home," chimed in Maria, the middle girl. "I need a kiss, Papa!" she pleaded. "And Rosa, too, and baby Aloisia, too . . . , but she's asleep now."

Unable to resist such sweet words, Franz turned from the door, but Franziska put one hand on his arm and raised the other to her lips. To the girls she said, "Shhh, now. Papa has to go out a moment."

Franz slipped out the door at that moment lest the little ones see his distress.

Father Fürthauer was the new parish priest at Saint Radegund and he felt his inexperience very painfully at this moment. "Oh, Franz, I know your reluctance. . . ."

"Not reluctance, Father. Refusal!"

"Yes, Franz, your refusal. And I understand your reasons, too, but I must . . . at least it seems better, to advise you to do your civic duty. You don't really have a choice, do you?"

"I do have a choice, Father. And I have made it."

"Please, think of your family, Franz! If you go against the authorities, what will happen to Franziska and the girls?"

Dropping both arms at his sides in an expression of dismay, Franz said, "I can't believe that by having a wife and children a man is then free to offend God by lying, and who knows in how many other ways as well. Didn't Christ tell us that 'he who loves mother, father, or children more than he loves me, isn't worthy of my love?'"

"No one is asking you to lie, my good sexton," the priest replied.

"But they are, Father," Franz continued. "Everyone wants a lie from me. Everyone wants me to serve a government that is a lie, in an army that is a lie, for a cause that is a lie! I will not serve this evil regime!"

His pastor tried one more tack, "Then please, Franz, try to seek out the advice of some other priests."

"All right, Father. I will have to set out soon, but I'll stop along the way. I promise. You know I don't want to abandon my family, either, but I see no other way in conscience." As he turned to take his leave, Franz said, "Father, one clarification. Not everyone wants me to lie. My Franziska understands my reasons. She accepts what I must do . . . at least as far as her heart will let her accept it."

"You are blessed, Franz. Truly you are. God be with you," the priest said as he watched his sexton head back toward his house.

Several days later, Franz had said his sorrowful goodbyes to family and friends. As he had promised Father

Fürthauer, he stopped in at another parish, and he also went to see Bishop Fliesser in Linz. Unfortunately, neither was familiar with Jägerstätter, nor was either very welcoming. It is believed they hesitated from the fear that this man with the unusual questions might be a plant of the National Socialist Party sent to trap them. Franz realized their fear, too, and this is how he excused them in a letter home. "Do not be bitter toward the bishop and the priests. They are only human, after all, and they must be much more cautious than a single man has to be, for their responsibilities are much greater."

On March 1, 1943, wearing his determination on his sleeve, Franz arrived at the headquarters of his company. He was several days later than expected. He explained his stand to the authorities, "My religious convictions do not permit me to serve as a weapon-carrying soldier. I will willingly serve as a medic, however. But I will not fight as a Nazi."

"I'm sorry to inform you, Jägerstätter," the commandant barked, "but you do not make the rules. It is military service or prison. And that is your final choice!"

Franz Jägerstätter stood his ground. The commandant stood by his threat as well, and Franz was placed in temporary holding at a former convent. Here he suffered greatly from his decision, both mentally and physically. What had he done? Was he really crazy as many people thought? Didn't the people of his own town think of him as a religious fanatic? It was true he was a man of strong convictions. Not just strong convictions, he told himself, but *true* convictions. What was he to do? Turn over responsibility for his actions to the Führer? Now that would be crazy! No, he would remain true to his conscience, to what God expected of a believing man.

Several months passed before he was transferred to a military prison in Berlin-Tegel. Again, at his court-martial, Jägerstätter offered to serve in a medical unit, but he was refused and sentenced to death. It was now July 6, 1943. He dedicated all his remaining time to reflection and prayer. He thought of the Bible study he had done over the past few years—how the word had been his strength and how it was his true food now. This word, along with the occasional reception of the Eucharist and a photograph of his dear little girls were what sustained him.

His wife and the parish priest were allowed to visit, a last effort to "put some sense into his head," the authorities thought. The visit was bittersweet. Franziska could see the human pain of parting in his eyes, but she also saw the light of promised peace and eternal joy that strengthened her husband. He thanked her for their life together and begged pardon for causing her this suffering. He repeated his love to his daughters and the family back in Saint Radegund. The priest gave him the last sacraments and the blessing of the Church. He was alone again with God.

On August 9 Franz Jägerstätter was moved to Brandenburg, Germany, where he was beheaded.

Franz witnessed to the integrity of the Christian vocation of every man. He was not an educated man, beyond the village school, neither was he a man of exceptional religious devotion—but he was a man with the conviction of his faith, the boldness of hope, and the all-encompassing love that embraces God's will in all things.

Prayer

Blessed Franz, man of God, witness to conscience,
you freely stood before the men of this world and before
God,
accepting responsibility for who you were.
You were a man of peace and integrity
who willingly pardoned and who humbly sought pardon.
You were a man who knew the truth and generously
witnessed to it despite the cost.
You were a man of the Church who served your parish
selflessly.
And you were a Christian husband and father
who loved your wife and children tenderly and wholeheartedly.
Intercede for us, Blessed Franz, so that we may imitate
your wisdom.
Help us seek truth through the study of Scripture and
the teachings of the Church;
practice fortitude by relying on God's grace and prayer;
and live zealously through our contemplation of heaven.
Amen.

About Blessed Franz Jägerstätter

Born: May 20, 1907, in Saint Radegund,
Upper Austria
Died: August 9, 1943, (beheaded) in Brandenburg,
Germany
Feast Day: August 9
Beatified: October 26, 2007, by Pope Benedict XVI
Patron: conscientious objectors, family, youthful
conversion

Notes on His Life

❧ His natural father, Franz Bachmeier, died in the First World War.

❧ His unmarried mother, Rosalia Huber, married Heinrich Jägerstätter, a farmer who adopted Franz.

❧ Franz worked in the iron ore industry from 1927 to 1930.

❧ He abandoned the faith, and in 1933 he had a daughter out of wedlock.

❧ In 1936 he married Franziska Schwaninger. The couple honeymooned in Rome, and Franz's faith was restored.

❧ The couple had three daughters, born from 1937 to 1940.

❧ Conscripted for military service in 1940, Franz refused to serve an unjust cause.

❧ In 1941 Franz became the sacristan, or sexton, of Saint Radegund.

❧ In 1943 he declared himself a conscientious objector.

❧ He was imprisoned and tortured, and nearly lost faith. The love of his wife sustained him.

❧ He was transferred to Berlin-Tegel prison in May 1943.

❧ On July 6, 1943, Franz was court-martialed and condemned to death. He was beheaded at Brandenburg on August 9, 1943.

❧ On June 1, 2007, the Church declared him a martyr.

Lesser-Known Facts

❧ It was customary for a man to be known by the name of his property, so in his town Franz was called "Leherbauer," the hereditary name of his farm.

❦ He often carried a backpack of food for the poor.

❦ Twice Franz was relieved of military service because of his necessary occupation as a farmer.

❦ Only Franziska stood behind his decision to resist service.

❦ While in prison he wrote a number of commentaries on the responsibilities of Christians.

❦ He was comforted in his final imprisonment by the Bible, the Eucharist, and a picture of his daughters.

❦ In 1938 he alone in his village voted against unification of Austria with Germany.

❦ His reply to "Heil Hitler" was "Pfui Hitler" ("phooey" or "shame on you").

❦ On May 7, 1997, his death sentence was annulled by a court in Berlin.

❦ Jägerstätter is considered a prophet of Christian truth.

In His Own Words

"From my own experience I can attest how painful life can be when one lives Christianity only halfway. It is vegetating, not living."

Saint Thomas More

Lawyer on Trial for Christ

*"Enter through the narrow gate; for the gate is wide
and the road is easy that leads to destruction, and
there are many who take it. For the gate is narrow
and the road is hard that leads to life, and there are
few who find it" (Mt 7:13-14).*

It was July 1535. A great yet hushed crowd had
gathered to see him leave the courtroom.
Whispers of "guilty" and "death" filtered through
the lines. Hands reached out; voices were raised to
promise prayers, to thank, to encourage, to cry. But
Sir Thomas More had to turn all his attention to
the struggle of walking, something very difficult in
his weakened condition. He followed the guards
along the familiar route back to the dread Tower of
London.

From the throng a voice cried out above all the
others: "Father!" Meg rushed forward to cling to
her father—her confidant, her inspiration. She could
not see his face through her tears. She clung to him

with such strength he could not move on. He took her face in both hands and gazed for the last time on his beloved daughter.

Heart full, thoughts racing, crowding upon one another, he kissed her forehead. What could he say to her? How, in the end, could he say goodbye to his family? *My dearest ones— God's precious gifts to me. I've tried to be a worthy husband and father, but what father would leave his family like this? My Meg could understand best, but it is she who will suffer most.*

This was his real trial—far more fearful than the one before the court that had just condemned him to death.

I can't do it, Sir Thomas thought. *I can't leave them to the mercy of the king.* He looked into Meg's eyes, so full of fear. *But I can leave them to the mercy of God, from whom all fatherhood on earth takes its name,* he thought, as the guards pushed him to move on. But he resisted.

"Meg," he whispered quickly to his daughter, "don't be troubled. However bad it seems, nothing can come but God's will, and it will be for the best. I trust him. Farewell, dearest Meg—"

Surely he saw the answer, the understanding in her eyes as the guards tore her away from him?

Then, a second time, Meg broke from the crowd, pushed her way past the guards and kissed her father. Her tears still flowed, but she was smiling! He gave her his blessing and tried to say something, but the words stuck in his throat. Later that day—his last before his execution—he wrote to her, "I never loved you more than when you kissed me last."

Thomas More's devotion and delight in his family were remarkable for the nobility of his day. Thomas himself had grown up with a close, affectionate relationship with his father. As a young lawyer, More would kneel before his father for his daily blessing.

Nothing pleased the young lawyer Thomas more than an evening full of rollicking fun with his wife, Jane, and their four children, followed by quiet conversation, storytelling, and prayer. Theirs was a family of love, but sorrow cut short their blissful years. When their oldest daughter Meg was five years old, and baby John near his first birthday, Thomas's sweet-natured Jane died. Thomas carried this shock and sorrow for the rest of his life. On her tombstone he had written: "Dear Jane, Thomas More's little wife."

There would never be another Jane in his life—the love of his youth, the one who shared his most secret dreams. His second wife, Lady Alice, was practical, staunchly loyal, and kind in her own way. She was reserved in her manner, but generous in her devotion to her family. Soon enough it was not hard to call her wife and mother.

After King Henry VIII took the throne of England, Thomas rose quickly in the king's service: member of Parliament, member of the king's Privy Council, speaker of the House of Commons, and eventually, Lord Chancellor—the second most powerful man in England after the king. Now Sir Thomas More, he relished the opportunities to exercise his lawyer's skills and serve his country, but he regretted not having more time with his family.

The youthful king was delighted with the wit and sparkle that Sir Thomas lent to conversation. The king even got into the habit of "dropping by" the More home for dinner. The imposition got so bad—in fact, Thomas saw his family so little—that he decided to try his best to become "dull" so as to be less in demand. Eventually, Henry called upon him less as the king realized he was a family man, but Thomas More never did succeed in becoming a bore.

Life at court was anything but upright. Thomas More's integrity stood in startling contrast to many of the practices at court. His reputation grew among not only the king and the entire court, but also the poor commoners.

One day an elderly woman came to court to complain that her little dog had run away and been taken in by a wealthy lady. The poor woman lamented that whenever she tried to get the dog back, the servants refused to let her see the lady of the house.

"Well, just who is this good woman?" More asked. "Perhaps they will let me see her."

"She is the wife of the lord chancellor," the woman smiled sweetly.

Sir Thomas sent for his wife. Lady Alice and the dog appeared shortly. At one end of the room stood Lady Alice. At the other end, the old woman waited. The lord chancellor walked to the center of the room with the little dog wiggling in his arms.

"Now, whomever the dog goes to may keep it."

He set the puppy on the floor, and it dashed toward the old woman.

"It's yours," Thomas said cheerfully.

The old woman was so amazed at his kindness that she made a gift of the dog to Lady Alice.

The kindness of Sir Thomas was not reserved for those in need who constantly sought his help. His first and last thoughts were for his own family. Many cares weighed on him; his worries were those of a nation, yet he never aired his problems at home. Only to his oldest child, his beloved Meg, did he sometimes confide his hopes and fears.

With Meg, he had tried to explain why he could *not* sign the Act of Supremacy, which established King Henry head of the Church in England instead of the pope. With her, he had confided his schemes—if he dropped out of public office, if he retired to his estate, if he made no public outcry—couldn't the king forget about him? Wouldn't the king allow him to live a quiet life dedicated to his family, to prayer, and writing, for the sake of their friendship?

But it was not to be. King Henry seemed to need his one-time friend's approval even though it be forced from him: isolation, imprisonment, trial, and now sentence of death.

Of all his sufferings, the most acute for Thomas was not the prison confinement, which he considered a gift to be able to prepare for death, nor the interminable interrogations, nor even the humiliation of being tried in court by friends and acquaintances over whom he had once held authority. The suffering that had broken his heart was that those dearest to him—his own family—did not really under stand his reason for dying.

Thomas didn't expect the practical Lady Alice to agree with his conviction and refusal to swear to the Act of Supremacy. She admired his virtue, but could not understand his holy stubbornness in refusing to act by human standards rather than God's. He understood that she feared what would happen to his children and herself after his death. When she pleaded with him to give in and come home, his answer was always the same: a gentle yet firm "no."

It was Meg whom he'd expected would understand. Of the few visitors Sir Thomas was allowed in prison Meg was allowed in more frequently than anyone else. The first time she actually saw her father behind bars and realized the seriousness of the situation, she cried and begged—really begged—her father to sign the act that declared Henry VIII supreme head of the Church of England. Words, usually at his instant command, failed him. Persuasive arguments reached only as far as his lips and then froze in icy silence. Only after she left did he break down, and muffled sobs filled the cell.

His pen dipped into his soul as he wrote to her: "None of the terrible things that might happen to me touched me so grievously as to see you, my well beloved child, in such piteous manner, labor to persuade me about the thing which I have of pure necessity, for respect for my own soul, often given you so precise an answer."

He had learned to pray from his own devout father, and it was to prayer that he turned night and day. God alone became his source of consolation, of much-needed strength to bear the trial that awaited him.

Though a lawyer, he did not consider himself fit to judge the consciences of others. He never questioned the integrity of those who did sign the act. "They have their conscience," he would say, "and I have mine." Remarkably, he held no grudge against those he encountered during his imprisonment and trial, nor against the king. He consistently repeated his desire for Henry's well-being.

On that fateful day in July, he faced his judges with his conscience at peace. Slowly and solemnly they pronounced his sentence: "Guilty . . . death!"

"I forgive you," replied the defendant with a sincerity that moved everyone in court. "I forgive you as Stephen forgave Saul. And just as now both are holy saints in heaven and shall continue there friends together forever, so I trust and pray that, though Your Lordships have been on earth my judges of condemnation, we may meet hereafter merrily together in heaven."

Thomas accepted his death sentence with such calm, it is surprising to know to what degree he feared death. He confessed to Meg that his fear of death was far greater than it should be for a Christian. But by the grace of God, his natural fear remained concealed beneath his sparkling wit.

As Thomas was led to his execution, he took comfort in knowing that Meg understood. Chiding the executioner to do his job well lest he lose his reputation, Thomas placed his neck upon the block. Then, to the astonishment of all, he stopped the executioner with a sudden exclamation. And drawing aside his beard so that it might escape the axe, Thomas said, "Spare this, for it has committed no treason."

At the end, he most eloquently explained his choice in his last words—for Meg, for Lady Alice, and for all the world who would grieve the loss of so holy and brilliant a man: "I die the king's good servant, but God's first."

Saint Thomas More—beloved husband, father, martyr for the faith—has rightly been called a man for all seasons. He chose to follow the narrow path, the path to which God had called him—the path of fidelity

Prayer

Saint Thomas More,
you used the gift of your mind to see clearly
beyond the mirage of success and admiration
to live what is most precious:
integrity, conscience, fidelity to Christ,
the Church, and your family.
In our time, the Church is misunderstood and devalued,
and integrity seems less important than appearance.
Give us the courage to stand in the truth of Christ
and to be faithful to the Church's teachings
both when popular and unpopular.
Help us to give prayer more importance in our daily lives

so that we have the strength to do what is right,
to treasure what is most important,
and to be faithful witnesses to the Gospel,
no matter the cost. Amen.

About Saint Thomas More

Born: February 7, 1477 or 1478

Died: July 6, 1535

Feast Day: June 22

Canonized: 1935, by Pope Pius XI

Patron: lawyers, politicians, civil servants, adopted children, widowers, stepparents, difficult marriages, large families

Notes on His Life

✿ Born the son of a lawyer, John More.

✿ Educated at Oxford and known for his brilliance, he studied law and literature, and continued writing and studying all his life.

✿ Married in 1505, Thomas and his wife, Jane, were very happy and had three daughters and a son. After Jane died in 1511, Thomas referred to her as "dear little wife."

✿ Thomas married again almost immediately to Lady Alice, a widow who capably managed the household and cared for his children.

✿ Even while he was a great success at court, Thomas sought to spend as much time with his family as possible without neglecting his duties.

✿ As a judge, Thomas was known for his impartiality and integrity.

❦ Thomas believed strongly in the education of women, and he gave his daughters the same education as his son.

❦ Thomas was at the height of his career when King Henry VIII decided to divorce his wife and, because the pope did not approve, declare himself head of the Church of England. Thomas immediately sought to resign.

❦ Due to the king's previous favor and Thomas's prudence – including his complete silence on the "great matter" of the king's divorce, Thomas was kept from earlier imprisonment and execution.

Lesser-Known Facts

❦ As a young man, Thomas initially discerned between a calling to religious life as a monk or civil service. Though he eventually chose the life of a civil servant, he continued the monastic practices of prayer and fasting throughout his life.

❦ Thomas was an immediate success in law, but offended King Henry VII, who retaliated by putting Thomas's father in jail. Thomas left public life, but returned to it after Henry VIII became king and quickly recognized his gifts.

❦ Thomas confessed that he feared death greatly, more greatly than a Christian should. But he seemed to find strength during his time of imprisonment, which he considered a blessed time for spiritual growth.

❦ Thomas was a prolific writer, and many of his writings can be read today, among them: *Utopia, Dialogue of Comfort Against Tribulation, Treatise on the Blessed Body* [the Eucharist], and *Treatise on the Passion.*

In His Own Words

"Whatever follows lies in the hand of God . . . take no thought whatsoever shall happen me. For I verily trust in the goodness of God."

— Letter written while in prison to his daughter Margaret

Saint Philip Neri

He Played the Fool

"To what then will I compare the people of this generation, and what are they like? They are like children sitting in the marketplace and calling to one another, 'We played the flute for you, and you did not dance; we wailed, and you did not weep'" (Lk 7:31–32).

A long, winding procession of three thousand people made its way through the streets of Rome in the mid-1550s. Although pilgrimages were common, this was a strange one. It began as usual, with sermons and Mass, followed by music and magnificent choral singing. But midway along the route, everyone stopped at a certain estate, sat on the grass and had a picnic.

A priest approached the obvious leader of the group and asked, "What are you doing here? This isn't the right way to conduct a religious procession."

"Oh, my good Father," replied the man, "what better way is there to honor God than with a happy heart?" With the same confidence, he jumped up and led the seated people in an incredibly beautiful song. Halfway through the singing, everyone rose up and continued their merry pilgrimage. Over his shoulder the leader called out to the astonished priest, "We are rebaptizing the Mardi Gras parades. You are welcome to join us, Father."

Who was this strange man behind the pilgrimages—this man with a snow-white beard and sparkling blue eyes? Rome was never the same after his first appearance. Philip Neri was born in Florence, but came to Rome to study and make his fortune.

Philip Neri always had an engaging personality. As the years passed, he was drawn to the priesthood. Although it had not been his original inclination, he realized that by embracing the vocation of priest he could reach out to many more people of the great city.

Philip was constantly on the go, popping up at market stalls, in shops, at schools, in the city squares. He would strike up a conversation with anyone he met, beginning with, "Well, my good friend, when shall we start to do some good?" He would continue by talking about God and spiritual matters. Won over by his vivacity, teenagers, businessmen, paupers, nobles, and craftsmen, individually or in large groups, often followed him to his bare room to continue their conversations and pray together.

These spiritual conversations quickly led them to desire to lead better lives, and Philip urged his friends to go to confession, for a good confession was the beginning of a reformed life. Through the act of confession they would secure that all-important virtue of humility.

Conversations might go like this:

"Father Philip, I have sinned greatly. I am lost," the woman confided.

Philip answered, "Heaven is yours."

"No, Father, I am afraid I'm going to be lost."

"All right, I'll prove it to you that you won't be lost. Tell me, for whom did Christ die?"

"For sinners."

"And who or what are you?"

"A sinner."

"Well then, heaven is yours, because you are sorry for your sins."

Philip Neri made himself available to those who would confess their sins. One day, he was approached by a young man whose many sins left him without the courage to open up his heart. He just stood before Philip with a bewildered look.

"Come," the priest urged. "You'll feel better soon."

"Father, I've made mistakes so often. . . ."

"They will all be forgiven you."

"Maybe, but at the cost of how much penance?"

"Nothing exceptional, only this," Philip assured him, "every time you fall, come right back and put yourself in the state of grace."

The young man promised. He confessed himself, received absolution, and went on his way. But he returned almost at once, head down, humiliated.

Philip Neri comforted him and encouraged him once, twice, three times; always the boy returned with bowed head, weary and dejected. But then he began to return less frequently; the falls were becoming smaller and further apart. Finally, aided by grace and virtue, the young man was well on his way to being a good Christian.

Father Philip Neri's success was the fruit of his inventiveness. Not one to abide by the usual, the conventional, the "proper" way to do things, he followed one course alone—improvisation and spontaneity. Philip and his retinue would often rise before dawn and begin a pilgrimage to the major basilicas of Rome. Along the route they would be joined by countless new companions drawn by the singing and happy faces of the pilgrims.

Word of the meetings he held at the "oratory," as his residence was called, spread rapidly throughout Rome. Many distinguished people came to investigate what was happening, and ended up joining in. These included musicians and well-known singers, whom Philip invited to lend moments of relaxation between the sessions of instructions.

After several visits, Orazio Griffi, a papal singer, found himself enthusiastically explaining the phenomenon of the oratory to a fellow singer. "It is such an easy approach. It is a perfect way of exciting that necessary fear of God while instilling great love and confidence in his mercy. People are lured by the wonderful singing. Then they are blessed by the moving words of Father Philip's sermon, which they can reflect on during the next musical piece. This leads to confession and penance, the reception of Communion, and a desire to engage in works of charity. It is ingenious!"

But all was not sweet for Philip. Many in Rome suspected him of trying to form a new sect, or of aiming for high positions in the Church, and of course, some envied him for the good he was doing. This was a time of reform in the Church. Under some popes true holiness was promoted; under others fear and acrimony prevailed. Father Philip, accordingly, was misunderstood and even persecuted by several, and encouraged and blessed by others. At one point things grew so bad that Philip thought of abandoning his work in Rome and going to Milan, or to India as a missionary. But he was told by his superiors that his India would be Rome.

This knowledge reinvigorated his apostolic zeal. Although he spent his time preaching, teaching, and tending the sick, he was primarily a confessor, a man accessible to all at any time of the day or night. "Come anytime, my friend," he could be heard saying. "I am here from daybreak to noon. If no penitents come, I will use the time to pray, read, say the office, or recite the Rosary."

"And sometimes, Father, you are just out here in front of the church walking back and forth," a young man added.

"Oh, yes," Philip replied with a chuckle. "That is my way of advertising that the sacrament is available."

Many times he heard confessions into the wee hours of the morning. Years later, when he was old and sick and his disciples begged him not to tire himself by hearing so many confessions, he retorted, "I tell you that those of my penitents who are now most spiritual are the very ones I gained to the Lord by being always accessible, even at night."

At times he could be severe and stern with those more advanced in the spiritual life, but was most tender and compassionate with the weak and sinners. He said, "If you wish to go to extremes, let it be in gentleness, patience, humility, and charity."

"I really must insist on humility *and* cheerfulness, he said. "I want you never to commit sin but always to be cheerful and full of joy. It is much easier for a happy person to reach perfection than someone with a gloomy attitude."

To him a serene spirit was a sign of innocence, whereas self-love caused most unhappiness. To bring about this spirit of joy and humility in his penitents, Philip would prescribe extraordinary penances, ludicrous ones that would help his disciples make fools of themselves for the love of God as he himself did. In fact, the more he found himself esteemed by men, the more Father Neri made himself ridiculous. His oratory became known as the school of Christian mirth.

Philip would go to any length to make others think less of him. When meeting notable persons, he would dress in odd ways, such wearing his clothes inside out while being half shaven, or wearing long white shoes. He might walk down the streets while piously carrying a handful of brooms. He would stop once in a while in a very conspicuous spot to smell them, as if to enjoy the fragrant scent! He would do anything to make people think he was foolish.

Through severe penance and constant prayer, Philip Neri attained great heights of holiness and contemplation. But although mystical and ecstatic, he was always at anyone's beck and call. He was the most sociable contemplative the world has ever known, for he had discovered how to pray even when he was talking with the greatest vivacity.

Favored by God with ecstasies and visions, he tried in every way possible to prevent them. If he felt an ecstasy coming on, he would try to distract himself with a joke or some humorous act. "It is dangerous to place our trust in visions," he would say, "for it is by being a good person and a good Christian that one reaches heaven." By his laughter and comical antics, he tried to prevent people from discovering his own union with God and God's favors to him.

But still, people knew.

Saint Philip Neri always distrusted himself. Once when ill, he was heard to sigh, "If I get well, I intend to change my life. Ah, poor me, how many ignorant peasants and poor girls of the street will be far above me in heaven. Lord, beware of me today, lest I betray you. Let me get through today, and I shall not fear tomorrow."

But if Philip was stern toward himself, toward sinners he was gentle, even whimsical. Overcome with grief and sorrow, one man broke into uncontrollable sobs at the end of his confession. Philip let him cry, saying, "Go ahead and weep. God understands you are sorry. Didn't you ever cry on your father's shoulder? Well, let me embrace you in God's name." After some moments, Philip continued, "Now then, you must stop crying. You must rejoice because your sins have been forgiven. And I shall give you a special penance: You are to go the city square and stand there and laugh for one full minute. If anyone stops to ask what you are doing, simply reply that you are rejoicing because you are a son of God."

Finally the day came when Philip Neri met his Lord. It was Corpus Christi of 1595, and he had spent the better part of it in the confessional. At midnight one of the priests heard him tapping his cane on the floor. The priest rushed into Father Neri's room to find him sitting on his bed, very pale and stooped. With a weary smile the holy man announced, "It is time." After hearing the prayers for the dying and giving his blessing to his spiritual sons, Philip quietly breathed his last.

In his long life, Philip Neri made a great mark on the spirituality of the day by helping people seek God in joy.

Prayer

> Good Saint Philip, you were a true father to souls after
> the very heart of God.
> You went out to the street searching for the wanderer,
> in imitation of the Gospel father who welcomed home
> his straying son.

How many reluctant hearts returned to God because
of your generous and joyful spirit.
Make us serious enough about our own sanctification
that we take ourselves lightly.
And let us follow your example of availability and
ingenuity
so that anyone can find in us a willing guide
and a gentle companion on the road to the kingdom.
Amen.

About Saint Philip Neri

Born: July 21, 1515, in Florence, Italy
Died: May 26, 1595, in Rome
Feast Day: May 26
Canonized: March 12, 1622, by Pope Gregory XV
Patron: Rome, US Special Forces, the Oratory

Notes on His Life

❖ The youngest child of noble family, Philip received his early schooling from the Dominicans at San Marco Monastery.

❖ At the age of eighteen, he was sent to be an assistant to a wealthy uncle near Monte Cassino.

❖ In 1533 Philip had a religious conversion and moved to Rome.

❖ He became a tutor, then studied with the Augustinians.

❖ He cared for the poor, the sick, and the prostitutes of Rome.

- In 1548 he founded the Confraternity of the Most Holy Trinity of Pilgrims and the Infirm.
- Philip was ordained a priest in 1551.
- In 1556 he began the mission of the Oratory.
- In July 1575 he officially began the Congregation of the Oratory at Santa Maria in Vallicella, Rome.
- In 1587 he was elected superior for life.
- In 1593 he was instrumental in having Pope Clement VIII lift the excommunication of Henry IV of France.
- Philip suffered a hemorrhage and died on May 25, 1595, and he was buried in the church at Vallicella.

Lesser-Known Facts

- Called the Apostle of Rome, Philip was compared to Socrates, who traveled about engaging people in conversation in order to challenge them to better their lives.
- He desired to be a missionary to India.
- The most famous members of the Oratory are the 19th century contemporaries John Henry Cardinal Newman and Frederick Faber, who wrote the hymn "Faith of Our Fathers."
- Philip was modern and urbane, yet simple and pious.
- He wrote *laudi spirituali*, spiritual poems, that were put to music (called oratorios) and included in prayer services at his Oratory.
- He was canonized with Saint Ignatius of Loyola, Saint Francis Xavier, Saint Teresa of Avila, and Saint Isidore the Farmer.

In His Own Words

"Let every one stay at home, that is within himself, and sit in judgment on his own actions, without going outside to investigate and criticize the actions of others."

Saint Peter Claver

Slave of the Slaves

"Whoever gives even a cup of cold water to one of these little ones in the name of a disciple—truly I tell you, none of these will lose their reward" (Mt 10:42).

The harbor of the white-walled city of Cartegena, Colombia, steamed in a blanket of tropical humidity in the summer of 1616. Boards creaked as three men made their way up a gangplank. On deck, a swarthy sailor pointed to an open hatch. Slowly, the three men descended the ladder leading down into the dark recesses of the slave galleon.

As Father Peter clung to the ladder, a wave of heat and stench overwhelmed him. Dizzy and sickened, he prayed for strength as he continued his descent. His superior, Father Sandoval, preceded him. Just a few rungs above, Teodoro, their interpreter, followed.

Peter Claver reeled when he reached the bottom, where the odors stifled his breathing. Sweat poured down his face and he swallowed hard as his stomach churned with nausea. His thoughts shrieked wildly, "I need air—air!" He wanted to run back up the ladder. But shame shackled his feet. Had he not prayed for this opportunity to help the poor slaves?

Father Claver's eyes adjusted to the dim light and he faced a sea of human beings, lined up on different levels of shelves, all chained together. Ebony bodies—half starved, naked, bleeding, and feverish—stirred as the strange visitors approached. Peter looked long at their terror-stricken faces. Suddenly a thud and the jangling of keys diverted his attention. A sailor brushed by Father Claver, mumbling some sort of apology about the slaves still being fettered. They should have been loosened of their bonds before the padres arrived. . . .

In a corner, Father Sandoval was already bent over a lower-level bunk. He was pouring water on the head of a man whose labored breathing indicated death's approach. Father Claver crossed the room, knelt and joined Father Sandoval in prayer as the poor dying man breathed his last. "We came not a moment too soon," sighed Father Sandoval.

For the next two hours the Jesuits and their companion ministered to the men and women in the ship's hold. They washed their feverish, dirt-caked bodies, soothed their wounds, and slaked their thirst.

Although an interpreter was needed to communicate words, the unfortunate bondsmen and women understood the language of love silently spoken by the strangers. Father Sandoval gathered a small group around himself. He held aloft his large crucifix. Teodoro translated Father's simple statements: "This is Jesus Christ, who loves you very much and will take care of you. I, too, am your friend, and I will be back tomorrow, and I will tell you more about Jesus."

Grateful hands reached out to stroke the arms and garments of the two priests and their interpreter as the three turned to leave. Tears filled Father Claver's eyes. "This is probably the first compassion these poor people have experienced in months," he thought. Back on deck, a long draught of fresh air cleared his head. He timidly broached the question, "Father Sandoval, what do you feel every time you approach a slave ship?" Looking young Claver straight in the eye, the veteran missionary answered, "Son, every time I hear that another slave galleon has docked, and think of what I'll have to encounter, I tremble from head to foot."

A sense of deep reverence and awe filled Father Peter's heart. He prayed that he, too, could be so heroic!

The following year, Father Sandoval was transferred, and Father Claver took over the full responsibility of working among the black slaves. He felt apprehensive. He had only been an apprentice. How could he continue all alone in a task that never ended? More than ten thousand slaves spilled into the city every year!

"Father Rector," he ventured, "with your permission may I look for some slaves to act as interpreters? The language barrier is the greatest obstacle; they speak over sixty different dialects. . . ."

Permission received, Father Claver set out immediately to find helpers. Soon he had fifteen well-trained interpreters.

Despite the enormous task, not only would Father Claver meet the slaves on board ship, he would also accompany them to the filthy, one-windowed slave sheds where the poor Africans awaited market day. Torn from their homeland and loved ones, the men and women responded to Father Claver's love with gratitude. They could not doubt his love for them. His eyes soft with compassion, his body taut with fatigue, his hands calloused with work—all these proved that he loved them! Once

Peter Claver had soothed their aching bodies, he taught them about Jesus Christ, of his love for them, of his own life of hard labor, suffering, and execution on a cross. He told the slaves they were not alone in their misery, that although coerced to serve human masters, they could be children of God through the waters of Baptism. The often inhumane owners could never own their souls, never steal them from God's hands, nor rob them of their personal worth in God's eyes.

With eagerness and joy at this good news, most of the African natives embraced the new-found faith. Father Claver kept track of each of the baptized. He visited them on the plantations, in the prisons, and in the hospitals, and personally provided a decent burial for those who died.

After working among his beloved slaves for six years, he solemnly pronounced his final vows in the Society of Jesus on April 3, 1622. On the official document, he signed his name, "Peter Claver, slave of the slaves forever."

The days and months flowed into years. When Father Claver was in his mid-fifties, a young brother of the society, Nicholas Gonzales, was assigned to assist him in his work among the slaves. Nicholas was strong and generous. But his nature often recoiled at the prospect of making the daily rounds with Father Claver.

One exceptionally humid and still day, the horrifying thought of the filth, sickness, and misery filled Nicholas with loathing. He performed his duties of sacristan with hands that flew and a mind that raced even faster. *Maybe,* he thought, *if I just keep myself extra busy today, Father Claver won't call on me to accompany him. I can't do it any more!*

Suddenly, through the thin ceiling, Nicholas heard a familiar voice ring out from the room directly above. "Nicholas! Nicholas! It's time to go. Come and give me a hand with this pack."

Reluctance quickened Nicholas's pulse and bathed him in a cold sweat. *Oh, my, now what am I going to do?* he desperately asked himself, as he pushed open the door to Father Claver's cell. Father Peter did not raise his eyes, but Nicholas could see a smile playing on his lips.

As the brother handed the various herbs, medicines, sweet cakes, and trinkets to the priest to be packed, he thought, *how happy he is to go out everyday, and I. . . .*

Soon the two were making their way to San Sebastian hospital, Brother Nicholas's eyes riveted on Father Claver's face. *After so many years, how can a man keep on at this pace day after day with the same energy and enthusiasm?* he kept asking himself. *My own body constantly cries out with weariness and nausea. . . .* Their arrival at the hospital increased his anxiety, and he stared blankly into the eyes of the brother who answered the door. *Somehow,* he concluded, *love for others must make everything easier.*

Brother Nicholas decided that Father Claver was just so full of love that he didn't feel human weakness any more.

He must be some superhuman, untouched by selfishness or temptation, thought Brother Nicholas naively: *I wish I were made of the same stuff.*

Little did Brother Nicholas know then of the interior battles waged by his confrere. Only later, much later, would he dip into the soul of the "slave of the slaves" and glean something of Father Claver's heroic self-conquest. Father Peter Claver was no superhuman being. In fact he shuddered within himself at the repulsiveness of his tasks. He was sickened by his duty many times, but he did it anyway. Whenever he felt hesitation, he would increase his acts of mortification and humiliation. He had to conquer his weakness! He pushed on, praying intensely and reducing his sleep to the minimum, though often he dragged himself home, faint with exhaustion.

He sat in his stuffy confessional for hours on end, listening to confessions. He spent hours teaching catechism and traveling great distances—pleading, always pleading, for his dear slaves.

Many self-righteous men and even some members of his own community disapproved of Father Claver's activities. A tremendous wave of criticism threatened to submerge his work and bury it forever. Humbly, but fearlessly, Claver accepted what he felt was his due. Others could step on him, frustrate him, humiliate him, just as long as he could share a little in the fate of his brother slaves. Had he not vowed to be their slave forever? Had not Christ emptied himself, taking the form of a slave?

In the small notebook he always carried over his heart, he wrote: "I must imitate the donkey. How does the donkey behave? When slandered it keeps silent; when forgotten, it is silent; no matter how much it is pulled, kicked, or maltreated, it never complains. So must the servant of God be. I stand before you, my God, as your donkey." These dispositions in the former Spanish gentleman were the fruit of much prayer and effort.

In 1650, Father Claver embarked on his last journey, through steaming jungles and swamps. He returned to Cartegena racked with fever and barely able to stand. He had contracted the plague. Although his life was spared, the disease left him broken, with partially paralyzed hands and feet and a body that trembled from palsy.

For four long years, the intrepid missionary lay helpless in his bare cell. A young man, Manuel, was assigned as his nurse. Rough and inconsiderate, Manuel caused untold sufferings to the gentle old man. Before bringing the food tray to the invalid, he himself would eat the choicest parts of the meals prepared for Father Claver. None of the priests, not even faithful Brother Nicholas, knew of Manuel's mistreatment of their reverend confrere. But one day Manuel did not show up to help Father Claver dress to go to chapel. The patient pulled himself out of bed, fumbled and fell. Brother Nicholas heard the thud and ran upstairs, shocked and grieved.

"Wait until I get my hands on that Manuel and tell Father Rector how he neglects you!"

"No . . . no . . . please don't do that. The poor boy tries his best," pleaded Father Claver with tears in his eyes. "He mustn't be punished on account of me!"

Brother Nicholas knew it was useless to say anything more.

It deeply pained Father Claver to be so useless and to have others wait on him. Feeling that he could still do something, he requested and obtained permission to have some of the children come to his room to receive the sacrament of Penance.

"Ah, Nicholas," he remarked one day, "it is good for the old donkey to be in the harness again!"

Just before two on the morning of September 8, 1654, Father Peter Claver died without a sign or movement.

Word rushed through the city like a strong wind. Suddenly everyone remembered him! They seemed to see him again as he embraced terrified blacks in the ship holds and slave sheds, as he cared for the sick and dying, as he walked fearlessly among the lepers. For nearly forty years he had been a friend and a father to the slaves. And after a life of selfless dedication, he had been helpless and forgotten in his own last years. But now they remembered, and the world would always remember Saint Peter Claver, the slave of the slaves, forever!

Prayer

Saint Peter Claver, you were a man of great strength and
compassion,
unafraid of confronting the powerful in order to assist
those trapped in slavery.
You selflessly spent your energies of body and spirit
to raise
those crushed and humiliated to a level below personal
dignity and worth.
You tended the wounds of body and soul;
you applied soothing water to fevered brows
and bathed the willing in the waters of eternal life.
Raise our awareness of the dignity of all God's children,
and help us find ways to express this awareness in our
treatment of others.
Help us to deal lovingly with others,
especially those who are unable to respond to the love
we offer.
And from the Lord Jesus obtain for us hearts that see
and reach out
to break the bonds of sin that still afflict the world in
which we live.
Inspire us to serve wherever there is need. Amen.

About Saint Peter Claver

Born: June 26, 1580, in Verdú, Catalonia, Spain
Died: September 8, 1654, in Cartagena de Indias,
Colombia

Feast Day: September 9

Canonized: January 15, 1888, by Pope Leo XIII

Patron: slaves, racial harmony, Colombia, African Americans

Notes on His Life

❧ Peter was one of the four children of Pedro Claver y Mingüella and Ana Corberó y Claver. His father was a farmer and mayor of Verdú.

❧ His mother died when Peter was thirteen (two stepmothers followed).

❧ In 1596 he went to the university in Barcelona.

❧ Peter entered the Jesuits on August 7, 1602, and made his profession of vows on August 8, 1604.

❧ In 1610 he arrived in Cartagena, Colombia.

❧ He was ordained to the priesthood on March 19, 1616, and then worked as an associate of another Jesuit, Father Alfonso de Sandoval.

❧ Together they met each ship and ministered to the arriving slaves.

❧ At his final profession in 1622, he signed his vows "Peter Claver, slave of the Africans."

❧ He baptized 300,000 slaves within forty years, and visited prisons, hospitals, mines, and plantations, as well as the ships.

❧ He preached the annual mission in the city square for sailors and traders.

❧ During his last few years he was incapacitated by a tremor, which may have been a symptom of Parkinson's disease.

Lesser-Known Facts

⚝ Peter spoke Greek, Latin, Castilian, and limited Angolan.

⚝ He was canonized with Saint Alphonsus Rodríguez, the doorkeeper at the college of Palma de Mallorca and Claver's spiritual director when Claver was a student.

⚝ At first Peter doubted his call to the priesthood, but he was ordained at the encouragement of Saint Alphonsus.

⚝ Peter trained a team of interpreters to assist him, and when language failed, he used illustrations of the life of Christ.

In His Own Words

"Near the dying men we raked together some live coals on which we tossed some aromatics. Then with our own cloaks . . . we provided smoke treatment which warmed them. . . . The look of joy in their eyes was a beautiful sight. This is how we spoke to them: without words, but with our hands and our actions."

Saint John Vianney

A Pastor After God's Heart

[Jesus's] disciples asked him privately, "Why could we not cast it out?" He said to them, "This kind can come out only through prayer" (Mk 9:28-29).

The unusually tall lad, just turned twenty, knocked at the door of the rectory and waited. Despite his nervousness, fatigue, and worn shoes, nothing could dim his hope. Finally he had a chance to follow his impossible dream to become a priest.

The turbulence of the French Revolution had dominated John's short life. His parents, Matthew and Marie Vianney, peasants from a small country town called Dardilly, near Lyons, had continued to practice their faith despite the dangers. It was risky even to go to Mass, which had to be celebrated in secret. Priests were hunted down and executed, and those who hid them were killed, too. As their oldest son, perhaps John had understood best the risks his parents were taking to practice their faith.

That deep faith had led him here, to the doorstep of a new school in Ecully to prepare young men for the seminary. Hearing footsteps, John held his breath as he waited. Finally, a kindly, middle-aged curé opened the door. Eyes sweeping over John, he immediately extended his hand in welcome. "I am Father Balley."

"John Vianney. I want to become a priest!"

"Yes, that is what your pastor told me. I will help you in any way I can. Come in!"

John Vianney's quest for the priesthood launched very slowly. Due to his family's poverty, the instability caused by the French Revolution, and the persecution of the Church, John had not been able to study much at all. That first year, John found his studies excruciatingly difficult and slow. What really tested his faith was Latin. But Father Balley did not give up on him. During his first year, John was often discouraged.

"I should quit!"

Father Balley laughed and chided, "Over a little bit of Latin? Oh, no, you won't give up that easily."

John continued studying. Time passed and despite some major and minor setbacks, the young man clung fast to his priestly goal. Receiving news that his mother was dying, John went home to see her.

"John, I want you to be a priest so much. I want to see you a priest."

John stroked her forehead and she smiled. "Maman, you look as if your prayer is already answered, as though you know I will be a priest. But Latin seems impossible . . ." he trailed off, not wanting to disappoint her.

"Have faith!"

Tears danced in his eyes as he swallowed, "What will I do without the strength of your faith, Maman?"

Grieving his mother's death, John returned to his studies with Father Balley, more determined than ever. The priest sent him to the minor seminary at Verrières-le-Buisson, and then to the major seminary at Lyons. The major seminary was much more difficult: all the classes were taught in Latin. John tried his best, but after six months, the rector invited him to his office.

"Sit down, John. We need to talk about your studies."

John's face and shoulders tensed. He already knew he had failed.

"John, I want to do what is best for you. The studies required are far beyond your grasp. You are not meant to be a priest. Go home in peace and serve God as best you can. He will show you the way."

Somehow, John found himself back on Father Balley's doorstep. In halting phrases, confused and bewildered, he told the story of failure and discouragement. He concluded, "I've decided to become a brother."

Father Balley responded crisply. "You will become what God wants you to become, John. And I believe with all my heart that God wants you to become a priest!"

Father Balley tutored John privately and then presented him for an oral examination. By this time, John knew many of the answers to the questions they asked, but he panicked so badly that he could only stammer and repeat useless phrases. He did not pass.

Devastated, he returned to the waiting Father Balley. "Now you *have* to admit that God doesn't want me to be a priest."

The priest looked up at him with a questioning glance. "Why no, son. The thought never even occurred to me."

Father Balley's faith was like a rubber punching bag—the harder the punch, the more his faith bounced him right back into action. Taking heart from his mentor, John continued studying with greater intensity. When Father Balley felt that the young man was ready, he took the slowest seminarian in all of France to see the bishop.

The bishop looked at the tall, painfully eager young man before him. He thought of all his parishes left vacant by the Revolution, and then looked back to John. Turning to Father Balley, he asked, "Is John Vianney good?"

"He is a model of goodness."

"Very well, then, let him be ordained. The grace of God will do the rest."

John Vianney was ordained a priest on August 13, 1815. Because of his poor marks, at first he was not given the faculty to hear confessions. The bishop assigned him to assist Father Balley in Ecully. The whole town welcomed the young priest who had long ago stolen their hearts.

"Father John! Father John!" They kissed his consecrated hands. John tried to pull away as fast as he could. There was someone else he had to see!

One more time, John found himself waiting outside the rectory door. This time it opened quickly. The two priests simply looked at each other. Finally Father Balley managed to say, "Come in, son, come in. What did I tell you? I never doubted the will of God in your regard. He chose you to be his priest. And I said to myself: 'A priest he will be!'"

As Father Balley's curate, Father Vianney spent the happiest years of his life. During their three years ministering together, they lived an austere and prayerful life, completely dedicated to serving their parishioners. Then the saintly Father Balley became very sick and lay dying. Still his thoughts centered more on his curate than on himself.

"My life on this earth is over, John. But, you know, it's really the beginning. . . . And I will still be with you. You struggled to become a priest, my son! I tell you in the name of God, all your life you will bless that struggle, which will make you more sensitive to the needs of thousands of people hungering for God's peace through the sacrament of Penance."

Father John buried his beloved friend and mentor in a plain graveyard in that country town. The new pastor who arrived did not agree with Father Vianney's austere lifestyle or pastoral approach. Soon, the bishop gave Father Vianney a new assignment. Ars was derided as a "hole"—the town was too small to even have a real parish. But it was remote and the families who lived there needed a priest.

As he trekked the road to Ars, the words of the bishop rang in Father John's ears: "My friend, you have been appointed curé of Ars. It is a little parish where there is not much love of God; you must put some into it." Vianney felt the spirit of Father Balley with him. Grateful memories flooded John's mind of this good man and great priest. What would Father Balley do?

Father Vianney had big plans for Ars—spiritual plans. The town had seen a long string of priests who didn't stay very long, and spiritual life in the town felt stale, indifferent. The new curé sought the conversion and holiness of every person in his parish. He preached, taught catechism classes, and got to know every parishioner by visiting each family. He prayed late into the night and doubled his usual physical penances, fasting and praying for each parishioner. The townspeople quickly discovered that their new priest was different from the others. Spiritual victories, more than the curé dared hope for, gradually transformed Ars. But Father Vianney wouldn't be satisfied until every parishioner was living a holy life!

One night, loud noises disturbed Father Vianney. He asked a strong parishioner to stand guard for him the next night. But then he realized that the noises and physical attacks came from the devil. Noticing that the worst disturbances usually happened the night before a big conversion, the curé dismissed the attacks as unimportant—even the physical attacks on his person. (Once he confided that the devil would "drag him around" by the feet.) Others who heard the bangs and shouting at night could not disregard them as easily. But all Father Vianney cared about was the salvation of his parishioners. He knew that the devil was attacking him out of frustration that many souls were being won over to Christ!

After a while, Ars was not able to keep its holy pastor to itself. Some people came to hear the holy priest preach, others thought his preaching unremarkable. In a shrill voice, he condemned the vices of his times: carousing, blasphemy, working on Sundays. He demanded much of his parishioners, but not nearly as much as he demanded of himself. The weight of his gaze as he preached, and the conviction with which he spoke, touched his listeners deeply. Above all, people sought him for the way he advised and heard their confessions.

Pilgrims began coming to see the holy curé and make their confession to him. He seemed to know just what each penitent needed—encouragement, gentle prodding, or admonishment. He himself would perform the penances he would not give them. Stories began to spread about his miraculous gift to see a person's spiritual state without being told a word. The curé asked one penitent, "But, my friend, why did you come from such a great distance to Ars?"

Through muffled sobs, the man stumbled out, "Father, I settled on hell a long time ago. And I made up my mind that my sins were too rotten to tell anybody. . . . Then some people passed through my town. They said that there was a priest who could straighten out anybody's life. And I made up my mind to find you if I had to walk the length of France!"

The curé began to spend sixteen to seventeen hours a day in the confessional. Sometimes people sought him out of curiosity; they'd return out of necessity. Some tried to hide the state of their soul or to conceal a sin and he would weep at the offenses against God, saying after each sin, "What a pity! What a pity!"

The prayers of Father Vianney followed each person as he or she left the church and went back to daily life. He never forgot a single person.

The years of extreme physical penances, fasting, and total dedication to his parishioners—which had expanded to include the 20,000 pilgrims who came to see him each year—took their toll on his health. He said with a smile, "I can do no more. Sinners will kill the sinner." But he refused to rest. He wanted to die still living his dream of serving as a priest.

"Hear my confession!"

"And mine. . . ."

"Bless my children. . . ."

"Pray for me!"

The curé smiled and carefully fulfilled each request. In 1859, the last year of his life, more than 100,000 pilgrims journeyed to Ars. They came to find a man who resembled Christ as much as any human being could, and they were not disappointed.

After forty-five years of priestly dedication, the curé of Ars lay dying, heart flooded with gratitude for the gift of his life and his priesthood. He made his last confession, and then a group of priests, each bearing a lighted candle, filed in solemn procession to his room. They brought with them the most beautiful gift that Father Vianney could ask for: he could no longer come to the Master, but the Master had come to him. He whispered softly, "It's sad to be making one's last Communion."

The humble curé of Ars died silently and serenely, and woke up in the loving embrace of the Master whose image he had tried to be while on earth.

Prayer

Saint John Vianney
you appreciated so much
the tremendous gifts of the sacraments:
the Eucharist, Reconciliation, and priesthood.
Help me to share that same appreciation,
to receive the sacraments of Eucharist and Reconciliation often and with fervor.
In your time, the priesthood was not always valued
and priests were persecuted.
I ask your intercession for priests today.
Help them to live their vocation to holiness
with joy and gratitude.
Bless especially those priests who are struggling
with the demands of continual self-giving,
and bless my family and me with the grace to grow in
holiness. Amen.

About Saint John Vianney

Born: May 8, 1786, in Lyons, France
Died: August 4, 1859, at Ars, France
Feast Day: August 4
Canonized: May 31, 1925, by Pope Pius XI
Patron: priests

Notes on His Life

⚜ John Vianney was born and raised on a farm during the French Revolution.

⚜ He started his studies at the late age of twenty, which may explain some of his great difficulties in school—so great that he repeatedly failed Latin and was sent home from the seminary.

⚜ With the persistent support and tutoring of Father Balley, he was finally accepted for ordination.

⚜ His assignment to the small country village of Ars was considered by some in the diocese to be a punishment. It was too small even to be a "real" parish.

⚜ By 1855, some 20,000 pilgrims came to Ars each year to see the curé or make their confession to him. He spent sixteen hours in the confessional every day.

⚜ The "hauntings" or visits from the devil quickly ceased to frighten the curé once he realized that it was the devil protesting the conversion of a sinner the next day.

⚜ The last year of his life, some 100,000 pilgrims came to visit the city of Ars.

Lesser-Known Facts

⚜ Father Vianney worked hard for the conversion of his parish, but during his first years he was often ignored, ridiculed, or taunted by his parishioners.

⚜ His shrill voice was not always pleasant to listen to; many did not consider him to be a good preacher. Yet one of Father Vianney's penetrating glances could sometimes be enough to convert someone.

❧ Father Vianney founded an orphanage for girls and gave them catechism classes. The classes became so popular they were eventually moved to the church.

❧ Three times Father Vianney attempted to flee his parish for a secluded life of contemplation. All three times he was convinced to turn back because God had entrusted the people of Ars to him.

❧ Father Vianney became a Secular Franciscan during his lifetime.

In His Own Words

"The priesthood is the love of the heart of Jesus."

Venerable Matt Talbot

The Thirst

Jesus said to his disciples, "Occasions for stumbling are bound to come, but woe to anyone by whom they come!" (Lk 17.1).

The year was 1869; the country, Ireland. A burly stock man called: "Hey, errand boy! Come over here!"

The young boy stopped what he was doing and looked up at the man.

"What's your name? How old are you?"

"Matthew Talbot," he replied, "and I'm thirteen, sir. Do you have a message for me to take somewhere?"

"Well . . . no, but tell me, how long now have you been working here?"

"Two weeks, sir. But it's a little boring," Matthew sighed. "There aren't many messages to deliver."

The man laughed to himself and rubbed his chin. "Some of us have decided to initiate you and make you one of us," he said, handing something over to the boy. "Here's a bottle. This is what we men do around here when we're bored."

"But where did you get that?" Matt asked.

"This is a wine place, isn't it? A case broke and this is what's left over."

Matt started to turn and go. He didn't want anything to do with this drinking business. The Talbots never drank at home. What would his mother and father say?

The man chided him saying, "What's the matter? Eh, Matty? Maybe you're still too young to drink!! We could put some milk in a cup for you instead."

Matt stopped and turned. His face was scarlet as he blurted out, "I'm not afraid to drink. It's just that I don't care for it right now."

The man just laughed. The boy debated within himself and then said,

"I'll take one drink, okay? Just to be social and prove to you I'm not afraid."

Within a year, Matthew Talbot was not only drinking to be sociable, he was drunk most of the time. Rumors started to spread throughout the city.

"Did you see that young Talbot boy yesterday? Why, he's a disgrace, such a little drunkard. I just happened to look out the window; there he was, reeling and staggering right past my house."

"Imagine it's heartbreaking for his good parents! I've known that family for years. They never miss Mass, and they pray the Rosary every night together. It's a real shame."

"His father took him out of school. Mr. Talbot earns so little money at his job, and he has twelve mouths to feed. Matt was supposed to help, but I don't think he'll be giving much money to the family now."

"I heard that, too, but I also heard Matthew is the messenger boy at the wine merchants' warehouse."

"Poor Mr. Talbot . . . he probably blames himself."

"Well, you know that all the men at that place drink heavily. It's their bad example that induced the boy to drink."

The tongues kept wagging until the gossip reached the ears of Matt's parents. Mrs. Talbot whispered to her husband, "It's almost impossible for me to believe that Matt is resorting to the 'awful drink.'"

Then one evening their son stumbled into the house drunk. Early the next morning, Mr. Talbot changed his son's place of work. He took Matt with him to the Post and Docks Board. Matt became the new messenger boy there.

Without realizing it, his father had exposed him to greater temptations. Now the boy found whiskey instead of wine. Everyone knew it now. The gossip spread all over the piers. His father scolded him, beat him, begged him to stop, but nothing helped. Matt's parents were truly heartbroken.

The boy changed his place of work on his own the next time. In this way he planned to save his father the agony of seeing him at work every day in a state of perpetual drunkenness. Matt became a bricklayer.

As his parents witnessed their son's steady downward slide, they suffered and walked their way of the cross, station by station. They prayed. . . . Oh, how they prayed! Surely God would help him. Meanwhile, the years passed.

Every weekend after work Matt followed the same schedule. The quitting whistle pierced the air on Saturday evening. It signaled time to get paid. As the money was passed out, several friends usually gathered.

"Come on, Matt. Quit counting your money and let's get going. I'm so dry, there's fire in my mouth and only a shot of whiskey can quench it."

"You're right!" Matt replied. "It's just too bad our money only lasts until the beginning of the week. And your money, Pete, runs out quicker than mine."

"That's okay," Pete said, "If mine outlasted yours I would buy you a drink. That's our pact, right?"

Another friend joined in. "Sure, that's right. Whoever has leftover money is obliged to buy drinks 'on the house.' That's what friends are for. Let's get going. This money's so hot I think I'll buy the first round of drinks."

At that they all quickly walked to their favorite pub.

No price was too great to pay for a drink. One time Matt sold his boots. Another time he and his buddy tricked a drinking companion. The buddy kept the poor man busy while Matt stole his fiddle. They pawned it and bought drinks "on the house" for everyone. When the poor man realized the drinks were being served at the cost of his livelihood, he became hopelessly dejected. That didn't matter to Matt. The fiddle had bought a few drinks. What mattered beyond that?

Yet, at times he wanted to stop drinking . . . to take the pledge and become a good Catholic . . . but he didn't have the courage.

Finally came a week when Matt didn't work, and by Monday he had drunk up any money left over from the previous week. He craved whisky with all his being. His whole body seemed to be on fire. Only one thought kept him going: Saturday was approaching and his buddies would help him out. They knew what it was like; they would buy him a drink. *Sure*, he thought. *Of course, they'll help me out.*

Matt trembled with eagerness as he waited on the familiar corner across from the work yard. The whistle blew. A few men hurried out, laughing and joking. When one noticed Matt, he signaled the others. They fell silent and tried to ignore him, scurrying past without a word. A few more came out of the yard and crossed the street. Matt called to them. They were his best friends!

"Hey, Jim! Pete! It's me, Matt."

"Oh, Matt," one replied heartily. "How have you been? We missed you this week. Didn't we, lads?"

Then Pete chimed in, "Well, we've got to be going, Matt. Come to see us when you're working again."

Not one of my friends invited me to come and have a drink, Matt thought in disbelief. It wasn't like this before.

Something icy swelled in his stomach and crept into his throat. He was humiliated. "My friends?" he choked. "Some friends they are!"

Things were different now. He was broke. It didn't matter to them one bit how badly he needed a drink.

"I always bought drinks for the others when I had money. I see how it was. They just took advantage of me!" he realized as he talked to himself, pacing back and forth. "Friendship?" he fumed. "To them it is only as important as the amount of money in your pocket. No money, no friends! It's that simple!"

Now he saw clearly that each was wrapped in his own vice. To share a drink with someone who has no money, no matter how bad off he is, only deprived the lender of another shot of whiskey. Who wants to share a drink with a bum?

His heart filled with anger and then remorse. It seemed that everything his drinking habit had smothered inside him for years was now bubbling to the surface. Slowly he made a decision. He *would* take the pledge to stop drinking, and with God's grace, he would keep it. God was the Friend who stuck by you. God would be his Friend, the only Friend he could be sure of, the Friend who would never betray him.

Matt was now twenty-eight years old. He had spent more than half his young life drunk. He went home and told his parents, to their great astonishment and joy, about his resolution.

"Son, I am so pleased," his mother said, "but don't take the pledge if you don't intend to keep it. You know you can count on my prayers. May God give you the grace to succeed."

Then Matt went to a nearby chapel, made a good confession, and took the pledge for three months. It seemed impossible to Matt that he could abstain from drink for that long, "but with God nothing is impossible," he repeated to himself.

After his confession he started to attend daily Mass and Communion. By the end of the first three months, the man who had once let alcohol rule his life was now ready to take the total abstinence pledge. Giving up drink was by no means easy. Matt faced many temptations, and he had to fight constant battles. But he prayed and gradually, through grace, self-denial, and prayer, he became strong. He was known to spend hours huddled in a back pew of church begging Our Lady, "O Virgin Mother, I ask for only three things: the grace of God, the presence of God, and the benediction of God."

Until Matt Talbot's death, he never took another drink. He became a Franciscan Tertiary and lived a most austere, penitential life. This man whose tremendous "thirst" had once led him far from God learned through self-denial and prayer that the only "thirst" that leads to happiness is the thirst for God, who has made us for himself.

⟨❦⟩

Prayer

We praise God for the life and example of Venerable
Matthew Talbot,
who lived the life of a common laborer.
As a boy he was led into addictive behavior; as an adult
he was given completely to alcohol.
Through his intercession, we beg you, dear God,
to give our children and young people the strength
to resist those temptations that would enslave them
to vice.
For ourselves and for all adults, we ask Matt Talbot's
help
in ordering our lives according to the eternal plan
of God.
Give us balance, grant us peace.
Help us to rely on God's grace and take advantage of
the sacramental life,
that we may live as your true children. Amen.

About Venerable Matthew Talbot

Born. May 2, 1856, in Dublin, Ireland
Died: June 7, 1925, in Dublin
Declared Venerable: October 3, 1975, by Pope Paul VI
Patron: recovering alcoholics, penitents, addicts

Notes on His Life

☙ Matt was second of the twelve children of Charles and
Elizabeth Talbot.

☙ He lived alone most of his life.

❧ In 1884 he took the pledge to abstain from alcohol, and remained sober for the last forty years of his life. Later he also gave up tobacco.

❧ Matt made amends for his previous life and paid all his debts.

❧ He had a good reputation as a loyal, industrious worker.

❧ He belonged to the Irish Transport and General Workers Union, but opposed going on strike.

❧ He attended daily Mass and spent his life in prayer and works of charity.

❧ He practiced many penances, including wearing a chain, sleeping on a board with a block of wood for a pillow, abstaining from meat, milk, and butter most of the year, rising at two in the morning to pray, and kneeling on church steps a half hour before Mass.

❧ In 1890 he became a Franciscan Tertiary.

❧ His spiritual life was guided by Monsignor Michael Hickey of Clonliffe College.

❧ Matt died of a heart attack in Granby Lane, Dublin, while on his way to Mass.

❧ He was buried in Glasnevin Cemetery and later transferred to Our Lady of Lourdes Church in Dublin.

Lesser-Known Facts

❧ He worked as a hod carrier (one who hauls mortar and brick for bricklayers).

❧ At the time of his death, he worked at a lumberyard.

❧ He loved singing and joking.

❧ He was hot-tempered, given to swearing and fighting before his conversion.

⚜ He died without any identification, but was identified by the penitential chains he wore.

⚜ His tomb has a glass panel exposing a view of his coffin.

⚜ He was buried in his Franciscan habit with his penitential chains.

In His Own Words

"There are three things that I cannot escape: the eye of God, the voice of conscience, the stroke of death. In company, guard your tongue. In your family, guard your temper. When alone, guard your thoughts."

Blessed Victoria Rasoamanarivo

Princess of Madagascar

"But as for what was sown on good soil, this is the one who hears the word and understands it, who indeed bears fruit and yields, in one case a hundredfold, in another sixty, and in another thirty" (Mt 13:23).

The young woman stood quietly, waiting to speak with the priest. When the old Jesuit looked up he noticed how tense she appeared as she fidgeted with her hands. He motioned her over.

"Victoria," he began, "do you remember the story Jesus told about the man who sowed seeds?"

"Of course, Father. The man was walking along scattering seed all over the ground around him," replied the young woman.

"Well, I expect you to be like that man, Victoria. I'm sure you already know this, but it seems that all of us priests, and the sisters, will have to leave Madagascar soon. You must keep a great supply of the good seed on hand, and whenever you are among the people you must sow it generously."

"I promise you I will do everything in my power to keep the Church together while you are away, Father."

"Not just away, Victoria," he said with a deep sigh. "We are being exiled from Madagascar. It is hard to predict when we might return. You must be strong for everyone."

Victoria solemnly promised the priest she would do her best. And Victoria Rasoamanarivo had a distinct advantage over most of the island's other Catholics. She was a member of the royal family of the Hovas. She had been raised by her uncle, Rainimaharavo, who was commander-in-chief of the Malagasy army. Under Queen Ranavalona I, who reigned from 1828 to 1861, Victoria's grandfather served as prime minister. Although she was still young, Victoria was a woman of prestige among her people, and she fully intended to use her influence to protect the Church.

She had faced trials before. A few years earlier Victoria had worked hard to convince her uncle that allowing her to receive Christian baptism would be an advantage, not a burden, to the family. When she enrolled in the first school of the newly arrived Sisters of Saint Joseph of Cluny, the young princess, then known by her given name Rasoamanarivo, discovered a wonderful treasure in the Catholic faith. She marveled at the idea of a religion that encompassed the whole world.

"Tell me again, Sister," she pleaded, "is the Christian God the ruler of the whole world?"

"Yes, Rasoamanarivo, the God we are speaking of is the ruler and the maker of the whole world, of all people, of every country, even of this mighty land of Madagascar."

"And this God is good, Sister?"

"He is very good, and *only* Good, little princess. And if we love him, he will make us always good, too."

"That is what I want to be," Rasoamanarivo declared. "I want to be always good. I want to be a daughter of the Christian God."

This was blessed news for the French missionaries in Madagascar. If such a child as Rasoamanarivo were to be baptized many more would follow her example.

When she told her uncle of her desire, he first threatened her, "I will remove you from that school immediately." Then he appealed to her pride, "We must all uphold the beliefs of our tradition." He even pleaded, "Rasoamanarivo, do not ask to do something that will make us indebted to the French." Eventually her cajoling won his assent. After all, what harm could it do for his favorite niece to embrace this new faith?

How reverently she bowed over the baptismal font. As the priest spilled the saving water over her brow and pronounced her a daughter of great Trinitarian God, her heart felt it would burst. With her baptism, Rasoamanarivo received a second name. She was now Victoria Rasoamanarivo. Her baptism was truly a victory for the young woman and a victory for her God.

Everyone agreed that not only was her new name beautiful, but the girl herself became more beautiful in her ways. She was even more obedient and respectful, but she also gave herself generously to the service of the poor and needy. The family began to think of her future. She would make a fine wife for some young man.

In her own mind, however, she pictured herself joining her teachers as a sister of Saint Joseph of Cluny.

"This is my dearest wish, Father," she announced to her confessor. "I want to become a spouse of Jesus. I want to enter the convent."

"That would be wonderful, Victoria. You would be the first religious from among your people," the priest confirmed. "But, you must consider some things. . . ."

"Consider what, Father? My heart is ready," Victoria declared.

"Now, Victoria," her confessor stressed, "I think you should not set your heart on becoming a religious. Do you really think that your family would understand this desire of yours? We would not want to give them any cause against the Church, would we? I recommend that you follow the normal path of your people. Be a truly religious wife and mother, an example to the other women."

Not without a tinge of disappointment, Victoria had to agree. "Yes, Father. I can see the wisdom of your words. May God see that I be wed to a good man."

This, however, would be the second big disappointment of her young life. Radriaka Rainilaiarivony, the husband chosen for her, was a relative of her uncle, but he would prove to be a poor choice. Radriaka was a young man of poor character and loose morals, an alcoholic, and a violent man. Even his parents recommended that she leave him.

"Victoria," her mother-in-law said. "I certainly give you my permission to leave my son. He is not living up to his obligations to you. Too much anger rages in Radriaka."

"No, he is my husband," she answered. "Perhaps he will change in time. I pray for this every day."

Meanwhile, in her heart she knew that she must stay with him, not just because of their marriage bond, but because she, as a princess and a Christian, had to give an example to everyone of the sacredness of Christian marriage.

In God's Providence these disappointments and struggles had prepared Victoria for the day of trial for the Church in

Madagascar. France had set its sights on the large island of Madagascar for a number of years. Now on May 17, 1883, the French navy took possession of the northern port of Mahajanga. This, of course, was seen as an act of war by the queen and her prime minister. And so, by June 11 Queen Rasoherina expelled every French citizen, including the missionaries who had been working successfully for many years. The priests debated whether or not to go into hiding so as not to abandon their converts.

"Please, fathers, do not resist the Queen's command. If you try to stay, things will go badly for us," the leading Catholics said. "If you submit, it may be easier to return after the tensions cease."

Several Catholic laypeople took on the leadership of the Church once the priests left, none more effectively than Victoria. As a member of the ruling family and a relative of the prime minister, she made herself responsible for all negotiations between the government and the Church.

On the first Sunday after the priests had gone, soldiers guarded the doors to the cathedral in an attempt to discourage the faithful from assembling. Unafraid, Victoria led the rest of the Catholics right up to the door. To the guard she boldly announced, "If you must shed blood, begin with mine; but fear will not keep us from gathering for prayer."

She saw to it that the parishes sang the high Mass despite having no one to consecrate the Eucharist. Religious instructions continued. A system for transmitting messages was devised so that news and instructions could be shared among the parishes. This was an invaluable tool for maintaining unity, which insured survival.

When the Queen questioned her, Victoria had a convincing proposal. "We will go ahead on our own, my queen. You will see no influence of the French. Yes, we will take care of the schools and the parishes ourselves. It will be no burden on you or the government. All we ask of you, Queen Rasoherina, is your permission to go ahead," Victoria pleaded.

Although the government would not back down, officials could not help but admire the Catholic community's strong faith and commitment. Catholic practices continued as fervently as possible in that restrictive atmosphere. Even Victoria's husband was impressed by the character of this woman who stood by him so faithfully and lovingly through all his selfish years.

When the priests were allowed back into the kingdom in 1886, Radriaka was ready to seek that secret source of strength Victoria possessed. With great joy she witnessed his deathbed baptism in March 1888.

Victoria Rasoamanarivo humbly continued her service of the Church through her frequent prayer and her constant acts of charity among the poor, the lepers, the sick, and the abandoned. She was truly a mother of the Church in Madagascar in good times and in bad.

Prayer

Blessed Victoria Rasoamanarivo, princess of your
    people,
mother and apostle of the Church in Madagascar,
we ask your intercession for all those who are called
    upon by circumstances
to rise above their natural desires and to place their
    future in God's providential hands.
We ask you to watch over the people of Madagascar.

Help them overcome the difficulties that stem from years
of war and domination,
and the problems that progress itself presents.
Beg the Lord for the blessings of justice, peace, freedom,
and prosperity for everyone.
But ask the good God especially for hearts attuned to
the heart of God
so that faith, hope, and love may guide the lives of all.
Amen.

About Blessed Victoria Rasoamanarivo

Born: 1848 in Antananarivo, Madagascar

Died: August 21, 1894, in Antananarivo

Feast Day: August 21

Beatified: August 29, 1989, by Pope John Paul II

Patron: Madagascar, lay leadership, troubled marriages

Notes on Her Life

✿ She was born to the prime minister's daughter, Rambohi-noro, then adopted by her uncle.

✿ From childhood Rasoamanarivo practiced the local animist religion.

✿ At thirteen she attended Catholic school under the Sisters of Saint Joseph of Cluny.

✿ On March 1, 1863, she was baptized Victoria.

✿ She was discouraged from entering the convent, and on May 13, 1864, married Radriaka Rainilaiarivony.

✿ She was an exemplar of fidelity in a difficult marriage.

✿ In 1883 the Jesuit missionaries were expelled and Catholics were persecuted. She became a defender and inspiration of the Church in persecution.

  ❦ She saw her husband baptized before his death in 1887.

Lesser-Known Facts

  ❦ Rasoamanarivo spent hours in church at prayer, and was an apostle of charity to the poor, sick, and persecuted.

  ❦ When the priests returned after the persecution, they found 21,000 Catholics, many of whom Rasoamanarivo had ministered to.

  ❦ In the mid-1930s a brush fire threatened to consume the village of Antsirabé, but was halted when an image of Blessed Victoria was held up to the flames.

  ❦ Today about a quarter of the population of Madagascar is Roman Catholic.

In Her Own Words

"If you must shed blood, begin with mine; but fear will not keep us from gathering for prayer."

Saint Joseph Mukasa,
Saint Charles Lwanga,
and Companions

Radiant Lights for Africa

So again Jesus said to them, "Very truly, I tell you, I am the gate for the sheep. All who came before me are thieves and bandits; but the sheep did not listen to them. I am the gate. Whoever enters by me will be saved, and will come in and go out and find pasture" (Jn 10:7–9).

Heart pounding, Joseph made his way to the Catholic mission for morning Mass. He needed to get away from the Bugandan palace and clear his head of the paranoid screams of his king, Kabaka Mwanga, still piercing his heart. "How dare you undermine my authority—the pages no longer obey me as they should! You insulted my wisdom—I know what is best for my kingdom. Bishop Hannington was a threat—he had to die.

Whose side are you on—the white man's, or your king's? Give up this Christian faith or you will be sorry. Maybe I will put *all* Christians in my kingdom to death!"

Finally the king, worn out with his own rage, had dismissed Joseph. *If Kabaka Mwanga calms down, it might be as if nothing happened. But if the fire of his anger flares again . . . how I need you, Lord Jesus! What a gift to be able to come to Mass today, of all days. Help me!*

As he entered the chapel, Joseph felt distracted. He was grieved by the king's false accusations, and he was afraid of where the king's wrath would lead him. *I'm not just afraid for myself. What about the others? Today may be the day I face the ultimate test of my faith—like the first apostles. What if I am not ready? If I plead for the others, will it mean that I will die?*

As majordomo of the palace, Joseph Mukasa was a powerful and trusted aide to Kabaka Mwanga. Handsome and athletic, the twenty-five-year-old had earned his position of trust. As the faithful personal attendant of the previous king, Kabaka Mwanga's father, Joseph had saved him from the attack of a poisonous snake. Joseph had first encountered Christianity when the missionaries had been welcomed to teach at court. He had been one of the first royal pages to be baptized.

Kabaka Mwanga was still a young king; his father had died the previous year. During his short reign, Joseph had already thwarted one assassination attempt. Yet recently, Kabaka Mwanga didn't always remember Joseph's loyalty. He no longer trusted Joseph's advice and resented him whenever his counsel didn't match the king's personal agenda. Even though Mwanga had welcomed back the Christian missionaries—partly at Joseph's urging—the king remained suspicious of all the white colonists, and had started to distrust the Christians at court.

Kabaka Mwanga resented many of the Christian teachings, especially those on purity and homosexuality. In the past, the king had trusted Joseph enough to tolerate his pleadings to stop taking advantage of the boys and young men who served as pages. Privately, Joseph encouraged the pages—especially the catechumens—to resist the king's advances. But the king saw their refusal as disobedience. Joseph did as much as he could to help those in danger; when Kabaka Mwanga seemed to favor a certain page and called for him, Joseph would arrange for the page to be out of the palace. *Maybe Kabaka Mwanga realizes how I've tried to protect the pages—especially the catechumens and younger boys like fourteen-year-old Kizito—from his predatory ways. That would explain his rage against me.*

Distracted by his fears—for himself, for the other young men in his charge at court—Joseph couldn't concentrate at Mass. Then the thought that this might be his last Eucharist focused Joseph's attention. As he bent his head after receiving Communion, Joseph's worries fled. He offered his heart to the One who loved him so much that he had died to save him. *May I be worthy to offer my life for you, Katonda, my God.*

Joseph finished his prayer as best he could and turned to Father Simeon Lourdel, the missionary who had first introduced him to Christ. "Kabaka Mwanga interrogated me all night," Joseph said. "He was very angry."

"Is it safe for you to go back?" Father Lourdel asked.

"I would never desert Kabaka Mwanga. I am his loyal servant," Joseph answered. "But I need your blessing."

"Of course," Father Lourdel agreed. "My son, I will pray for you."

A page arrived from the palace, breathing heavily, with a message for Joseph, "Kabaka Mwanga demands that you come immediately."

"I am on my way," Joseph told the page. "Can you take a message to my friend Charles? Tell him what is happening, and to be careful today not to anger the king." Turning back to Father Lourdel, Joseph knelt and bowed his head. Deeply moved, Father Lourdel put his hands on Joseph's head in blessing.

As soon as Joseph entered the king's presence, he could tell that Kabaka Mwanga's rage had not died down but exploded. Not allowing him even to speak, Kabaka Mwanga furiously accused Joseph of betrayal, and finally ordered his immediate death by fire.

Relieved that he alone carried the brunt of the king's wrath, Joseph was led away to be executed. The royal executioner, who knew Joseph well, treated him with respect. Joseph prayed as he walked—untied—to the place where the pyre was being built. Wanting to give Joseph a less painful death, the executioner pulled out a knife. Joseph spoke to him, "Tell Kabaka Mwanga that I forgive him for having me die so unjustly, but that I pray that he repents for his sins so that God will forgive him." The executioner promised to give the king the message. As he lifted the knife to carry out his orders, Joseph knelt and prayed. *My God, I forgive him! I love you!*

Charles Lwanga received the news of Joseph's sentence and death with a heavy heart. He had not even been able to say goodbye to his friend, or receive his encouragement one last time. Joseph had been his mentor, friend, and protector. Together, the young men had worked closely to run the royal household and to teach the other catechumens.

Joseph's death could mean that we all die within the week, Charles realized. *We no longer have him to shield us from the wrath of the Kabaka. But I am not ready to die! Not without Baptism!*

Because the missionaries required a four-year catechumenate, Charles had not yet been baptized. He made a quick decision. With several other catechumens, Charles secretly ran to the mission. Father Lourdel had already heard the news of Joseph's martyrdom, and he agreed that they could receive Baptism, especially if they were to guide the other Christian pages in Joseph's place. Hearts overflowing with grief and joy, Charles and the others received Baptism that very day.

When Charles returned to the palace, he discovered that Kabaka Mwanga regretted his decision to have Joseph killed. Perhaps because of this regret, he didn't carry out his threat to kill all the Christians at court, although he forbade the royal servants to visit the mission. Even though Kabaka Mwanga seemed suspicious of him, Charles was entrusted with more responsibility after Joseph's death. A few days later, Kabaka Mwanga questioned him about his loyalty.

Charles replied, "My faith teaches me to serve you loyally. I was your faithful servant before. Now I am even more ready to lay down my life in your service." The king seemed satisfied. Five tense months passed.

Charles, whose charm and frequent triumphs in the wrestling ring already made him popular at court, used his popularity to continue to try to protect the Christian pages from the king's harassment. With great determination he tried to live up to his mentor's holiness and strength. It was hard not being able to go to the mission for Mass. On Easter, Charles confided to a friend, "It is too bad we could not celebrate Easter, but we will make up for it on the feast day of the Ascension!"

On May 25, Kabaka Mwanga's suspicions and hatred for the Christian Africans once again flamed out when a favorite page that he wanted was not available. On finding that one of his servants, Denis, was teaching catechism to the page, Kabaka Mwanga attacked Denis with a spear, then ordered his execution.

That night, Charles gathered the fearful catechumens around him to encourage them in their fidelity to Christ, and he baptized five of the most promising young men. Fourteen-year-old Kizito was shaken by the torture undergone by Denis, but still eager to lay down his life for Christ. At first, Charles advised him to escape, but Kizito refused to run, even though he was afraid. Charles took the hand of the young page in his own. "We will offer our lives for Christ side by side, hand in hand, as brothers," he promised Kizito.

The next day, Kabaka Mwanga called an assembly of all the royal servants, and demanded that the Christians give up their faith on pain of death. Then, he ordered all the Christians who refused to obey him to step forward.

Time stopped. *This is the moment we have both dreaded and longed for,* Charles thought. *But we are not alone.* Remembering his promise, he looked at Kizito's young face and saw fear mingled with determination in his eyes. Charles took a deep breath—it was harder than usual—and took Kizito's hand. As Charles and Kizito walked together to the spot the king had pointed to, Charles spoke clearly and respectfully to Kabaka Mwanga. "I cannot deny what I know to be true." After another moment of silence, the other

Christian pages followed him—in all, sixteen Catholics and ten Anglicans.

Infuriated, Kabaka Mwanga immediately condemned them all to death by being burned alive at Namugongo, several days' journey away. Executioners bound them tightly together—neck to neck and leg to leg—in two groups. Father Lourdel witnessed their departure and was deeply moved by their calm peace and the encouragement they gave to one another as they were led away. Their bonds chafed the men's skins raw during their death march. Several of the prisoners were executed along the way.

After reaching Namugongo, they were imprisoned in various places around the village as preparations were made. A week later, Charles Lwanga was chosen to be executed first, alone. Charles encouraged the others as he was taken away. His executioner made sure that the fire burned slowly, causing Charles great suffering, but Charles made no complaint. Just before he died, he called out, "Katonda—My God!"

Then the others were brought, group by group, to the large pyre. As each group arrived, they were greeted with cries of joy and encouragement from the others. After the pyre was set alight, they continued to pray aloud and encourage one another with the joy that they would see Jesus so soon. In all thirty-one young men died in the Namugongo holocaust, each of them with prayers on his lips.

It was Ascension Thursday. Charles Lwanga could not have anticipated that he would celebrate this feast day by offering his life for Christ, and then experiencing Christ's eternal embrace. The holocaust of Namugongo and the lives of each of the Ugandan martyrs have become a compelling, radiant light for the Ugandan people, and for young people of the world.

ໄ໑໑໑ວ

Prayer

O holy Ugandan martyrs,
under threat of persecution and death,
you were faithful to the Gospel virtues of purity,
of brotherly love,
of hope in eternal life.
You disregarded the sufferings of martyrdom
and joyfully gave your lives for the sake of Christ,
strengthening one another with encouragement
    and prayer.
In a world that desecrates
the dignity of human life and the virtue of purity,
teach us how to reverence every life
and the gift of our bodies.
Teach us also how to forgive those who do not
    understand us
or persecute us for our belief in Christ. Amen.

About the Ugandan martyrs

Twenty-two Catholic men between the ages of fourteen
    and fifty, most under the age of thirty-five, died as
    martyrs for their faith in the years 1885–1887, in
    Buganda (in southern Uganda), Africa.

Feast Day: June 3

Canonized: October 18, 1964, by Pope Paul VI (who
    made special mention of the twenty-three Anglican
    martyrs who also gave their lives for Christ)

All of the Catholic martyrs were recent converts.

Most were royal pages at court; some served the local chiefs.

Thirteen of the martyrs were burned alive at Namugongo; others were speared or dismembered.

The Martyrs

⚜ Saint Joseph Mukasa Balikuddembe ("Balikuddembe" means "the Christians are at liberty to worship"), twenty-five. The king's majordomo and leader of the Christians at court, Joseph was the first to give his life on November 15, 1885. The king had him killed because Joseph advised him not to kill an Anglican bishop, and he protested the king's sexual harassment and abuse of the royal pages. Patron of politicians and leaders.

⚜ Saint Matthias Mulumba Kalemba, the oldest martyr, age about fifty. Tortured for three days before he died, May 30, 1886. Patron of leaders and families.

⚜ Saint Noe Mawaggali, thirty-five. Speared and tortured on May 31, 1886. Patron of workers, artists, and technicians.

⚜ Saint Denis Ssebuggawo, sixteen. Baptized with Charles Lwanga. Killed by the king for teaching catechism. Patron of choirs and musicians.

⚜ Saint Pontian Ngondwe, between thirty-five and forty. Served as palace guard. Patron of soldiers, policemen, and militia.

⚜ Saint Andrew Kaggwa, about thirty. A favorite of the king, he served as bandmaster general. One of the first converts to marry in the Church, Andrew had a wife and daughter. Patron of catechists, teachers, and families.

Saint Jean-Marie Muzeeyi, between twenty and thirty-five. After his baptism, Jean-Marie took vows of chastity, poverty, obedience, and working for the sick. Out of obedience, he went into hiding during the initial persecution. Captured and martyred on January 27, 1887. Patron of doctors, nurses, hospitals, and clinics.

Martyred on the way to or at Namugongo, 1886

Saint Charles Lwanga, about twenty-five, baptized the day his friend and mentor Saint Joseph Muakas was martyred. Continued to lead the Christians after Joseph's martyrdom. Charles was the first to be martyred at Namugongo on Ascension Day, 1886. Patron of youth.

Saint Kizito, the youngest martyr, fourteen. Baptized by Charles Lwanga the week before his martyrdom, who promised to die at his side. Patron of children and primary schools.

Saint Gonzaga Gonza, about twenty-four. Was studying Islam when he converted to Catholicism. He collapsed on the way to Namugongo and was martyred immediately. Patron of prisoners and those who suffer.

Saint James Buuzaabalyawo, between the age of twenty-five and thirty. Baptized with Charles Lwanga, he refused the wine offered before his execution. Patron of merchants.

Saint Gyavira Musoke, seventeen. Gyavira became an outcast of his clan for converting from his training in witchcraft to Catholicism. He also risked his life rejecting the homosexual advances of the king. Patron of communications and travelers.

❦ Saint Athanasius Bazzekuketta, twenty. This royal page in charge of the king's treasury was martyred on the road to Namugongo. Patron of treasurers and bankers.

❦ Saint Luke Banabakintu, between the age of thirty and thirty-five. Walked forty-two miles to Mass every week, memorizing the homily and repeating it to his village when he returned. Patron of sailors, fishermen, and students.

❦ Saint Ambrose Kibuuka, eighteen. Convinced he would die a martyr, he took leave to say goodbye to his parents, who begged him not to return to court, but he did anyway. Patron of various youth groups.

❦ Saint Anatoli Kiriggwajjo, about twenty. Refused a prestigious post from the king to preserve his chastity. Patron of dairy farmers and veterinarians.

❦ Saint Achilles Kiwanuka, seventeen. Baptized the day after Saint Joseph Mukasa's martyrdom. Patron of clerks, journalists, and writers.

❦ Saint Mbaaga Tuzinde, seventeen. Son of the chief executioner by bloodpact, he resisted his family's pleas to renounce his faith and was executed by order of his reluctant father, who had him clubbed to death at Namugongo so he would not suffer by fire. Patron of religious vocations.

❦ Saint Mugagga, sixteen or seventeen. Not known as a Christian, because he had been privately instructed by Charles at night. He insisted on joining the others and died at Namugongo. Patron of clubs and tailors.

❦ Saint Mukasa Kiriwawanvu, between the age of twenty and twenty-five. The only martyr to die without Baptism because he was in prison for hitting another martyr, Saint

Gyavira. The two young men forgave each other and died together at Namugongo. Patron of hotels, restaurants, and bars.

❦ Saint Adolphus Mukasa Ludigo, twenty-four or twenty-five. Though he claimed to be descended from royalty, he would help the women prepare the meal for the gathering of Christians and catechumens. This women's work was considered beneath a man's dignity. Patron of farmers, herders, and hunters.

❦ Saint Bruno Sserunkuuma, thirty. Patron of penitents. After his baptism, Bruno took two pagan wives. With the help of friends Charles Lwanga and Andrew Kaggwa, he repented and went to live in penance and prayer as gatekeeper at the palace. Patron of penitents, those tempted against chastity, those tempted to drink or use violence.

Blessed Teresa of Calcutta

"Come Be My Light"

"Truly I tell you, just as you did it to one of the least of these who are members of my family, you did it to me" (Mt 25:40).

On August 16, 1948, Sister Teresa laid aside her beloved habit, put on a simple sari, and stepped out the door. After twenty years she was no longer a teaching sister of Loreto, but she was embarking as God's servant on a great adventure. Only a heart entirely on fire with love for the Lord would see anything beautiful or any promise in this new calling. In fact, all she knew of it was that God wanted her to go out into the streets of India and serve the poor.

It had all started on a train trip to Darjeeling. She was on her way to make the annual retreat at the Loreto Convent, when she was suddenly seized with an intense awareness of India's suffering poor. Jesus began to speak to her heart of his particular desire. *I thirst for souls. Do not deny me this. Go out and bring my light into the hovels of the poor. Serve me in them. Love me in them.*

Teresa had struggled with how to implement this "call within a call." She was a religious and always would be a religious, but Jesus wanted her to leave what she knew and begin to serve the country's masses of poor people in a new way. She had confided only in her spiritual advisor, Father Celeste Van Exem, SJ. He then sent her to the archbishop. When she approached His Grace Ferdinand Périer, he listened attentively as she pleaded for permission to begin, "It is the Lord who asks, who commands, that I go to the poorest of the poor, to shine the light of his love on all those in need."

"But your vocation is to be a Loreto sister," the archbishop explained. "You are a gifted teacher, and God knows we need them these days. Now I don't want to hear anything more on this matter until I return from Rome."

So Sister Teresa put all her desires—*and* Jesus's plans—on hold. However, the archbishop had given some hope. He instructed her to spend the coming months formulating answers to some important questions: What exactly do I want to do and how will I go about doing it? Who will follow me, and how will I form them? Would it be better to join an existing congregation or form a secular group? What success could I hope for? *I should also ask myself how the work will be supported,* Sister Teresa had thought. And she had prayed as never before. That was the easy part because Jesus was always there for her with his comfort and his encouragement. When the archbishop returned to Calcutta he listened again to her plans and this time gave Sister Teresa permission to set out to serve the poor.

But now, months later on the street, *she* must be the comforter. She had all the necessary permissions and had taken a basic nursing course; she was eager to begin. Realizing that she too was now poor, with no position, no home, no money, she quickly sought a place to stay. She was able to rent a little room that lacked everything, where she gathered a few children for reading lessons. These children would help her gain the trust of the neighborhood. *My neighborhood,* she reflected. *Here I am teaching children of the slum right in the streets behind our Loreto school, but I must expand out from here to find more of God's needy children.*

As she walked the streets, Sister Teresa came upon a woman lying in the trash. She was feverish and badly bitten by rodents and ants. "I have brought this poor woman to you for care," she announced to the local hospital staff.

"Sorry," they replied. "We cannot accommodate her."

"And why not?" Sister Teresa asked. "She is dying and needs to be cared for." The hospital attendants tried to make the little nun and the poor woman leave. Finally Sister Teresa sat down next to her charge and said, "I will not leave here until you admit her." Reluctantly they took in the woman. Sister Teresa later learned that the woman was restored to health. In her mind, however, she kept repeating what the woman had told her, "Imagine, Mother, it was my own son who tossed me there."

Who will take care of all these people? As Sister Teresa asked herself this question over and over she heard the voice of Jesus again insisting, *I thirst for souls. Serve me in them. Love me in them.* It became clear that what she must do is to seek out each needy individual. And, one by one, to show them the love of God, the face of Christ in her own smile and by her gentle touch. *After all,* she reflected, *hadn't Jesus assured us that what we do to others in reality is done to him?*

And so, Sister Teresa sought out the poor, the sick, the dying wherever she found them. She petitioned the local municipality for a place to shelter her charges. "They gave me a large building that had once been a hostel for pilgrims to the shrine of a Hindu goddess," she noted. Sister Teresa promptly turned this house over to Mary Immaculate, naming it Nirmal Hriday, "pure heart." This gesture of the government did not sit well with some of the local people. They wanted these Christians expelled from the property of the shrine. One day a politician who had promised action on the matter asked for a tour of the facility.

When he emerged outside to face the disgruntled crowd, he announced, "It is true I promised you that these nuns would leave, but that can happen only when you send your mothers, wives, daughters, and sisters to take their place. At the shrine there is a wooden goddess; here there are living goddesses."

With her work underway, Teresa's next big concern was how to do all this by herself. *Lord, send me helpers. You see how much need surrounds me,* she prayed. On a day in early 1949 Sister Teresa turned from the person she was serving to see a familiar face. It was one of the young women she had taught at the Loreto School.

Shubashini Das was an intelligent young woman from a well-to-do Indian family. "Mother, I am here to help with your work," she declared. Sister Teresa wanted to welcome her with a grateful embrace, but instead she sent the young woman away, telling her to think about it carefully. If she was still interested she could come back in a couple of months. Reluctantly her would-be companion walked away.

However, after two months had passed Shubashini Das was back. "Okay, Mother. Two months have passed and now I am here to stay." She became Sister Agnes, the first of many. Soon three more former students arrived to join their beloved teacher in her new work.

When a few more anxious new disciples arrived, Sister Teresa applied for canonical permission to form a new religious congregation "to serve the poorest of the poor." She explained, "We are to be called the Missionaries of Charity. In addition to the vows of chastity, poverty, and obedience, we will also take a vow of charity."

The constitutions she prepared in the evenings after caring for the sick were approved on the feast of Our Lady of the Holy Rosary in 1950. This allowed Teresa, now *Mother Teresa*, to begin her foundation within the Archdiocese of Calcutta. By 1965 the Missionaries of Charity had received approval from Pope Paul VI and had begun their worldwide expansion with the first house outside of India, in Venezuela. With God's blessing, the community and its works grew and prospered.

Often people are amazed at the poor living conditions of the Missionaries of Charity themselves. Mother Teresa was always ready to explain the sacrifices being made by her daughters:

> We must suffer with Christ if we are to share in the sufferings of the poor. Our Congregation would die out if we did not embrace the poverty of the poor Christ. This strict poverty is a safeguard. Otherwise, we might end up as did other congregations in the history of the Church who began by serving the poor, but ended up sharing the life of the wealthy. Living poorly helps us to understand the poor. The radical difference is this: those we serve are poor against their will; we, however, are poor by choice.

Mother Teresa had become well known throughout India and the world for her selfless charity to the poorest of the poor. Equally well known was her beautiful countenance, that serene and smiling face, which graced countless magazine and book covers. Almost no one knew, however, what lay behind that smile. Mother Teresa admitted that she "smiled at Jesus in order to hide, if possible, my soul's pain and darkness even from him." In her correspondence with her spiritual director and the archbishop, she revealed that although prayer used to be easy for her, she had been living in spiritual darkness since she started "the work."

Despite having many sisters and collaborators Mother Teresa lived with deep loneliness as her "traveling companion." And although she continued to encourage her coworkers to offer themselves as "cheerful victims" to God, God remained hidden from her.

Mother Teresa had often noted that the greatest poverty in the world is loneliness. Did it ever occur to her that this gift of darkness that dwelt in her soul was given to help her truly identify with the desperate state of "the poorest of the poor"—those whose material and spiritual lives were shrouded in darkness? Her darkness was her share in the lot of the poor. It was her mysticism, her offering of love to her Beloved Jesus Crucified who had died without the consoling vision of his Father.

Archbishop Périer tried to reassure her that she must not worry too much. "God's blessing is on your work; thank him for it." He added that she should "tell the Lord, 'Do with me as you see fit,' and then refuse him nothing." Somehow, despite her own struggles, Jesus was making her a source of enlightenment to millions as he had promised to do when he first invited her to "come be my light."

When her own strength finally failed and death was near at hand, Mother Teresa must have relived her many struggles and victories. Perhaps she recalled all the people who had been rescued from the streets and nursed back to good health; the dying accompanied lovingly to the gates of heaven; the unwanted children who found a home; the lonely and abandoned she had befriended; the many religious who shared her calling to cast the light of the Lord wherever they went; and the many coworkers who labored with such love along with her sisters. They had all done so much good. Did she regret this "call within a call," which had taken her around the world in search of the poorest of the poor? No, it was all done at the request of God himself. She often repeated these words to Jesus, "I have never refused you anything." How much light her spirit continues to bring to the world today in the wonderful work that began with her heroic "yes."

Prayer

> Blessed Teresa of Calcutta, mother of the poor, help us find in Jesus
> the light and the strength we need to face the trials and darkness,
> the poverty and loneliness of life. May we, like you,
> gift the world with a generous heart and loving deeds.
> May God's love radiate through our smile. And with you,
> may we find the courage to defend life in all its forms and at every stage.
> Ask for us from Jesus the desire to always serve the poorest among us. Amen.

About Blessed Teresa of Calcutta

Born: August 26, 1910, in Skopje, Albania (Macedonia)
Died: September 5, 1997, in Calcutta, India
Beatified: October 19, 2003, by Pope John Paul II

Memorial: September 5
Patron: World Youth Day

Notes on Her Life

✿ Her birth name was Agnes Gonxha Bojaxhiu, but she is commonly known as Mother Teresa of Calcutta.

✿ She entered the Institute of the Blessed Virgin Mary of Loreto in October 1928, in Dublin, Ireland.

✿ She arrived in India on January 6, 1929, and made her profession on May 24, 1931.

✿ She taught schoolchildren and did teacher training at Saint Mary's School in Calcutta.

✿ She became a citizen of India in 1948, and that same year she left the Loreto Sisters and began to serve the poor.

✿ She founded several congregations: the Missionaries of Charity (1950), the active Missionaries of Charity Brothers (1963), the contemplative Missionaries of Charity Sisters (1976), the contemplative Missionaries of Charity Brothers (1979), and the Priest Missionaries of Charity (1984).

✿ She also inspired the Co-Workers of Mother Teresa, the Sick and Suffering Co-Workers, and the Lay Missionaries of Charity, and she began the Corpus Christi Movement for Priests.

✿ She received many awards including:

— The Padmashri Award (1962)

— The Pope John XXIII Peace Prize (1971)

— The Jawaharlal Nehru Award for International Understanding (1972)

— The Nobel Peace Prize (1979).

⟨⟩ The great number of miracles reported after her death prompted the Holy See to open her cause within five years of her death.

⟨⟩ Monika Besra's cure of abdominal tumor was the recognized miracle.

⟨⟩ She was beatified six years after death.

⟨⟩ At her death, there were 4,000 Missionaries of Charity working in 123 countries.

Lesser-Known Facts

⟨⟩ She was fluent in Hindi and Bengali.

⟨⟩ Most of the first sisters were her former pupils.

⟨⟩ People referred to her as "Ma" (Bengali for mother).

⟨⟩ She lived with spiritual darkness for most of her religious life.

In Her Own Words

"It is not how much we do, but how much love we put in the doing. It is not how much we give, but how much love we put in the giving."

Saint Rose of Lima

What Can I Give a God
Who Has Everything?

And again he said, "To what should I compare the kingdom of God? It is like yeast that a woman took and mixed in with three measures of flour until all of it was leavened" (Lk 13:20–21).

Evening had already settled on the city of Lima, Peru. A sudden commotion broke out in the home of Gaspar Flores, as his wife Maria discovered that supper was not ready.

"Marianna, Marianna . . . where are you? Why aren't you preparing supper?"

Maria Flores opened the kitchen window overlooking the family garden. She motioned to Marianna, the Indian servant girl, who was standing at the gate.

"Come in now. What are you doing out there at this hour?"

Marianna hesitated and then spoke, "Its Señorita Rose, Señora. She heard the cry of someone in pain, and went to see if she could help."

"Out on the street?" the anxious mother asked. "What is that girl thinking of?"

She was about to slam the window shut and go down to the garden herself, when she saw the front gate slowly swing open. A young girl's voice called to her:

"It's all right, Mama. This poor woman was alone, and she slipped and fell on the walk. Her knee is badly hurt."

"But . . ."

"She's cold . . . and hungry, too, Mama. Can't we help her?"

Rose's gentle pleading muted her mother's objections. How could she refuse? Rose was always helping someone, either with food or clothing, not to mention all the prayers and sacrifices she offered daily. Mama Flores sighed:

"Ah, well . . . yes, bring her in. At least we can give her a good meal."

Attentively, her mother observed Rose as she carefully seated the woman at table.

"What a pity," Mama grumbled to herself, "Rose is such a beautiful girl, but she won't even think of marriage. All she worries about is those ragged people. Perhaps she'll change her mind some day."

Rose had a modesty and charm that won the hearts of friends and relatives alike, and her mother had looked forward with pleasure to a good marriage for her daughter.

But Rose had other interests. She had been greatly impressed by an incident that happened on her Confirmation day. She and two other children were confirmed in the parish church of a small mountain village outside Lima. Most of the villagers were Indians who were still a long way from being

Christianized. The cruelty of some of the Spanish soldiers who had overrun and conquered the land caused the majority of the Indians to distrust anything that came from Spain, including the faith the missionaries preached.

When the Confirmation ceremony was over, Rose and her mother left the church. A group of Indians gathered around them in the plaza. They began to shout angrily: "Look at the Christians!"

"They think their God is in that church!"

"Fools!"

Hearing the uproar, the archbishop came to the church door. He tried to calm the crowd, but they jeered and shook their fists at him. Finally Rose and Señora Flores fearfully made their way around the edge of the crowd and headed home. Rose never forgot that day! She explained to her mother:

"God inspired me to do something for the souls of those Indians. . . . I want to share with them the treasure of my faith."

"But how?" Mama asked.

"I can pray, and offer my whole day, every day, to God for their intentions. I can be patient about little troubles and ask Jesus to help these poor people."

Little by little as the days, weeks, and months passed, Rose grew in union with God, in her love for him and for his people. She realized more and more how much the Indians suffered materially and spiritually. And so, for the love of them, she increased her penances, fasting and rising at night to pray. At the same time she kept herself busy and useful at home, especially by growing flowers that Marianna, the Indian servant, sold at the market.

Mama Flores was getting impatient again. She wanted to distract her pretty young daughter from the life of hard work and prayer to which she was devoting herself. The anxious mother often invited friends to visit, and then she would ask Rose to sing and play her guitar. Mama would call, "Rose, come and join us!"

Although Rose enjoyed their company and wanted to please her mother by entertaining them, she always felt attracted to a more hidden life. As she explained one day to one of her closest friends, Doña Maria de Quinones, "Mother doesn't seem to understand that I don't care about pretty dresses and having a good time. Jesus has taught me how much he loves each person and he wants me to help him save them."

"Well, why don't you become a religious?"

Rose's eyes sparkled with joy as she replied, "I've thought about that, Doña Maria. Ever since I read about the life of Saint Catherine of Siena, I've wanted to be a Dominican Tertiary, just like her."

Doña Maria shook her head and whispered, "That is a difficult life, child. It takes a very special grace."

"You are right, Doña Maria. I've prayed and asked God to help me find out what his will is for me. Right now I believe that this is it."

"Well, we'll see," her friend replied.

When she was twenty, Rose obtained her father's permission to care for some of the city's many poor women who were ill and homeless. A section of the Flores home was set apart for this purpose, and it soon came to be called "the Infirmary."

Drawn by Rose's kindness and genuine concern, more and more women came to this new infirmary. Mama Flores sometimes lost her temper over the number of "patients," and would complain, "At her age! She should be thinking of marriage. It's a shame!"

Her husband would defend his daughter, "Now, Maria. Keep calm. You know that Rose has told us she intends never to marry!"

"Well, what is she going to do?"

That was a good question! Just a few weeks later, on August 10, Rose Flores joined the Dominican Order as a tertiary and received the longed-for religious habit. Although the circumstances and routine of her life had not changed, an interior change was taking place. Her thirst for souls and her love for solitude, prayer, and sacrifice grew daily. The great interior peace and joy that she felt were reflected even on her face and in her actions. She had wanted for such a long time to give her life more completely to Jesus.

On Palm Sunday of the following year, our Lord gave Rose a special sign that he had accepted her generous gift. She was kneeling in prayer after the procession of the palms, gazing at the statue of the Madonna and Child. Suddenly, right before the girl's eyes, our Lady smiled and turned toward the Infant in her arms. These words of Jesus himself sounded in the depths of her soul:

"Rose, be my spouse!"

The young tertiary could hardly contain her joy! From that day on these words echoed in her soul and she carried the treasured memory with her always. She increased the number and severity of her penances, sleeping only two hours a night and fasting for long periods of time.

Finally, when the young Dominican asked her parents' permission to live in a little hut in the garden, Mama Flores threw up her hands in despair and exclaimed to her husband, "I've tried threats . . . pleading and tears to persuade Rose to cut down on her fasting and to take better care of her health. She always listens so respectfully, but. . . ."

Señor Flores stared at the floor in silence as Rose responded: "Mother, I know that you are concerned for me. But . . . this is the best way for me to please God and to help my brothers and sisters in Christ. Please let me continue."

And her mother always had to give in. But the hard life Rose had freely chosen began to affect her health. She became pale and very thin. When she was just twenty-nine, her physical condition caused her confessor much concern, and he placed her under obedience to go and live with her friend, Doña Maria. Rose accepted this new sacrifice with her characteristic cheerfulness, despite the difficulty of leaving her family and her garden cell. In Doña Maria's home she made herself as useful as she could, sewing, doing housework, and caring for the younger children, even though her friend kept reminding Rose that she was a welcome guest.

Though Rose's health did improve, she knew that she would not live much longer. Shortly before her death she confided to Doña Maria, "Our Lord let me know that I will die soon . . . on August 24, Saint Bartholomew's feast."

On the night of August 1, Rose began the last and most painful part of her offering to the Lord. She lay dying of an incurable illness. Even breathing became almost impossible. Doña Maria and her family called in priests and doctors whom Rose knew. The young woman smiled weakly as she saw the efforts made to ease her mounting sufferings.

On the eve of August 24, she asked to see her parents. Rose whispered in her same sweet way, "I want to say good-bye. And I want to ask forgiveness of everyone for whom I may have caused trouble."

Many visitors came to see Rose throughout the day. She had befriended, helped, and encouraged many of them. Others had heard rumors of her years of intense prayer and sacrifice. They hoped to get a glimpse of "the young saint" as she was being called.

The hours ticked away. It was almost midnight. Rose looked around at the people gathered in the room praying and watching. She whispered with a smile: "Please don't be sad that I am leaving you. . . . This is really such a happy day."

Her mother wept at her bedside. She kept saying over and over: "Rose, forgive me, I should have tried to understand you better. Forgive me, child."

After a few moments of silence, Rose lifted a crucifix to her lips and whispered, "Jesus, be with me. . . ."

A thrill of suspense raced through all those in the room. Mama Flores dried her eyes. Then she stood and stared at her daughter.

"It's all over. . . . It's all over. My little girl has gone to heaven."

Rose of Lima died at the age of thirty-one. She has left us an example of prayer, penance, and heroic virtue practiced constantly and generously for the salvation of her countrymen, and for the souls in purgatory.

Prayer

Dear Saint Rose, you who were the first flower of
    sanctity in the New World,
we thank you for the generosity of heart and strength
    of character
that brought you to embrace the needs of the poor
    of Lima.

You sought justice for the oppressed Indian people, relief
for the poor,
care for the sick, conversion of heart for the sinner, and
the salvation of everyone.
You never denied Jesus anything and so were blessed
with the heights of prayer.
You patiently endured misunderstanding and censure,
offering all your suffering as a gift of love
to the One who claimed your heart from childhood.
Teach us the value of a life centered on pleasing God in
everything
and serving others, especially those in most need.
Help us realize that the little prayers and sacrifices of life
lead to the joy of heaven. Amen.

About Saint Rose of Lima

Born: April 20, 1586, in Lima, Peru

Died: August 24, 1617, in Lima, Peru

Feast Day: August 23 (August 30 in Peru)

Canonized: April 12, 1671, by Pope Clement X

Patron: Latin America, the Philippines, embroiderers,
gardeners, florists

Notes on Her Life

- Her birth name was Isabel de Flores y de Oliva, but was called by her Confirmation name, Rose.

- Her parents, Gaspar Flores, a Puerto Rican soldier, and Maria de Oliva of Lima, had eleven children.

- Her name as a Dominican tertiary was Sister Rose of Saint Mary.

❦ She received a gift of prophecy, i.e., she explained in every particular the future Monastery of Saint Catherine of Siena in Arequipa, Peru, including who would endow it, who would enter, who would be named prioress, and so forth. (She even foretold that her own mother would enter—which she did).

❦ She had great devotion to Saint Bartholomew because she knew she would die on his feast.

❦ She was buried in the chapel of the Dominican convent, and in 1619 her incorrupt body was moved to an alcove of the cathedral sanctuary.

❦ Later her body was moved again, this time to the side chapel of Saint Catherine of Siena in the cathedral.

❦ Countless miracles were attributed to her in life and after her death.

❦ Appearances of Saint Rose to various persons have been recorded.

Lesser-Known Facts

❦ She was confirmed by Saint Turibius of Mogrovejo.

❦ She was a contemporary of Saint Martin de Porres and Saint Juan Macias.

❦ She modeled her life on Saint Catherine of Siena.

❦ Rose fasted frequently and abstained from meat perpetually. She sustained her family and the poor by selling embroidery, lace, and flowers.

❦ She lived in a hermitage in her parents' backyard.

❦ She received the gift of many prophecies and ecstasies, and she performed constant penances.

Rose took a vow of perpetual virginity and joined Third Order of Saint Dominic when she was twenty years old. She was the first canonized saint of the Americas.

In Her Own Words

"I desire to love you, my God, as the saints and angels in heaven love you. And even more, God of my heart, of my life, you who are the joy of my soul, I desire to love you, if it were possible, as much as the Blessed Virgin, your Mother and my sweet Lady, loves you."

Saint Hildegard of Bingen

"The Sybil of the Rhine"

"Therefore every scribe who has been trained for the kingdom of heaven is like the master of a household who brings out of his treasure what is new and what is old" (Mt 13:52).

Hildegard remembered little of life outside of this monastery. It has been some time since the death of Mother Jutta. Hildegard, the new "magistra," or teacher, was resolute. She had been at this foundation since its beginning. She had literally grown up here. When she was only eight years old her parents had placed her first with Uda, for her early education, and then as a helper to Jutta. Actually, Jutta had intended to live as a recluse, but over the years others had sought out her counsel, and so she formed a monastery. Now the time had arrived for a bold new move.

Hildegard announced to the assembled community: "I want to move our whole monastery away from the dominance of the men's monastery. I appreciate their help all these years, but I want our monastery to have independence."

"Mother Hildegard, you will not be granted that release. It is unheard-of," said one sister.

"The situation is not that trying," another suggested.

"I will find a way," Hildegard replied. "It is not my will alone. It is true that I say, 'I want . . . I will have it . . .' but it is not only my will, it is God who wants it!"

How would a woman in a twelfth century Benedictine enclosure even consider such a move? It is probably enough to say that Hildegard of Bingen was by no means a typical medieval nun. She was a visionary, both in the literal sense of having had visions from her early childhood, and in the sense of being a forward-thinking woman.

The older members of the community anxiously asked, "Where shall we go, Mother? If we leave Saint Disibod, where will we reside?" The nuns knew little of the land beyond the area where they had spent most of their lives.

"I have made inquiries, through various friends, and I am told that a former monastery—now in ruins, by the way—exists near Bingen. We will relocate there," Hildegard stated.

"It's now a ruin? How can we occupy a ruin, Mother?"

"Do not distress yourself," Hildegard responded, attempting to reassure her flock. "Remember I told you this is God's will. Has he ever failed us? In time we will find ourselves in Bingen. For now, let us carry on our way of life in peace."

Ten years earlier, Hildegard had received a very significant personal command concerning the secrets of her spiritual life. "Since my childhood," she wrote to a priest, "I have been subject to many deeply mysterious visions. I don't see anything with my bodily eyes, but within my soul a whole world opens up."

For years she did not understand what was happening. She did know, however, that it was God's work, not anything she could control. "This happens," she noted, "as I am standing, fully awake, in the midst of my daily life."

Now God had decided, it seemed, that Hildegard was to begin publicizing what she saw in these visions.

"But, I am loathe to bring this attention to myself. How will it affect my own religious life, and that of my sisters?"

She worried about discussing her visions. Did God really want this, or did it spring from her own pride? She had to know for certain. So Hildegard sent a letter to the well-known Cistercian writer Bernard of Clairvaux. She wrote to him explaining that she saw in these visions the meaning of the Old and New Testament, but had no way of interpreting what she saw. She even revealed to Bernard that she had seen him in her vision two years earlier and told him, "you looked into the sun as one unafraid, as a very brave man. I beg you to explain these things to me. I have kept silent about them out of fear, but now God has struck me down with a serious sickness until I should speak. Advise me, please."

Hildegard had been extremely ill, and she believed it was due to her unwillingness to make her visions known. She had written them down with the help of Volmar, the Benedictine monk assigned by the monastery to be her adviser, and a nun, Sister Richardis von Stade, who was also a dear friend. Her great writing project took ten years to complete.

Bernard of Clairvaux had, in fact, already heard of Hildegard the Seer from her bishop, Henry of Mainz. And Bernard, in turn, had the opportunity to consult Pope Eugene III.

"While Your Holiness is here in Trier for the synod of bishops," Bernard ventured, "would you be able to give an opinion on a particular nun, a visionary?"

"Tell me, Bernard, what is your own estimation of her? After all, you are more the man of the spiritual realm than I am. I may be pope and a Cistercian, but I am afraid my duties keep me somewhat preoccupied."

"Holy Father, may I suggest that you send for a copy of her mystical experiences and we can review them together. I will then give you my insights as well."

The pope asked, "You say she has copies? Has it been published already?"

"Oh, no, Holy Father. She does have a bound copy, but it is the work of her secretaries. I believe it is called *Know the Lord's Ways* or by just the abbreviation, *Scivias*."

Since Trier was close to Saint Disibod, the manuscript arrived quickly and the two men scrutinized the visions.

Not long after, Hildegard was standing in the monastery great room surrounded by the community. "Look here, sisters. Not only has Pope Eugene III given a positive opinion of the visions, he has also sent us his blessing. Now we can go ahead," Hildegard declared. She was grateful for such public recognition. Now she could share freely with others what God had revealed to her.

"Mother Hildegard, could we celebrate this by singing some of the 'Symphony of the Harmony' that you composed?" Sister Richardis suggested.

"Oh, yes, that will be a perfect song of gratitude, Mother," another interjected. "Of course, sisters," Hildegard concurred. "Let us go into the presence of our Heavenly Lord and sing out a song of praise."

Soon the whole house was ringing with the joyful sound of their abundant thanks.

In monasteries of both nuns and monks all over Europe, religious quickly began to adopt practices that were now common among the sisters of the new foundation at Bingen, which was christened for Saint Rupert. Hildegard's reputation grew so great that many women came to join her in Rupertsberg. Soon she needed to found another monastery, and she chose a site across the Rhine in Eibingen.

When the nuns heard of this plan, they marveled anew at Hildegard's courage and stamina.

"Have you noticed that our magistra lives out of an amazing balancing act?" asked a particular nun.

"Do you mean her remarkable creative spirit, despite her terrible migraine headaches?" replied a second sister.

"Exactly! How do you think she does this?"

The second sister, after looking carefully up and down the corridor, whispered, "I have heard some think her visions are really products of those headaches."

"Oh, well, I think her prayer life and her dependence on our superiors guarantees that she is not dreaming up anything she says. I really believe we live with a prophetess. One other thing that speaks in her favor," she went on, "is certainly that the Church authorizes her preaching ventures."

"She will certainly have much to relate when she returns at the end of the month. This is her fourth preaching tour."

The nuns were impressed that she had official permission to leave the monastery for a preaching tour around Germany. Actually, she was doing the whole Church a favor by firing up the fervor of her hearers and also by addressing bad practices such as simony. Hildegard was definitely a woman of prodigious talent. She wrote a number of books on a variety of topics such as medicine, herbal cures, sexuality, poetry, aestheticism, virtue, music, cosmology, botany, drama, and liturgy. Besides these activities, Hildegard also kept up a voluminous correspondence.

Everything was going well until she made a fateful decision near the end of her life. When a man who had been excommunicated died, Hildegard authorized his burial in the cemetery attached to the Rupertsberg monastery. At least that was what the clergy of Mainz contended.

"I will not allow his body to be exhumed from our cemetery, reverend fathers. Please inform the lord bishop that I believe it would be sinful to remove him from his grave," Mother Hildegard insisted.

"But we have been told that he was never reconciled to the Church. He cannot be buried in a blessed spot. Surely, Mother, you are aware of this?"

"I am aware of the Church's disposition. I am also knowledgeable about his soul. He did make his peace on his deathbed," Hildegard responded.

"We have no proof of what you say, Mother, and so I am authorized to pronounce an excommunication on you and your house. I suggest you reconsider," the bishop's representative told her.

Because Hildegard knew what she knew, she did not retract her intention regarding the deceased man. The excommunication went into effect and lasted six months. The whole monastery stood with Mother Hildegard in her judgment and together endured the loss of Mass, the sacraments, and other liturgical activities. When the diocesan authorities at last relented, for reasons lost in history, the whole Rupertsberg community rejoiced that God had brought them through a difficult time with a courageous leader.

Not long after this incident, Hildegard fell into her last illness and went on to the ultimate vision of God.

Prayer

Dear Saint Hildegard, as a woman you were inspired
to advance knowledge of the needs, the roles, and the
abilities of women
as well as the spirituality of the feminine.
You also formed a balanced life for nuns in your
monasteries.
Your contributions to a wide-ranging field of arts and
sciences
enriched the basis of human culture.
We are grateful to you for all of this, but we are
especially indebted
that you allowed God to fill your soul with the visions
of salvation history.
Blessed be you, our God, for gifting this woman and
with her all of us,
by allowing her to glimpse your glory.
May the hope of this glory sustain us in the trials
of this life
and lead us to the triumph of your holy home. Amen.

About Saint Hildegard of Bingen

Born: 1098 in Bermersheim, Rhineland, Germany

Died: September 17, 1179, in Rupertsberg

Feast Day: September 17

Canonized: May 10, 2012, by Pope Benedict XVI by the
process of equivalent canonization (in which the pope
extends to the universal Church the feast of a holy
person who has been venerated as a saint but not
officially canonized)

Patron: women's education, vocations to monastic life

Notes on Her Life

- Her parents were Hildebert and Mechtildis, probably of the nobility, but the family surname is unknown.

- The youngest of ten children, she was a sickly child who received little education.

- At the age of eight she went to live with Uda of Gölklheim, and later with Jutta of Sponheim, a recluse in Speyer.

- Hildegard began having visions as a child.

- She learned Latin for singing the psalms at an early age although she could not yet read.

- In 1112 with Jutta and companions, Hildegard made profession as a Benedictine in Disibodenberg.

- Jutta died in 1136, and Hildegard became superior or "magistra."

- She wrote a theological trilogy (1141–1151): *Scivias* ("Know the Lord's Ways"); *Liber vitae meritorum* ("Book of Life's Rewards"); and *Liber divinorum operum* ("Book of Divine Works").

- Her other works include: *Ordo virtutum* ("Order of the Virtues"); *Physica* (on the physical world or natural sciences); *Causae et Curae* (natural cures); and the Dendermonde and the Riesenkodex manuscripts (treating music, literature, and science).

- She wrote often to popes, bishops, abbots, emperors, nuns, and others, and she made four preaching tours in Germany.

- In 1148 she moved the convent to Rupertsberg, and in 1165 she established a convent in Eibingen.

- She was declared a Doctor of the Church on October 7, 2012, by Pope Benedict XVI.

Lesser-Known Facts

- She created a twenty-six-character-alphabet known as Lingua Ignota.
- She learned to play twelve-stringed psaltery.
- She was reluctant to publicize her visions until she was struck with illness.
- The monk Volmar, who was appointed as her secretary, was succeeded by Godfrey, who wrote her biography (*Vita*).
- Her writings were approved by her local bishop and by Pope Eugene III.
- She is credited with introducing harmonic fifths into music.
- Her music and poetry are often performed and recorded.
- Four previous attempts to canonize her failed due to faulty documentation; however, she was listed in the Roman martyrology (official list of saints).
- Her relics are now in the parish church in Eibingen.

In Her Own Words

"And I, poor little woman, how could I not know that I am so? God chooses to work as he wills, for his own glory, and not for ours. Yes, I am full of trepidation having no confidence in my own ability. I stand with my hands opened up toward God, that he might support me. I am a feather that has neither weight nor will, but which is carried on the wind. I am incapable, in my bodily state or in my invisible soul, to understand what I see. It is not an ability of the human state. Yet, ever since I was a child, I have seen this vision in my soul."

— From a letter to Guibert of Gembloux

Saint Francis Xavier

Set the World on Fire!

"I came to bring fire to the earth, and how I wish it were already kindled" (Lk 12:49).

It was November 1552. A dejected figure stood on the shore, staring off into the distance. Only six miles away lay the Chinese mainland, its rugged coastline barely visible through the morning mist. Again, this morning, as on so many other mornings, Father Francis Xavier waited for the promised Chinese merchant junk—that again never came. His jaws tightly set, Francis wrapped his paper-thin cloak around his shivering body and trudged back to his makeshift hut.

Sorely disappointed, he sank down onto his mat and buried his head in his hands. How lonely and frustrated he felt! Now he would never be able to bring the Gospel of Christ into China.

Francis suddenly felt a tide of anger welling up within him as he remembered the painful circumstances that had brought him to the lonely island of

Shangchuan. "That meddlesome man, d'Ataíde," he muttered to himself. "It's his fault that I'm here. . . . He is jealous of Diogo Pereira because Pereira was appointed ambassador to China instead of him." Dom Álvaro d'Ataíde da Gama, son of the famous explorer Vasco da Gama, was appointed captain of Malacca's fleet in the 1540s, and captain of Malacca itself from 1552 to 1554.

But then, before his pride could get the upper hand, Francis reacted. "Father, forgive him," he mumbled half aloud. "And forgive me. It is your will that I am here. Forgive me, dear Lord, for my lack of confidence and love. Forgive me for my weakness." Yes, the captain had upset all of his plans and offended Francis. What of it? It was God's will, and God would straighten things out in his own good time.

The cold November winds ripped the priest's wasted body as fever raced through him and his strength continued to seep away. Pulling himself over to the low table, Francis penned his last letter. "It's a long time," he wrote with a shaking hand, "since I felt so little inclined to go on living." As he wrote, the faces of all his friends and converts passed before him. He gave advice and counsel to the missionaries he had left behind in India, Malacca, and Japan. Tears welled up in his eyes as he recalled their affection for him, their loyalty to the Gospel and to the person of Christ. How good they were! How unworthy he felt. Slowly and painfully, Francis folded the letter. He walked to his mat and fell on it. For some reason sleep wouldn't come. Perhaps it was the bitter cold, or the fever, or perhaps . . . He felt that his end was near and he should review his life. So much had happened to him in forty-six years.

Real living began for Francis in 1534 when he surrendered to a lame soldier, Ignatius of Loyola. Ignatius constantly pounded him with the question, "What does it profit a man to gain the whole world but lose his soul?" (Mt 16:26)

Now Francis mused, "My, how I fought Ignatius, and how I fought God, who was using Ignatius to call me to himself. Didn't Ignatius tell me that I was the toughest dough he ever had to knead? My God, thank you for the grace to surrender to you and to the guidance and advice of my father in Christ. Thank you for leading me to embrace a life of poverty, humility, and obedience. Where would I be now if Ignatius had given up on me?" Beads of perspiration rolled down Francis's face as he remembered the wayward deeds of his youth. Only much prayer, sacrifice, and self-discipline had enabled him to dominate his impetuosity and his vain and pleasure-loving spirit.

Quiet returned to Xavier as he recalled his ordination day. How anxious and impatient he had been to start working for Christ! By dint of sheer will power and generous response to God's grace, he had learned to wait patiently on the will of God.

And through the fruit of his own experience, he was able to advise his comrades, "Each one should strive to win the battle of his own heart before setting out to reform others. The way to conquer fear is to find courage totally in God. The road of true progress for a man is to show his greatness in little things."

As his fever rose higher and higher, Francis tossed and turned on his bed of pain. Days passed. This fever reminded him of his power idea, the command Ignatius had given him when he had assigned him to the mission in India and the Orient: "Go and set the world on fire!" Yes, even as fever consumed his body, his life had already been consumed by the fire of the love of God and men that burned unceasingly there. God had given him so much love that at times in his life he had to tell Christ, "Enough, O Lord, enough! My heart cannot stand all the love you are giving me. Do not take these crosses away from me unless you give me heavier ones."

Eleven years before he lay dying on Shangchuan, Xavier had embarked on a staggering adventure for Christ. The sufferings of the thirteen-month voyage to India had tempered the steel in him and enlarged his heart. Once ashore, he had spent and overspent himself to bring the Gospel both to those who knew it but didn't live it, and to those who had never heard of it before. His mornings had been a ceaseless round of visits to the sick and imprisoned; his afternoons, a series of intensive catechism classes; his evenings, a round of Bible storytelling; his nights, a preparation of prayer and penance for the apostolate of the following day.

Xavier hadn't mastered all the Indian dialects, so he had simply acted as a Christian should. He knew how to smile. He had been firm when necessary. But rather than drive people away by pouring vinegar on their spiritual wounds, he had striven to draw them to Christ with the honey of compassion, understanding, and kindness.

It had taken a great deal of courage to walk through the crowded streets, ringing his little bell and preaching in halting, imperfect speech. But he had made charts, diagrams, and pictures to convey the Christian truths. He had even set these truths to catchy tunes and simple melodies that made them fly from village to village and port to port.

After three short years in India, Francis could count 20,000 new Christians in thirty different villages. Then he had moved on to the Maluku Islands and beyond to continue "setting the world on fire." He couldn't rest as long as even only one person in the world didn't know Christ and the Christian message! Despite the tropical heat, despite surviving three shipwrecks, and despite constant danger from pirates and cannibals, he had labored for two years in that seething maze of islands and could number one hundred converts there.

Back to India then, and off to Japan! Japan had never before met Christ. Francis endured many hardships and disappointments along with success. His success, however, had been won at the cost of great personal sacrifice. But after two years in Japan, the fruits of Francis's mission had been consoling—more than 2,000 converts.

It had all passed now. And as the hours slowly ebbed by in the little hut on the island of Shangchuan, Francis's fever turned into delirium. He babbled incoherently. In his lucid moments, he would gaze out his door at the Chinese coast and heave deep sighs. "Oh, if only I could enter China! But it is not your will, Lord. Your will be done. How many souls there are to reach yet! How many do not become Christians simply because they have no one to preach to them! Sometimes I wish I could run through the hallways of the universities in Europe and cry out like a madman to those educated people who aren't using their learning to do good. If only they realized how many souls lose heaven because they sit by and do nothing about helping. They should be required to take a course on using one's God-given talents for you. If only more people realized how they could make this world a better place, and help people know you, Lord!"

As Francis lay dying, his faithful companion, Paul, a young Chinese Christian, kept his sorrowful vigil. He would one day give a detailed account of the last days of his dear father in Christ. But now he tried to shelter Francis from the piercing winds as best he could and knelt close to him so as not to miss a word.

Between his spells, Francis prayed continually, gazing at his beloved crucifix and murmuring, "Jesus, Son of David, have mercy on me. Mother of God, remember me!" Humanly speaking, it was a strange and sad end to his heroic labors for Christ. But what did that matter? "In you, O Lord, have I hoped!" he exclaimed. "Let me never be confounded."

On December 3, 1552, Francis Xavier went to the Christ he had loved so much on earth. Francis was a torch lifted high to dispel the darkness of error and sin. From that happy day in 1534 when he had said yes to God, this man of fire had striven to conquer himself. Because of this God had blessed his labors and used him to bring the light of truth to thousands who otherwise would have remained in darkness.

Prayer

Saint Francis Xavier, you lit the world afire
with your intense love of God and zeal for souls.
Despite the dangers and inconvenience of travel
you sought out those who needed the saving word
    of God.
You devised clever philosophical arguments to convince
    the learned,
and charming songs and games for the children.
In your lifetime and throughout the centuries since, you
    have inspired many
to generously dedicate themselves to the missions of the
    Church at home and abroad.
Obtain for us from the Lord you served so completely
a strong, vibrant, and constant love for the kingdom
    of God.
Inspire many today to give themselves generously to the
    work of evangelization
in far-flung missions, in classrooms, at home, at work, at

every moment of their lives.
May God light our hearts on fire, too.
We want to be men and women in love with God
and touched by the same flame of love that burned so
brightly in you. Amen.

About Saint Francis Xavier

Born: April 7, 1506, in Xavier, Navarre (now Spain)

Died: December 3, 1552, on Shangchuan Island, China

Feast Day: December 3

Canonized: March 12, 1622, by Pope Gregory XV

Patron: foreign missions, the Apostleship of Prayer, India
and the Far East, Navarre, Spain, tourism

Notes on His Life

❧ Born Francisco de Jasso y Azpilicueta, he was the son of
a privy counselor to King Juan III of Navarre.

❧ His first language was Basque.

❧ In 1516 the family castle was conquered by the duke of
Alba for the kingdoms of Castile and Aragon.

❧ In 1525 he left to study at College Sainte-Barbe in Paris,
where he met Ignatius of Loyola.

❧ In 1530 Francis received a master of arts degree; to many
he was known as "Master Francis."

❧ In 1534 he took vows in Montmartre with Ignatius of
Loyola and others, marking the beginning of the Society
of Jesus.

❧ On June 24, 1537, he was ordained to the priesthood in
Venice, Italy.

* He became a secretary of Saint Ignatius of Loyola.

* In 1541 Francis was appointed apostolic nuncio to Portuguese India; he traveled to Goa with two companions.

* In April 1542 he began work with pearl fishers on the east coast of India, establishing many parishes.

* In 1545 he arrived at Malacca in Malaysia.

* In 1546–1547 he worked among the people of the Maluku Islands of Indonesia.

* He landed in Japan on July 27, 1549, but at first was not welcome and was forbidden to preach.

* Eventually he had some success in Hirado, Yamaguchi, and other places in Japan.

* Ignatius of Loyola appointed him as provincial of India and the East in 1551.

* He returned to Malacca and Goa from 1551–1552.

* In August 1552 he arrived on the Chinese Shangchuan Island. It was here that he died awaiting entrance to mainland China.

* He was buried on Shangchuan; in 1553 his incorrupt body was moved to the Basilica of Bom Jesus in Goa.

* In 1614 the relic of his right forearm was brought to the main Jesuit church, Il Gesú in Rome.

Lesser-Known Facts

* An empty tomb is maintained in Malacca where Francis Xavier was buried for two years.

* Francis preached harshly against the practices and teachings of other religions.

* He requested the king of Portugal to set up the Inquisition in Goa.

❧ After death he was instrumental in many miracles, especially Father Marcello Mastrilli's cure of a brain lesion.

❧ In 1622 he was canonized with Saints Ignatius of Loyola, Teresa of Avila, Isidore the Farmer, and Philip Neri.

❧ The novena of grace in honor of Saint Francis Xavier is prayed in preparation for his feast day.

❧ Thousands of books and articles have been written about him, and numerous works of art depict him.

In His Own Words

"First and above all, pay attention to yourself and your relationship with God and your conscience, because this is what makes it possible to be of use to others. Remember to make the particular examination of conscience at least once, if not twice, a day. Take care of your own conscience with much more care and concern than you care for anyone else's. If one isn't attentive to be good and holy, how can he expect to lead others to be so?"

Blessed James Alberione

Apostle of Communications,
Founder of the Pauline Family

"Therefore whatever you have said in the dark will be heard in the light, and what you have whispered behind closed doors will be proclaimed from the housetops" (Lk 12:3).

Before opening the front door Papa Michael turned around and asked, "Is everyone ready to go?"

"The air is chilly this evening. Make sure you all have your scarves," Mama Teresa reminded them.

With a chorus of yeses the Alberione family set out for their fields. Michael had told his sons that every hand was needed in order to cover the seed. Hoeing would protect it from too much rain. Mama Teresa had packed some bread in a small basket. Outside the house they each picked up what they would need for the work ahead of them, and then they set off.

Michael and his older sons arrived at the field first. When Mama and little James arrived, James enthusiastically called out to his father, "What shall I do, Papa?"

"James, I have a very important job for you," his father replied. Papa Alberione picked up the kerosene lamp and handed it to his youngest son. "You are going to hold up the lamp so we can see what we are doing in the field."

"I wanted to help you hoe, Papa," James offered.

"I know, son, but someone has to lead us. We will all go wherever you direct us."

"That's important, isn't it, Papa?"

"It certainly is, James. Now you go up ahead in the row . . . Okay, that's good! And turn around to face us. Very good!"

It wasn't long before the small boy grew tired. The lamp was heavy and he had to hold it high enough to shine on the rows.

His mother was keeping an eye on her youngest son. Every once in a while she would call out to him, "James, give us some light!"

A dozen years later, James reflected on that time. His mother had not said "bring us the light," but "*give* us some light." Somehow he would have the light to give; he would be light. Now he was kneeling before the Blessed Sacrament in the Cathedral of Alba, Italy, on a very significant night, the night between 1900 and 1901. James was a seminarian, and he and his classmates were encouraged to spend as much time as they liked in adoration to mark the turn of the century. Everything from his studies, his reflections, his prayers, his experiences, and his hopes were coalescing in his soul here before Jesus Host in the great monstrance on the high altar. The hard, honest work of his parents and his brothers passed through his mind. They were good, pious people of

Piedmont. His own desire to be a priest—something that had suddenly occurred to him in the second grade when Miss Cardona had asked what the children wanted to be when they grew up—was deepening in his heart. The light he now carried was this call to priesthood.

James frowned slightly as he thought of how he had almost put down that particular lamp the year before. Last year he had been sent out of the seminary of Bra where he had studied for three years. *How foolish I was,* he thought. *And stubborn! I almost let my pride and ambition get the best of me.* He had been reading books of faulty theology, and the ideas were interfering with his studies.

But, thanks to the perseverance of his pastor, James had been admitted to the seminary of Alba and was at peace.

While he was looking up at the high altar, the candles brought back another memory from his childhood. This one was about his mothers: the Blessed Mother and his own dear mother. At the end of second grade he had raced home to announce to Mama that he had passed. *And* about his promise. . . . "What promise?" Mama had asked.

"I promised Our Lady of the Flowers a candle if I passed," he had replied. His mother scolded him for making a rash promise, but she gave him enough money to place a large candle at Our Lady's shrine.

As his prayer continued on this night between the centuries, James also reflected on the new century that was dawning. What would it bring? All the seminarians had read Pope Leo XIII's latest encyclical, *Tametsi futura.* In it, he challenged Christians to dedicate themselves anew to Christ, the Redeemer of the human race. He urged the Church to address the social issues of the day, and to bring the Gospel to everyone. And professor Giuseppe Toniolo had spoken about the need to join forces around Jesus, to organize in order to accomplish great things. To Alberione these were battle cries urging the Church to carry out its mission to evangelize, and he felt an obligation to respond. *What if we used the very same means that some use to oppose the Gospel, such as the press, to spread the Gospel?* the young seminarian pondered.

As these thoughts raced through his mind, James was drawn into the light reflecting off the great monstrance. The Host seemed surrounded by light. "I am with you always until the end of time," Jesus seemed to say. "Come to me. . . ." These words from the Gospel of Matthew penetrated the heart of the young seminarian. Jesus was offering new light, nourishment, comfort, victory, and purpose to James. His future was not clear, but he had found his purpose and moti-vation. From then on James directed all his reading, study, and prayer toward the light that had embraced him that night.

Shortly after James was ordained, his bishop appointed him spiritual director at the seminary of Alba. His assign-ments also included master of ceremonies, librarian, and professor of liturgy and art. From these responsibilities he gained valuable insight and experience for his central calling. In prayer James began to understand more clearly what the light of the night between the centuries would lead him to. He began to see a way to put the Gospel in the hands of everyone. The idea of "an organization of Catholic writers, technicians, book dealers, and salesmen" was formulating within him. In time, he found himself the managing editor of the diocesan newspaper, the *Gazette* of Alba. This was another invaluable shaft of light for his future mission.

While continuing all his diocesan assignments, Father Alberione began accepting boys, most of whom he had met in the parishes or at the seminary, to become the nucleus of his Little Worker School of Typography. The first thing they printed on their secondhand press was a catechism prepared by Father Alberione himself. With the school for boys underway, Father Alberione soon opened a workshop for women in May 1915. The original purpose of this initiative was to provide the local church with good catechists. The young women also ran a small shop that carried books and religious articles. Alberione told them that the day would come when they too would be apostles of the good press: writing, editing, printing, and binding God's word, which they would also carry to homes and schools across Italy and even in other lands. In the beginning, however, they concentrated on making army uniforms to support themselves.

Father Alberione had asked Teresa Merlo, a holy young woman and a professional seamstress, to lead the group of young women. In December 1918 they took over the publication and distribution of the weekly newspaper of the diocese of Susa. With their success and enthusiasm, Father Alberione began to see in them the foundation for a religious congregation. This vision of religious apostles, both men and women, would anchor all his initiatives through the years. Religious congregations would guarantee stability and continuity to whatever God inspired. Two new communities were born: the Society of Saint Paul (priests and brothers), and the Daughters of Saint Paul (which developed out of the women's workshop).

As Father Alberione contemplated the inspiration he had received, he later founded three other congregations of women religious: the Sister Disciples of the Divine Master (liturgical apostolate), the Sisters of the Good Shepherd (pastoral apostolate), and the Sisters of Mary Queen of Apostles (vocational apostolate). The Pauline Cooperators, a lay association, complemented these congregations. In his later years,

Alberione added four vowed lay groups: the Institute of Jesus the Priest (for diocesan clergy), the Institute of Mary of the Annunciation (for single women), the Institute of Saint Gabriel the Archangel (for single men), and the Institute of the Holy Family (for married couples). This tenfold foundation came to be known as the Pauline Family because of its devotion to Saint Paul the Apostle, which inspired the members to imitate his apostolic zeal.

If someone had asked Father Alberione, "How do you motivate so many people?" he would have replied, "I tell them, first of all, what God expects of the Pauline Family: that we lead millions of people to heaven. We do not confide in ourselves, or in our own strength, but we are to place all our confidence in God and pray. We rely on God for everything: health, study, providence, piety, *everything*. The most serious injustice God receives from our house is lack of confidence in him, when it is evident that it is he who is doing everything. So, let us take heart, pray much, and be courageous."

His Pauline Family seemed like a microcosm of the whole Church. It encompassed everyone and it wove into its mission many aspects of the Church's mission. This was to be expected of a man whose original inspiration came from a desire to spread God's word to every person throughout the world. The word is communicated through every apostolic work, and every ministry is interconnected to evangelization.

His greatest joy was to see his Paulines correspond to the grace originally given to him, to see them becoming apostles and saints. He said, "Holy people are simplifications of sanctity, luminous reflections of the divine perfection, seen from a particular angle, which matches the mission the Holy Spirit has entrusted to each one of them. Every holy person is a genuine and practical school—a stimulus and an instructor for good." He always maintained that "the first concern of the Pauline Family should be holiness of life; the second, holiness of doctrine."

This school of sanctity came directly from Jesus, who had manifested himself to James Alberione in a particular way around 1923. Recalling a "dream" in which he saw Jesus "walking among us," Alberione said, "Jesus assures us with these words: 'Fear not; I am with you.' Then Jesus motioned toward the tabernacle and said, 'From here I want to enlighten you. Be sorry for sin.'" The whole Pauline Family treasures these words, which are found in every Pauline chapel near the tabernacle. For Father Alberione, Jesus is the Divine Master (Teacher), the Way, the Truth, and the Life. In other words, Jesus presents himself as transformer of our entire being, our mind, our will, and our heart. He wants to teach us how to say with Saint Paul, "it is no longer I who live, but Christ who lives in me."

Alberione himself always taught by example. His mind was always actively seeking new means for evangelization. He had no patience with indecision or procrastination. So much good had to be done! "Is it possible," he would say, "that one day is needed for decision and another for execution? No! Let's do it in one day." He only "relaxed" when the weakness of old age forced him to slow down.

Father Alberione summed up his life in these words:

> Before God and man, I feel the gravity of the mission entrusted to me by the Lord, who, had he found a person more unworthy and unfit, would have preferred him . . . just like an artist who picks up a paintbrush worth a few cents to use for his work.
>   I have accomplished part of God's will, but I must fade from the scene and from people's memories, even though,

because I was older, I had to take from the Lord and give to others. So, too, at the end of Mass, the priest removes his vestments and stands before God as the person he is.

Prayer

Blessed James Alberione, you were a man called to work
modern "wonders"
through the consecration and use of the means of
communication.
You saw these inventions, the work of human ingenuity,
as the most fruitful means to proclaim the word of God.
You attributed all of your works to the inspiration of
Saint Paul the Apostle.
To him you entrusted your entire religious family.
We look to you for guidance in the ever-new world of
electronic communication.
Intercede for us so that we may use these means wisely
as tools of evangelization,
to broadcast the word of God across the globe.
Jesus, Divine Master, Way, Truth, and Life,
continue to inspire many men and women to live
the charism
you placed in the heart of Blessed James.
Make us seekers and sowers of truth,
so that our lives may bear fruit in an abundant eternal
harvest. Amen.

About Blessed James Alberione

Born: April 4, 1884, in San Lorenzo di Fossano, Cuneo, Italy

Died: November 26, 1971, in Rome

Feast Day: November 26

Beatified: April 27, 2003, by Pope John Paul II

Patron: workers in social communications, founders of Catholic religious congregations and other initiatives

Notes on His Life

.⚗ Born Giacomo Alberione, he was the fourth of five sons of Michael and Teresa (Allocco) Alberione, farmers.

.⚗ His family moved to Cherasco, Cunio, Italy, when he was a boy.

.⚗ From October 1896 to April 1900 he studied at the seminary in Bra.

.⚗ In October 1900 he entered the seminary in Alba.

.⚗ During the night between 1900 and 1901, at the cathedral of Alba he experienced an inspiration to form the Pauline Family.

.⚗ He was ordained to the priesthood on June 29, 1907.

.⚗ In 1908 he earned a doctorate in theology and he became associate pastor in Narzole, Cunio, Italy.

.⚗ He also served as spiritual director and professor at the seminary.

.⚗ On September 8, 1913, he became director of the diocesan weekly, the *Gazette* of Alba.

.⚗ In July 1914 he opened the Little Worker School of Typography in Alba.

榃 He founded several religious institutes: the Society of Saint Paul (1914), the Daughters of Saint Paul (1915), the Sister Disciples of the Divine Master (1924), the Sisters of Jesus the Good Shepherd (1938), and the Sisters of Mary, Queen of Apostles (1958).

榃 He also founded the Union of Pauline Cooperators (1917) and several lay institutes: the Institute of Saint Gabriel the Archangel (1960, for single men), the Institute of Mary of the Annunciation (1958, for single women), the Institute of Jesus the Priest (1959, for diocesan clergy), and the Institute of the Holy Family (1960, for married couples).

榃 He contracted pulmonary tuberculosis in 1923 and was given a year to live, but he was cured "by Saint Paul."

榃 He started publishing *Famiglia Cristiana* in 1931; this magazine apostolate spread to many nations.

榃 In 1939 he established a film production apostolate, Romana Editrice Film, later called Saint Paul Film.

榃 Pope Paul VI visited him on the day Alberione died, November 26, 1971.

榃 He is buried in the subcrypt of the Sanctuary of the Queen of the Apostles in Rome.

Lesser-Known Facts

榃 At age six he decided to become a priest.

榃 Because of his theological degree he was commonly called "the Theologian."

榃 On December 24, 1918, the Little Worker School of Typography burned down.

榃 He introduced a prayer called "The Secret of Success," to which he credited the success of his institutes to a deep trust in God.

- Among his writings are: *Notes on Pastoral Theology* (1912), *Woman Associated to Priestly Zeal* (1915), *Donec Formator Christus in Vobis* (1932), and *Abundantes divitiae Gratiae Suae* (1954), the charismatic history of his work.

- The first priest ordained in the Society of Saint Paul was (now Blessed) Timothy Giaccardo.

- Alberione's horarium was from 3:30 AM to 9:00 PM.

- He began establishing Pauline Communities outside of Italy in 1931.

- Other works inaugurated: radio in Japan (1951); three large churches built in Italy.

- He attended every session of the Second Vatican Council.

- On June 28, 1969, he received the *Pro Ecclesia et Pontifice* cross from Pope Paul VI.

In His Own Words

"A special light came from the Blessed Sacrament, a greater understanding of the invitation extended by Jesus: 'Come to me all of you. . . .' He seemed to understand the heart of the great Pope (Leo XIII), the calls sent out by the Church, the true mission of the priest. It appeared clear to him what (Blessed) Toniolo had said regarding the duty of being apostles of the times, using the means exploited by adversaries. He felt deeply obliged to prepare himself to do something for God and the people of the new century in which he would live. He had a sufficiently clear awareness of his nothingness and at the same time he heard: "I will be with you until the consummation of the world," in the Eucharist; he felt that in Jesus Host he could find light, nourishment, comfort, and victory over evil."

— Written in the third person on the night between the centuries, December 31, 1900

Saint Joan of Arc

Child of God

"When they bring you before the synagogues, the rulers, and the authorities, do not worry about how you are to defend yourselves or what you are to say; for the Holy Spirit will teach you at that very hour what you ought to say" (Lk 12:11-12).

On December 23, 1430, the young French maiden known as Joan of Arc glimpsed the English-held city of Rouen for the first time. Fear and uncertainty clutched at her heart as her captors rudely dragged her through the streets while a menacing crowd mocked her. They had no sympathy for the Maid of Orleans. Even her own king—the king she had fought to place on the French throne—had not attempted to rescue her from enemy hands, So what could she expect from her enemies?

The procession came to an abrupt halt. One of the guards shouted: "There, you witch! Look up there! That's your new home. You'll stay there until you admit that you never really heard any holy voices." A formidable gray mass loomed high in the distance. Its towers cast long, eerie shadows over the entire city. Joan shuddered at the sight. But she could not escape. Would her voices send her a rescue, or would this be the end for her? Joan knew her fate because her voices had already told her she would die, and die soon.

When the procession reached the castle entrance, Joan cast one last look out across the horizon toward far-off Domrémy. There her mother and father were thinking of her and praying for her. Did they know about this terrible turn of events? Did they know that the Burgundians had sold her to their English allies? These thoughts raced through her mind and stopped cold in the face of the inevitable: she was now a prisoner of the English. She would never again be free; she would be a captive until her death.

"And do you know how a witch dies?" The Earl of Warwick's question still rang in her ears. "By fire!"

Heart in her throat, she could still hear her own gasping, startled reply: "Fire?"

"Yes, fire. Now we'll see how long you'll continue this foolishness. Your trial is scheduled for February 21. Until then you will reside at the castle of Rouen. Now, witch, get out of here!" With these words he gave her a rude shove. "The English soldiers are waiting for you," he continued. "They are all very anxious to see the pretty young maiden that cost them so dearly. You mean a lot to them. Remember, they paid no small price for you. Now, get out!"

The *castle* in which Joan was to reside, as the Earl of Warwick had so carefully phrased it, was nothing more than a dungeon. The guards escorted her to a dirty, dismal cell, threw her on a bed, and chained her wrists and ankles to the four bedposts.

The stark realities of prison life were a horrifying experience for Joan. A mere teenager, as pure as an angel, attractive, kind, and compassionate toward everyone, even her persecutors, she was roughly mistreated. Yet never once did she succumb to the taunts and crude advances of the rough men. Her only love was Christ, and she was faithful to him to the end. Her only consolation was the joy of knowing that she was suffering for her Savior, who had once suffered for her.

Joan had plenty of time to think. She traced and retraced the events that had reduced her to this condition. She never regretted one moment of them. She lovingly thought of her early years in Domrémy with her brothers and sisters and her dear parents. Then she turned over and over in her mind the first time she heard the voices of Saint Michael the Archangel, Saint Catherine of Alexandria, and Saint Margaret of Antioch. How insistently they had commanded Joan to carry out the mission they had told her about. They had described the difficulties of the beginnings, the scorn and ridicule, the hardships of military life, the repugnant nature of battle, her nausea at the sight of blood, the hard-won victories. They spoke of the coronation of the dauphin at Reims, and then his sudden change of attitude toward her. In time they had revealed her capture by the Burgundians, the king's refusal to ransom her, and even this last lap of her journey in Rouen.

It had all been so hard to believe. Yet Joan knew that God was leading her in mysterious ways. She only needed to follow. God would guide and protect her. When the time came, he would tell her what she should say.

The weeks passed, the seasons changed. Fear and anxiety filled her days and nights, alleviated only by fleeting consolations that followed fervent prayer. Her trust in God could come only from him. Joan had no one else to console or encourage her.

When February 21 arrived, a worn and haggard Joan confronted the stern faces of her accusers. She listened and hoped, but the verdict was a foregone conclusion—everyone knew that. However, the authorities went through the charade of a whole legal pageant. They knew the trial must look good for those consciences that her accusers called "overly scrupulous."

And so it began—three long months of torture for that poor peasant girl who knew neither how to read nor write.

If only they could discredit her as a heretic, her accusers thought. If only they could make her say her voices were a fraud! But no matter how cunningly they phrased their questions or in what manner they tried to confuse her, Joan gave clear and straightforward answers. At one point they asked her, "Do you believe that you are in the state of grace?"

Her reply stunned them, leaving them momentarily speechless: "If I am not, may God put me there; and if I am, may God keep me there."

Thus she foiled her accusers, this wisp of a girl who would not back down before any man. "My voices told me to answer boldly," she stated as the trial began. And she did indeed speak boldly, almost audaciously at times. She steadfastly refused to speak about certain things, saying that the saints had forbidden her to do so.

All these learned men, the bishops and theologians who accused her, could not rattle her determined spirit. Their defeat at the hands of the young peasant drove them to exasperation.

"Admit that your voices were a hoax!" shouted one accuser.

"Admit that you lied!" said another.

"Confess that you practice witchcraft and that your success comes from the devil."

This constant bombardment wore on Joan. Her once sparkling eyes grew bloodshot and tired. Her body had been reduced to a skeleton. Although the tortures had alarmingly weakened her physical stamina, her willpower and convictions only intensified. Her voices still spoke to her and encouraged her to carry on with fortitude.

One day the court again seriously threatened her with death by fire. Joan was terrified at the thought of such a fate. Her accusers took advantage of this moment of weakness to offer her a way out. If she would sign a document they had drawn up denouncing her voices as coming from the devil, and if she promised to avoid wearing the male clothing she had adopted for her own protection on the battlefield, she would receive a lesser sentence. Joan, who could neither read nor write, was persuaded to make a sign on the document indicating she agreed that what it said was true. When this document was presented before the assembled court, however, it was much longer and more involved than what they had shown to Joan. In this supplanted version, she was asking pardon for all sorts of sins and crimes that were not on the paper she signed. Joan was overcome with grief. By giving in she had denied God's calling. She had sinned, as her voices now told her, and she must clearly rectify her stand or face rejection by her Lord.

At her next court appearance, Joan again wore men's clothing, remonstrating with those who had tried to trick her. She resumed her confidence and stated that she would stand firm no matter how they threatened her.

At last when the court asked for her final statement, the Maid of Orleans categorically declared: "God truly sent me and my voices are from him."

Now they had her. They had a definite, indisputable charge on which to convict the girl. By going back on her recantation, she had, in fact, declared herself guilty. And nothing could be more evil than a recalcitrant heretic. Her accusers thought Joan was a witch because of her unnatural success in battle, and the voices she so relied on; this was also a crime worthy of death.

Finally, the verdict was delivered: "guilty" on all charges. Joan's days were numbered. In her cell she prayed for strength, mercy, and peace. She prayed also for her spineless king and for those jealous men who had sold her to the enemy. She prayed for her family, her little village, for all the beauty for which she longed. "For you, my God, for you," she repeated over and over.

On May 30, 1431, Joan of Arc was led to her execution. Hailed by her heavenly voices as Maid of France and Child of God, her human accusers instead burned her as a heretic and a witch. They brought her on a cart to the place of execution and helped her mount the scaffold, where she was securely bound to the stake. Then they lit the fire. As the flames rose higher and higher, the girl kept her gaze fixed on a crucifix that a compassionate priest held before her eyes.

"Jesus, Jesus," she whispered, "Jesus, Jesus."

Suddenly the onlookers realized that an awful crime was being committed. Some cried out, "We are burning a saint!" But it was already too late. Joan's pure soul was winging its way to heaven.

Prayer

> Dear Saint Joan, you are the model for those who hear
> the call of God
> and generously follow wherever he may lead.
> You had no standing in the world of your time,
> nor the advantages that come with education.
> You listened, however, for the voice of God.
> He asked you to accomplish a seemingly impossible task,
> yet you did not question but went out with faith and
> confidence.
> When you had completed your task, you remained before
> God in humility and trust.
> Be an example for us as we listen for the voice of God.
> Intercede for us that we may accept life's challenges
> with humility and faith, so that we may confidently speak
> God's Word
> and serve his kingdom with generosity and conviction.
> Amen.

About Saint Joan of Arc

> *Born:* ca. January 6, 1412, in Domrémy, France
>
> *Died:* May 30, 1431, executed by the English in Rouen,
> France
>
> *Feast Day:* May 30
>
> *Canonized:* May 16, 1920, by Pope Benedict XV
>
> *Patron:* soldiers, France, captives, martyrs

Notes on Her Life

> ⸙ She was one of five children of Jacques d'Arc and Isabelle
> Romée, farmers.

- Joan was illiterate, but skilled at sewing and spinning. She first heard her voices in 1424.

- In May 1428 she made her first visit to Vaucouleurs, where her campaign began.

- Charles VII was crowned at Reims on July 17, 1429.

- Joan was wounded in an attack on Paris on September 8, 1429, and on several other occasions.

- On December 29, 1429, she was invested with nobility (and her family name became *du Lys*).

- She was taken prisoner by the Burgundians on May 23, 1430, in Compiègne. They later handed her over to the English.

- Her trial began on January 9, 1431, with a preliminary inquiry. The full proceedings began on February 21. She signed a confession, but recanted on May 24, 1431.

- On May 30, 1431, she was burnt at the stake as a heretic.

- Her rehabilitation trial began in 1450.

- In July 1456, Pope Callistus III revoked her sentence and declared her a martyr.

Lesser-Known Facts

- She was known as the Maid of Orleans or La Pucelle.

- Joan has been the subject of many literary, musical, theatrical, and artistic works including those by George Bernard Shaw, Mark Twain, Giuseppe Verdi, and the sculptor Emmanual Frémiet.

- She had to outfit herself in borrowed knight's clothing and gear.

- Her voices helped Joan to identify the dauphin (the heir-apparent who became Charles VII) despite his attempt to trick her.

- The original records and transcripts of her first trial and the trial of rehabilitation still exist.

- Joan's work helped to bring an end to the Hundred Years' War and establish peace between France and England.

In Her Own Words

"I would rather die than do a thing which I know to be a sin or against the will of God."

Saint Anthony of Padua

Humble Miracle-Worker

"On the last day of the festival, the great day, while Jesus was standing there, he cried out, 'Let anyone who is thirsty come to me, and let the one who believes in me drink'" (Jn 7:37–38).

Brother Anthony scanned the crowd around him, looking for the superior whom another friar had pointed out to him earlier. Perhaps this superior would agree to take him. Brother Anthony knew he was in an unusual situation, and he wasn't surprised that the last couple of superiors had not wanted him. Though he had a sturdy build, Anthony was still frail from his illness. Most of the superiors obviously thought he would be a burden.

And I would be, Anthony reasoned to himself. *My life in the order has been a failure so far.*

A part of Anthony bristled at calling himself a failure. He tried to quash it. But he still felt it. As he looked back over his life, he wondered where he had made his mistake. . . .

Anthony came from a noble family in Lisbon. Though his life could have been one of wealth and luxury, he wanted to dedicate his life to God and entered the Canons Regular of Saint Augustine. He loved his studies, and was ordained early to the priesthood. For some time, he was content with life at the monastery.

But then visitors came to his community in Coimbra—five friars from the new Order of Friars Minor. They went on to Morocco to preach the Gospel, and were martyred when they refused to stop preaching. Their bodies were brought back to Anthony's monastery. Something deep stirred in Anthony at the witness of their lives. After deep prayer and great resistance from the prior of the monastery, Anthony had received permission to transfer to the Friars Minor. One desire burned within Anthony—to go to Morocco and preach Christ and, if worthy, to give his life as the ultimate witness to Christ.

Almost everyone in his Augustinian community told him he was crazy. Life in a monastery was strict compared to the lifestyle of a nobleman, but these begging friars wore rags and lived in hovels. Worst of all, they weren't allowed to study theology. Their founder, the holy Francis of Assisi, worried that education would lead to pride.

But Anthony could not resist the call resounding in his soul. Shortly after, he and another friar set out for Morocco. But instead of preaching Christ, Anthony fell seriously ill. With no resources and unable to recover, Anthony had no choice but to return home. The two friars boarded a ship for Spain, but never arrived. Instead, their boat was blown off-course and finally landed in Sicily. The friary in nearby Messina took them in and nursed Anthony. When the holy Francis himself called a meeting (known as a chapter), Anthony was recovered enough to make the trip to Portiuncula, near Assisi. The meeting of the friars was so large that many of them slept outdoors on reed mats, so it was called the Chapter of Mats.

Brother Anthony was deeply impressed seeing Francis, hearing his admonitions, and witnessing his great joy despite his illness. Anthony didn't talk to Francis—he was just one of thousands of friars there. New to the friars and far from his home, Anthony was a foreigner and a stranger, easily ignored. Though he enjoyed the companionship of the many friars, Brother Anthony hoped to receive an assignment when the Chapter of Mats was over. But so far, he wasn't able to find a superior who would accept him.

Where are you leading me, Lord? What is your will for me? Brother Anthony was still struggling to accept what had happened. He had thought he was seeking God's will when he had joined the friars, and then again in going to Morocco to preach. *Was I seeking God's will, or mine?* Anthony asked himself. *Is that why I failed, Lord?*

He finally spotted Father Gratian, the superior that another friar had recommended to him. Steeling himself inside for rejection, Anthony approached him. *This time, I only seek your will, Lord. Do with me whatever you wish.*

"I am Brother Anthony and not yet assigned. Father Gratian, would you accept me and assign me to a place where I could learn the spirit of Francis?"

Father Gratian squinted at the gaunt friar. "Where are you from?"

"Coimbra."

"Ah, yes. You have been ill?"

"Yes, Father."

"What can you do?"

"I will do anything you ask of me. I seek only to do God's will. I am happy to beg, to clean, whatever is needed. I am new to the friars, but I was ordained in the Order of Saint Augustine."

Father Gratian smiled. "Our hermitage near Forli needs a priest to celebrate Mass. It is a remote area, but you could learn the spirit of Francis there. If our minister general gives permission, you may go."

Anthony bowed humbly and gratefully.

Almost a year later, Anthony had recovered as much of his health as he ever would. At the hermitage, his was a life of humility, seclusion, contemplation, and manual labor. Since Francis did not encourage the friars to study for fear of pride, Anthony had not studied or written much. He had not even preached to the little community when he had celebrated Mass. The superior came to count on him for his obedience, and invited the humble friar to accompany him to a nearby ordination, where both Franciscans and Dominicans gathered to celebrate. But due to an absence or oversight, no one was prepared to give the sermon at the reception.

Father Gratian asked several of the Franciscan priests present, but none wanted to speak unprepared. He then asked the Dominicans, but they also refused. As Father Gratian searched the room for somebody—anybody—to preach, he saw Anthony.

"We need someone to preach," Father Gratian told Anthony bluntly. "Would you?"

Anthony demurred. "Surely someone else is better suited, better prepared—"

"No one is prepared. Just speak a few words, as the Holy Spirit inspires you."

As Father Gratian had hoped, Anthony bowed his head in obedience. He walked to the front, thoughts whirling but more importantly, heart seeking the Lord. *Speak, Lord, your servants are listening*, he prayed.

Anthony began slowly, but as his voice gained volume, it also grew in confidence. The fruit of his prayer and studies came pouring out of him. Anthony was not just a competent speaker—he was eloquent, passionate, and learned, yet accessible. His words pierced the hearts of his listeners, perhaps as much for his inner conviction as for his eloquence. When he finished, Anthony stood in the absolute silence for a moment, then stepped down and joined his brothers.

Father Gratian was stunned. All the friars present were amazed. As Father Gratian came to speak to him, Anthony's anxious eyes met his.

"I think you've learned the spirit of Francis," Father Gratian sputtered. "Your time in the kitchen is over. You will be assigned to preaching."

Anthony nodded, a deep peace settling over him. Now, in obedience, he could be certain that his mission was to preach. Even Francis confirmed Anthony's tremendous gifts by writing Anthony a letter that not only approved his preaching and his studies, but also authorized him to teach the other friars, as long as their humility and devotion were not endangered.

For the next nine years, Anthony constantly traveled, preaching all over Italy and southern France. He quickly gained popularity with his brilliance, his holiness, his breadth of knowledge, and his prophetic challenges of the evils and errors of his time. Eventually, thousands—even tens of thousands—would come to hear him. When word got around that he was in town, the church was often too small to hold the crowds, and Anthony would preach in his booming voice outside, from a platform built for the occasion. People would sometimes arrive hours early to be near the platform.

Anthony's style was popular and engaging, convincing and eloquent. He frequently called for conversion and repentance, and the friars and priests in the area would have long lines of people waiting to go to confession afterward. In the style of his time, he explained the Scripture text with other passages from Scripture. He quoted the Bible so often in his homilies that some scholars suspect that Anthony had memorized the entire book. When Pope Gregory IX heard Anthony preach, he called Anthony the "Armory" of Scripture—which in contemporary terms might be the "Reservoir" or "Repository" of the Bible.

But the secret of Anthony's preaching was his deep prayer life. He had spent his life trying to listen to the Holy Spirit, and now the Holy Spirit was using him to draw countless people closer to Christ.

After the death of Saint Francis, Anthony was among the delegation sent to Rome to consult with the pope about the rule for the Friars Minor. The controversy over the rule for the friars had been a painful one even before Francis died. But now the question of the rule became more urgent and a source of heated division: should the friars follow the original rule that Francis wrote, which took literally the demand of the Gospel to live in an absolute day-to-day dependence on God for the next meal? Or should they live the revised rule that the pope had worked on with Francis, which offered more stability to the rapidly growing order? Many friars felt strongly about the matter and fanned the flames of division. Though Anthony was one of the delegates sent to Rome and his opinion was obviously respected, he refrained from adding to the division, and sought only to do God's will.

The friars entrusted Anthony with many other responsibilities of leadership. But Anthony's health had never been strong since his missionary trip to Morocco. As his health started to decline, he asked and received permission to dedicate himself only to preaching and teaching.

Anthony developed a special love for the city of Padua, where his preaching led to conversions, reform, and even a new law mitigating the punishment for those in debt. In 1231, he preached a daily Lenten retreat. Padua quickly became overwhelmed by the huge crowds of people coming to hear Anthony—as many as 40,000 people daily. Because of the demands of the crowd, Anthony had no time to eat or rest during the day. After preaching, he and many other friars and priests heard confessions until dark, when Anthony could finally break his fast. Several strong men began acting as Anthony's bodyguards, to protect him and prevent his clothes from being shredded by the crowds eager for a relic of the living saint. Reconciliations, reforms, conversion—the fruit of the Holy Spirit at work in Anthony—were evident to everyone.

After the retreat, Anthony was exhausted. Realizing that his life was truly ebbing away, Anthony withdrew nearby to rest and prepare himself for death. He died at the young age of thirty-six, in the company of several friars who helped him to sit up to be able to breathe. His last words were, "I see my Lord!"

☙✿☙

Prayer

Saint Anthony,
you humbly sought to do God's will
throughout your entire life.
Deeply devoted to living and preaching the word of God,
you allowed the Holy Spirit to work freely in you,
to touch thousands of people through your preaching
and example.

Give us that same love for the Scriptures,
so that the word of God may quench our thirst,
and flow through us to others.
Do not let us lose our way,
but help us to follow Christ always more closely,
and live the Gospel call
to generously provide for others' needs. Amen.

About Saint Anthony of Padua

Born: 1195, in Lisbon (at the time in Spain, now in
Portugal)

Died: June 13, 1231, near Padua, Italy

Feast Day: June 13

Canonized: May 30, 1232, by Pope Gregory IX

Declared Doctor of the Church: January 16, 1946, where
Pope Pius XII gave him the title Evangelical Doctor

Patron: finding what is lost, expectant mothers and
women who want to conceive, sailors, those who are
poor

Notes on His Life

⁞ Anthony was born into a noble and wealthy family.

⁞ Baptized Fernando, he first became a canon regular of
Saint Augustine, and then transferred to the Franciscan
order, taking the name Anthony.

⁞ Numerous miracles were attributed to Anthony during
his lifetime, including: preaching to a crowd in which each
person understood in his native tongue what Anthony
was saying; receiving a vision of the infant Jesus, whom
Anthony held in his arms; healing the amputated foot of

a young man who, after confessing to Saint Anthony, so deeply repented of his sin of kicking his mother that he cut off his own foot; when one town refused to listen to Anthony's preaching, he went and preached to the fish, who gathered, came to the surface, and appeared to be listening.

❧ Anthony's canonization was one of the fastest in the history of the Church—he was canonized less than a year after his death.

❧ Saint Anthony is rightly called the miracle-worker. Within the year of his death, countless miracles were reported, and fifty-six miracles were approved for Anthony's canonization. All but one of them occurred after Anthony's death.

❧ Anthony is one of the most popular and beloved saints of the Church.

Lesser-Known Facts

❧ Though Saint Anthony preached to hundreds of thousands, he was a Franciscan friar for only ten years and died at the young age of thirty-six.

❧ We don't know what illness Anthony suffered as a missionary to Morocco—it may have been malaria, hepatitis B, or a number of others. This illness may have caused the later edema (swelling) that Anthony suffered, which eventually led to his early death.

❧ None of the sermons that Anthony preached exists today. His "sermons" that do exist are instructions and outlines intended as resources for scholars or for preachers to help them to prepare a sermon.

In His Own Words

"Attribute to God every good that you have received. If you take credit for something that does not belong to you, you will be guilty of theft."

— From his sermon notes

Saint Zita

God's Own Servant Girl

"For all who exalt themselves will be humbled, and those who humble themselves will be exalted" (Lk 14:11).

Busy tending the family garden, a young girl looked up at the sound of her mother's voice calling, "Zita! Zita, come in the house a minute."

Zita leaned the hoe against the little fence surrounding the garden and started to run across the farm yard. She dashed through a flock of chickens that cackled noisily as they flew out of her way. She bounded up the stairs, threw open the door, then stopped a minute to straighten her apron when she saw the visitor.

"Come in, Zita, and sit down." Her father smiled broadly at her and indicated an empty chair at the table. "Father Antonio has some good news for you."

"Good afternoon, Father Antonio," Zita said as she slid into her chair.

The venerable old priest at the head of the table nodded in acknowledgement. "My, how you have grown, Zita. How old are you now?"

"Twelve, Father."

"And I'm sure you're still a big help to your mother and father."

"She certainly is," her mother joined in. "She's always ready to do anything we ask of her."

Zita blushed and looked down at her hands folded on her lap.

"Well then, Zita, how would you like to accompany me to Lucca? You could have a good position with the Fatinelli family."

The girl looked puzzled and turned to her parents.

"You see, Zita," her father explained, "things are not going very well for the family. The crops grew poorly this year, and with your older sister now in the convent, we have very little income. Your mother and I thought it would help if you took a position with Pagano de Fatinelli. He is a prosperous wool and silk weaver in Lucca."

"And very respectable," the old priest added.

"They will provide you with whatever you need. You'll be like one of the family, helping to do the chores around the house."

"And Lucca is only eight miles away," her mother said, consoling herself more than her daughter. "You can come and see us once in a while."

Zita felt excited about the new venture but a bit apprehensive about leaving her family. "If it's what you want," she agreed.

The next morning Zita said goodbye to each member of her family. Then she climbed into the cart that was waiting for her. Her father put her bag next to her, smiled, and gave her a little tap on the cheek. Father Antonio waved to everyone and motioned the driver to go. Mama quickly gave Zita a last hug before the cart rumbled down the road to Lucca.

Zita continued waving to her family standing in the road. But soon they faded out of sight. She felt a tear slide down her cheek. She knew she was going to miss them, but her tears soon turned into a prayer. Her mother had taught her that if she ever felt sad or alone, she should start to pray. She smiled a little now as she remembered the time she had very innocently asked her mother if she could talk to God only when she was sad.

"Oh no," her mother had laughed. "You can talk to God whenever you want."

From then on, Zita had formed a warm friendship with God. She turned to him for every need. So prayer came naturally now. The family she was leaving behind was poor, but Zita had received from them a priceless spiritual inheritance.

When she arrived at the home of the Fatinelli family, she was very happy to see the Basilica of San Frediano next door. At once she resolved to go to Mass daily, a resolution she kept for the rest of her life despite the obstacles to come.

It would seem that Zita could have settled down to a comfortable life. But that was not Zita's way. She treasured work just as she treasured her relationship with God—in fact, she saw work as her way to God. She could go to church only in the morning, and had no opportunity for hours of contemplation. She was a servant and had her duties to perform. But she could offer this daily labor of hers to her Friend and God. Often through the years she was heard to remark, "A servant is not good if she is not industrious. Work-shy piety . . . is sham piety."

The beginning of Zita's life at the Fatinelli home was hard. Her determination to do every single task with precision and care caused considerable friction with other servants. They resented her daily attendance at Mass and her constant good-natured serenity, both of which were a silent reproach to some of their own habits. Why, this girl from Monsagrati never grumbled or complained—even when she was given the most revolting assignments. They couldn't understand her and strongly disliked her. Some even went to the point of misleading Signor Fatinelli for a time.

But no one could believe unfavorable reports about her for long. The master could see for himself the responsibility she displayed and the quality of her work. And even her fellow servants soon found that her love of God and Church was not smug and self-satisfied as they had thought. Her actions held no pretense, no aloofness. She was always ready, always available to help out in a tight spot. If something was needed in a rush and no one could be found, Zita would arrive to help, simply, quietly, without fanfare. So she spent her teen years, her young adulthood—her life—doing housework from morning to night, nothing but housework.

The other servants came to rely on her good judgment, ready smile, and unaffected helpfulness. Gradually she was given more responsibility. With full confidence, Signor Fatinelli placed his children under her care, and his wife entrusted to Zita all the details of the household. These changes placed her in a position of some authority, a situation that always caused her embarrassment. But she never lost her uncomplicated disposition or her habit of doing her job thoroughly and completely.

She had a secret, of course. No one can buck the relentless tide of life's daily problems for long by herself, and this was where Zita's secret lay. She was not alone. The God she had known and loved during childhood had not faded into a dim and distant memory. He became daily more real and more loved. And he often made his presence and approval of this servant girl very apparent, too.

One Monday morning, Zita was up early, since it was baking day. She planned to prepare the dough for the week's bread before she went to Mass, so it would have risen nicely by the time she returned. It could then be formed into loaves and baked soon after.

Humming softly, she kneaded the mound of white paste to just the right point, set it in a corner of the kitchen and happily left for Mass. However, Mass was a little longer than usual that morning, and Zita was a little more wrapped up in the eternal. Consequently, when she stepped out of the church door, she was stunned to see people already in the streets. Normally she was home long before anyone else was even stirring. She rushed up the back steps of the house, ran through the door and pecked sheepishly into the kitchen. Instead of a gooey cascade of dough on the shelf, she saw one of the other servants standing, hands on hips, shaking her head at a row of neat, even loaves already formed, in the pans and ready for the oven.

The girl turned when she heard Zita enter. "I just don't know how you do it, Zita," she exclaimed. "I got up early this morning to help you out—and look, you've finished it all!"

"But, but . . ." stammered the astonished Zita. "You mean you didn't. . . ."

But the girl wasn't listening. She was trying to balance two of the mysterious loaves on a large wooden spatula, to place them in the oven. Zita whispered a silent thanks to the One who had been watching out for her so carefully.

Other instances occurred of inexplicable help given to this unassuming maidservant. One day Signor Fatinelli decided to check on the stock of food in the storehouse. Zita always had permission to help the poor, but she suddenly realized she had been overly generous with her employer's goods. She told Signora Fatinelli about it. Both women trembled, for Signor Fatinelli, though a kind man, had a terrible temper. However, Zita soon recovered her calm as she felt certain that God would not let her suffer for helping his poor.

And her confidence was rewarded. When the master inspected his granary, all was as it should be. No supplies were missing or even diminished.

Another time Zita was preparing to go to the Christmas Midnight Mass. She had been ill earlier that winter and Signora Fatinelli was concerned about her. But Zita was determined to go, so the mistress gave Zita her own fur coat to wear. As Zita pulled its warm folds tightly about her on the icy road, she whispered a prayer for her kind employer.

At the door of the church, a happy, jostling group of worshipers worked its way in. As she joined them, Zita noticed a hunched old man off to the side, shivering in his threadbare rags. She could not resist her impulse to help, and, with the understanding that she would retrieve the coat on the way out, she placed it gently around the beggar's shoulders. After a beautiful sung Mass, Zita made her way to the door where she had seen the old man. But her heart stopped—he was nowhere to be seen.

Trembling as she ran home, more from fear and remorse than from the cold, Zita prayed with all her might. As she had known he would be, Signor Fatinelli was beside himself with fury—and he had every right to be, thought Zita. She went to bed feeling sad and sick inside that night. She knew she could never even pay for the coat.

The next morning, she heard a knock on the front door. Trying to smile, Zita opened it. For the second time in two days, she was gasping for breath. The man at the door was surely the same one who had looked like a beggar the night before. Now he stood tall and healthy . . . with the fur coat draped over his arm. Without a word he walked into the house and handed the coat to an equally astonished Signor Fatinelli. The mysterious man turned quickly and left. Zita closed the door slowly, blinking hard to keep back her tears. Surely, she thought, God is never outdone in generosity.

As the years passed, Zita became dearer to the family with whom she lived. Daily she strove to serve them better, and through them, to serve the Lord.

At the age of sixty, Zita lay dying. She had lived in calm, productive serenity, and this was how she prepared to meet the Lord to whom she had given her entire being through a life filled with ordinary duties, ordinary tasks, worries, and joys. Christ's own words could easily be addressed to her. She truly was the faithful, farsighted servant whom the master set over his household (cf. Lk 12:42). Her comfort was the Lord's promise, ". . . your reward is great in heaven" (Lk 6:23).

Prayer

Dear Saint Zita, teach us the fine art of service.
Help us recognize that in everything we do for others
we are imitating Jesus, the true Servant.
Teach us trust in the power of prayer and confidence in
his friendship.
Let us find consolation in work well done, and through
your intercession
Help us always strive to purify our intentions that all
may be done for God's glory.

Work gives dignity to life. We want always to appreciate
our jobs, our duties,
our professions, and our ability to provide for our needs
and those of our families. Amen.

About Saint Zita

Born: 1218 in Monsagrati, Italy

Died: April 27, 1272, in Lucca, Italy

Feast Day: April 27

Canonized: September 5, 1696, by Pope Innocent XII

Patron: housekeepers, maids, domestic workers,
waitresses, finding lost keys

Notes on Her Life

- At age twelve, Zita was sent as a servant to the Fatinelli
family in Lucca.

- She considered her life as a servant as God's will for her,
and a way of penance.

- She also served the poor and the imprisoned.

- Miracles were recorded during her lifetime.

- Her body, exhumed in 1580 and found incorrupt, is now
enshrined in Saint Frediano's Church in Lucca.

Lesser-Known Facts

- She is also known as Sitha, Citha, or Scytha.

- She spent forty-eight years as a servant in the Fatinelli
family.

- Because of her position of trust, she is often invoked to find lost keys.
- She has been depicted in many stained glass windows and other works of art from the fifteenth century.

In Her Own Words

"Unless we are industrious, we cannot be called a good servant. In our position, if one does shoddy work, it is a sham."

Saint Pio of Pietrelcina

A Man on the Mountain

"You do not know what you are asking. Are you able to drink the cup that I am about to drink?" They said to him, "We are able" (Mt 20:22).

Padre Pio trudged up the hill to the building being used as a military headquarters. When he reached the door he had to stop to catch his breath. He opened the door and stepped into the dimly lit room. After searching for the soldier in charge, he slowly walked over to the desk.

The sergeant looked up at the figure before him. *Pretty sad-looking recruit,* he thought. Then, with his best military command voice, he asked, "Name?"

"Forgione, Francesco Pio."

"Age?"

"Almost thirty-one, sir"

"Thirty-one?" the sergeant yelled. He looked over at the other soldiers present. "This one is *only* thirty-one," he announced.

Padre Pio was embarrassed. He tried to muffle his cough.

"So, *young* man," the sergeant said sarcastically, "where have you been? Usually men are called up at an earlier age than *thirty-one!*"

"Yes, sir. I . . . cough, cough . . . realize that."

"So, where were you, man?"

Coughing badly, Padre Pio tried to explain. "Studying . . . cough . . . twice before . . . cough."

"Studying twice before? What are you talking about? Are you a professional student?"

"No, sir," Pio said, clearing his throat. "No, I've been in the seminary, but now I am a priest, a Capuchin. And, by 'twice before' I wanted to say . . . cough . . . I have been called up on two previous occasions."

Overhearing this, another soldier dashed over before the sergeant could speak again. "I recognize you, Forgione, but you are thinner now. Yes, Sergeant, he has come in twice and was deferred, or actually discharged from camp. Bad health, it seems."

"Well, we must really be getting desperate," the sergeant commented. "Forgione, here, is like a bag of bones . . . with a cough to boot."

"Listen, Padre, I'm sending you up to the camp with reservations. You will probably flunk out again, but we want to look good down here. Got to keep up our quota. Just one more thing: What town are you from?"

"Originally, Pietrelcina, but now I live in San Giovanni Rotondo."

"All right, then, that's all we need from you," the sergeant noted. "Off to the camp now—and good luck!"

As could be expected, Padre Pio was soon sent back to the monastery. Finally, the army issued him a permanent exemption due to severe bronchitis. Padre Pio made a mental note: maybe he should pay more attention to his health. The superiors were always saying that he went too far with his austerities. His own mother, also, kept on encouraging him to be more careful, to eat better and sleep more. He would pray over this to see what God would like him to do.

Six months later, the young friar received an extraordinary response to his prayers. Padre Pio was left alone in the monastery with the student friars. He was relieved that he would no longer have to fear the call to military service. He sincerely felt he would die simply from the horror of having to raise a weapon against another man. Now, in the chapel, he prayed fervently for an end to the war. So many on both sides were dying for no good reason, the Italians and the Austrians. No one could win. And the people left behind—wives, mothers, children, the elderly—were falling into despair.

As Padre Pio prayed and supplicated God to put an end to the madness of war, he sensed the presence of another person in the chapel. Maybe one of the younger friars needed something. He raised his head and caught a glimpse of someone in the corner of the choir. Pio's eyes adjusted to the shadows, and he noticed that the man was bloody. *A soldier hiding here,* he thought. But then the stranger approached Padre Pio and rays of light shot from his hands into the young priest's hands. Rays also came from the feet of the figure, and then a final shaft of light pierced Pio's side. He fell unconscious to the floor. When he revived, he raised one of his hands and felt the warm, moist sensation of blood. "Lord, what is this?" he cried and ran to hide in his room.

When the superior came home, Padre Pio presented himself and explained what had taken place. He unwrapped his wounds and showed them to the superior. Right away the superior went to consult the provincial superior. This resulted in a round of medical appointments at which doctors prodded and poked the wounds. They concluded that they could not explain the wounds.

Word slipped out to the press and soon the story of the friar in the mountains who had the stigmata of Christ spread like wildfire. The tide of war had turned and a semblance of peace had returned to Italy, so people could travel, and they wanted to seek out a sign of God's special benevolence. The people began to come on pilgrimage to San Giovanni Rotondo. Meanwhile the authorities, both civil and ecclesiastical, began debating the possible source of this phenomenon.

"Perhaps it is supernatural or paranormal, but not of God," suggested one expert.

"I am more inclined to think he is delusional," another stated. "Perhaps he rubbed some acidic solution on his skin or inflicted the wounds on himself by another means."

Despite applying the best medical remedies, the wounds on Padre Pio's body showed no signs of healing. As time went on the calm of San Giovanni Rotondo was shattered. The police came to protect the young stigmatist from overzealous crowds of the faithful. And while the monastery attempted to keep Padre Pio secluded, the pilgrims clamored to see him.

In the midst of all the turmoil surrounding him, Padre Pio was allowed to minister to the faithful. As had been his practice since ordination, his celebration of Mass always lasted at least two hours. He spent most of his other time for ministry in the confessional. Yet disputes continued to arise. Was this priest a hoax or a holy man?

Dissention reached another notch and by 1922 the Congregation of the Holy Office had declared that Padre Pio must limit himself to private devotion only and cease ministering to the faithful. For his part, Padre Pio humbly obeyed.

Constant dissension took place among the Church authorities, the civil leaders, and the faithful believers. Observing this, Padre Pio said, "Truthfully, I am nothing and whatever good you see in me, is God's. In our own great presumption, we often ruin the good that God gives us. When I observe what people are expecting of me, I do not dwell on what I can do, but on what I am incapable of doing, of that which causes doubt in many."

Padre Pio was often put on trial in the opinion of those in authority. And often the groups of political partisans considered him as the cause or the cure of all Italy's troubles. He constantly faced forfeiting his faculties as a priest. Sometimes it seemed a punishment more for his devotees than for himself. Nonetheless, his soul was constantly buffeted by the powers of this world, as well as the assaults of the devil.

Despite all my own worries, I cannot stop pleading with God for the end of the suffering inflicted on the poor, Padre Pio thought. *The war is over, but so many are sick, injured, or worried. What can I do, dear Lord?*

One day a great plan came to him. Many people sent monetary gifts to him in thanks for his prayers or advice. Why not engage all these good-hearted people to establish a hospital? He presented this idea to his superiors and together they approached the Church authorities and civic leaders. As long as he could raise the necessary funds, Padre Pio had everyone's backing. The project began in 1947, and by 1954 the new hospital was ready to accept the first patients.

At the convention of cardiologists that inaugurated the Home for the Relief of Suffering, some doctors were speaking together.

"You can tell this facility was the design of a man who suffered much."

"How is that?" another doctor asked.

"Well, look at it. the walls and furnishings are all in bright, cheerful colors, the 600 rooms are perfectly appointed, and the hospital even has a movie theater."

"And," added a third doctor, "a helicopter landing pad."

"Too bad there isn't another Padre Pio or two in this world. We could definitely use more hospitals like this one."

Padre Pio himself had the highest expectation for his hospital. He told the doctors who would serve there "that the hospital was the gift of Divine Providence, but their mission was to bring God to the sick." How could they do this? "You accomplish this at the patient's bed by bringing to him or her the warmth of loving care. If you do not do this, I believe medicines will also fail the patient."

In 1958 Padre Pio himself fell seriously ill again. This time he was bedridden.

"Father," the doctor told him, "it's pleurisy again, but virulent. You will need chemotherapy."

His own physician, Dr. Sala, disagreed, saying the illness was bad, but not something that chemotherapy would help. He refused to allow anything more aggressive than the medicines he prescribed for pleurisy. "We'll put him in the *Casa.*"

"No, doctor," the priest feebly protested. "Not the hospital. I just want to return to the monastery. If I am going to die, I want it to be there."

He managed to get up from bed to visit the statue of the Pilgrim Madonna of Fatima. To her, he prayed, "My dear Mother, I have been sick ever since your statue came to Italy. Now you are leaving. Will you say a word of comfort to me?"

At that moment he felt a surge of energy and was completely cured. The skeptics scoffed at the idea, saying that his illness was a big hoax.

Padre Pio responded, "I know how I felt. I know that I was very ill. I prayed to the Blessed Mother and she healed me. Some don't want to believe this, but to them I say: you can then put the Madonna on trial. After all, it was she who healed me."

It seems that Padre Pio was cured just in time for his final period of trial. Many bishops and cardinals had already made unfavorable judgments about the holy friar. But now they also grew dissatisfied with the way the hospital was being administered, and with the handling and distribution of funds. They also looked askance at the numerous prayer groups that often seemed fanatically devoted to Padre Pio, and at the influential women who were attached to his ministry. Some people invented rumors insinuating sexual impropriety as well. In July 1960 the Vatican sent a visitor to investigate these charges. All this scrutiny led to new sanctions. Once again, Padre Pio was to avoid all public ministry. These restrictions were not lifted until June 1963, when the newly elected Pope Paul VI restored all of Padre Pio's priestly faculties.

By now Padre Pio was an old man, and his strength had been greatly diminished by his constant illness and the interminable persecutions. On September 20, 1968, he observed the fiftieth anniversary of receiving the stigmata. He managed to celebrate Mass for the crowds who came to mark this significant date. He also joined in the public recitation of the Rosary, but did not make any further appearances at that time. He again celebrated Mass on September 22, and was able to bless the crowds. People noted that the wounds in his hands had disappeared. Later that day he went to bed saying of himself, "I belong more to heaven now than to earth. Pray that the Lord will let me die soon."

God was listening to his humble, suffering servant. At about 2:30 the next morning, Padre Pio quietly died while whispering the names, "Jesus . . . Mary . . . Jesus . . . Mary."

Prayer

Dear Saint Padre Pio, thank you for being for us a living icon of our crucified Lord.

Through you we are given a glimpse into the many layers of suffering

taken on by our Savior during his life, his passion, and his death.

You also modeled for disciples how to accept and live out in humility and confidence

the will of God as it is designed for each one individually.

Jesus Lord, you infused your own heart into the soul of the young Francesco Forgione.

We ask you, through his intercession, that we, too, may recognize your voice

and offer you an uncompromising yes, as he did. Amen.

About Saint Pio of Pietrelcina

Born: May 25, 1887, in Pietrelcina, Benevento, Italy

Died: September 23, 1968, in San Giovanni Rotondo, Foggia, Italy

Feast Day: September 23

Canonized: June 16, 2002, by Pope John Paul II

Patron: civil defense volunteers

Notes on His Life

⊛ Baptized Francesco, he was the son of farmers, Grazio and Maria Giuseppa (Di Nunzio) Forgione.

⊛ He had a brother and three sisters.

⊛ In 1892, at the age of five, he dedicated himself to God.

⊛ He spent his youth as a farmer and shepherd.

⊛ The Forgione family attended daily Mass and were devoted to Our Lady of Mount Carmel.

⊛ Francesco had ecstasies and visions even as a child.

⊛ In 1903 he entered the Capuchin order in Morcone.

⊛ He received the Capuchin habit at sixteen and was named Fra Pio (Brother Pius).

⊛ On January 27, 1907, he professed solemn vows.

⊛ On August 10, 1910, he was ordained to the priesthood.

⊛ He remained with his family as a religious until 1916 due to poor health, then was assigned to the community friary at San Giovanni Rotondo in Foggia.

⊛ Between 1915–1918 he was called three times for military service, but each time was discharged for health reasons.

⊛ He returned to community in March 1918.

⊛ On September 20, 1918, he received the stigmata in the choir of the church of Madonna delle Grazie.

⊛ He became a spiritual director and confessor.

⊛ In the 1920s and early 1930s he was denounced as a fraud, and even questioned by the Vatican; he was not allowed to publicly exercise his priestly ministry.

- In 1933 his ministry was reinstated.
- In 1959 he became gravely ill.
- In 1961 restrictions were again placed on his ministry.
- He celebrated his last Mass on September 22, 1968.

Lesser-Known Facts

- His father came to the United States seeking work to help Francesco fulfill his dream of entering the Capuchins.
- Pio took his religious name in honor of Saint Pius V, the patron saint of Pietrelcina.
- Because of his illness he could only eat cheese and milk.
- In 1905 he was sent to the mountains in hopes of a cure for his asthma.
- He was often accosted by the devil in various disguises.
- He possessed many spiritual gifts, including bilocation, prophecy, healing, and levitation.
- In 1956 he opened the Home for the Relief of Suffering, a hospital at San Giovanni Rotondo.

In His Own Words

"When Jesus wants me to understand that he loves me, he allows me to savor the wounds, the thorns, the agonies of his passion . . . When he wants to delight me, he fills my heart with that spirit which is all fire; he speaks to me of his delights. But when he wants to be delighted, he speaks to me of his sorrows, he invites me—with a voice full of both supplication and authority—to affix my body [to the cross] in order to alleviate his suffering."

Blessed Miguel Agustín Pro

Escape Artist

"But he passed through the midst of them and went on his way" (Lk 4:30).

The cab had been weaving in and out of the afternoon traffic for only a few blocks, but the tense ride seemed to last forever. "Señor," the cab-driver asked anxiously, "why are we trying to lose that car?"

"I am a priest, my friend," the man barely whispered the words as he tapped his chest.

The driver responded with a solemn but tiny sign of the cross. "Okay, my friend," the passenger said, leaning closer to the driver. "You are doing very well, but slow down by that corner up there."

"Hey," the driver mockingly retorted, "don't try to tell me how to drive this. . . ." Then he heard a sudden "click," "swoosh," and "bang." *Did he just do what I think he did? YES, good for you, Señor Padre,* he thought. His passenger, like Houdini, had just jumped out of the cab and disappeared.

The policemen pursuing him didn't even notice that marvelous escape. They continued their chase, glancing at the people on the street: the mother with the stroller, an elderly bicyclist, a couple arm-in-arm, a bit agitated, yet together. . . .

"Oh, my goodness, Padre, you gave me quite a fright," the young woman was saying between nervous giggles.

"So sorry, Señorita! We almost didn't pull that off. I thank you for being such a good sport." Padre Miguel Pro had very quickly explained his reason for jumping from a cab and grabbing her arm so tightly. "I am a priest, being chased by the police, in need of a cover . . . please!" he had whispered into her ear. She turned to see the pleading look in the stranger's eyes. She comprehended immediately and patted his arm with her free hand.

"Let's keep going for a few more blocks," he suggested. "Just in case, someone else is watching."

"Certainly, Padre," the young woman agreed.

"Just call me 'Miguel.' "

"All right, Miguel, of course," she replied with a smile.

"You are good at this," Pro conceded. Then he lowered his head and mouthed, "God bless you."

A few months passed. And now Padre Pro was sitting in a cell with his brothers, Humberto and Roberto, awaiting his fate. Since returning to Mexico he had played out many "holy escapades." *I've been a very successful policeman,* he told himself, *bringing Communion to the prisoners. That was actually fun! And then I pretended to be a street cleaner. . . .*

Miguel Agustín Pro had been away from Mexico for twelve years studying, first in California, then in Spain, Nicaragua, and Belgium. Finally the great day of ordination arrived—August 31, 1925. He was overjoyed to be entrusted with Christ's own mission, the care of souls. His heart also ached, however, because none of his beloved family could travel to Belgium. His dear mother would witness the special day from heaven, but no one else was near. While the other newly ordained priests spent time with their families, Padre Miguel Agustín went to his room, laid out all the pictures of his family and blessed each one in a very special way.

He still had to complete further studies. However, Miguel felt more at home among working people than with his books. He was a good student, and sometimes even excelled, but he longed to serve. As he finished his studies, he often spent vacation time with the coal miners in Charleroi, Belgium, going down into the mines with them, listening intently to their concerns. He did the same with factory workers, youth laborers, and even socialists and communists. He did all this in view of his future assignment in Mexico among the communist workers in the city of Orizaba. His superiors thought the young Jesuit would be perfect for the mission to those hardened hearts.

Miguel always enjoyed a challenge. One day while serving in Charleroi, he boarded a train car full of obviously unfriendly men. Feeling the Spirit's urging, Pro approached one man and made some small talk. The man grew tense and curtly stated, "Listen, Padre, we are all socialists."

"How wonderful," he replied. "I, too, am a socialist! It is true, but I bet not even one of you actually knows what being a 'socialist' means."

"What do you think we are? It means that we take all the rich men's money."

"Very good," Miguel returned. "However, who then will protect those monies from thieves?"

Not to be deterred, the socialist went on to declare with a sneer, "Many of us are communists!"

"Well, now that is stunning news," the Padre replied with a smile. "I, too, am a communist." Allowing for a dramatic pause, he continued, "It is now lunchtime and I am starving. Which of you would like to share his lunch with me?"

Then they all began to laugh. The man who first challenged Padre Pro asked him if he had been afraid of them.

"Why should I be? I am an armed man."

Startled, they watched him fish through his pockets as if to find his weapon. "Ah, here it is!" he said, as he pulled out his crucifix. "This is my weapon. With him I fear no one." For the rest of the trip he spoke to the men about the love of the Crucified for each of them. Afterward, Padre Pro often recalled this incident to illustrate the humanity and openness of all men to the power of truth.

During these years of formation-in-exile he often suffered from stomach pain. Foreign food and climate, as well as pre-occupation for his family and compatriots living amidst the Mexican revolution, exacerbated his ulcers to the point that he experienced constant pain. He did not like to complain, and would make light of his suffering whenever the subject came up. After his ordination he underwent surgery for the ulcers, but he never recovered his health. Those ulcers became a blessing in disguise, however, because they provided him with early passage home to Mexico. His superiors thought his best chance at some recovery would be to return to his native land. "Better he go home and do some good before he dies," they thought. No one imagined that God would give him a full sixteen months of fruitful ministry amidst the most dangerous conditions.

Padre Pro arrived in Mexico City to find the revolution raging. No sooner had he set foot in his new parish than he became a prisoner of the confessional. In that nearly round-the-clock ministry, he became a very good "sin-sifter," as he put it. He also set up "Communion stations" around the city where people knew they could come to receive the Eucharist. This gave him great joy and consolation because the devout Mexicans made great sacrifices to receive Communion in reparation for the sins against religion that surrounded them. These stations had to constantly change location to avoid detection by the authorities, who tried to suppress all religious practice.

"Thanks to you, Lord, for enabling me to carry out an effective ministry. Now protect me and my brothers," the priest prayed as he sat in the cell. He had escaped from the authorities many times. Lately he had carried out his ministry on a bicycle. He dressed like a young rogue and dashed through the streets whistling, singing, and joking. He sported a very unkempt mustache. In his travels he would salute the policemen and pretend to flirt with the young ladies. The bicycle was an effective cover and a valuable asset for dashing among furtive Masses, baptisms, instructions, and visits to the sick. He even delivered much-needed food and clothing to the poor.

But now prison. Yes, it seemed that his game of cat and mouse had finally ended with the cat as the apparent victor. Some youths had attempted to assassinate the former president, Alvaro Obregón, by throwing a homemade bomb into his car. Though no harm came of it, the police had to produce the culprits. Suspicion fell on both Humberto and Roberto. One night the police stormed in, woke up all three brothers and arrested them.

Now this was their fifth day in the dirty, wet, and smelly cell. They had an abundance of time for prayer and reflection, but Miguel Agustín knew that his brothers and the other prisoners needed something more, something to enliven their spirits. So every evening they said the Rosary together, and they said it loud and clear. They wanted everyone to hear them. And they sang even louder. First Padre Miguel led them in religious songs and then in popular, well-known tunes. The group also spent time exercising each day in the cramped, uncomfortable quarters. The dark cells had almost no ventilation. In fact, on the last night the guards had nailed boards over the windows so the prisoners could not see what was happening outside. However, they could hear a lot of commotion in the courtyard and the sounds of many feet tramping during the night.

The next morning, November 23, at 10:20 AM, a soldier appeared in the dim light. He barked out Padre Pro's name. Roberto, who shared Miguel's cell, jumped at the noise.

"My brother," Miguel said, "let us ask God for the grace we will need." He then shook Roberto's hand and blessed him.

Other men had already confessed to the assassination attempt, but Plutarco Calles, the fanatical president, took this as the opportunity he had long sought to rid the city of this troublesome priest. He had notified prominent men of the city, as well as the press, to come for the story of the day. He wanted to terrorize the citizens who stubbornly adhered to religion. Little did he realize that he was documenting for history the martyrdom of this heroic Jesuit.

Quickly, Padre Miguel put his jacket on and stepped out of the cell. He was marched out between two guards into the courtyard, where he could clearly see the markers lined up against the wall for the firing squad. As the procession drew near the fated spot someone meekly asked pardon of the young priest.

"Of course," Pro generously replied. "Not just my pardon, but also my thanks."

The major then asked a rather farcical question. "Do you wish anything?"

"Only that I may pray," stated Padre Pro as he dropped to his knees. He slowly blessed himself and repeated the offering of his life. Then, serenely, he rose to his feet. Clutching his crucifix in one hand and his rosary in the other, he stood before the gunners with his arms outstretched in the pose of his crucified Lord. As he stared out at the rising rifles, he took a deep breath, opened his mouth, and declared the immortal words, "Viva Cristo Rey!"

Prayer

Blessed Martyr Miguel Agustín Pro, we come to you
    begging your intercession
for all the people of your beloved Mexico and for all
    peoples of the Americas.
May we all seek to live as Christ's disciples in this world,
that God may be glorified and that the civil rule of our
    countries
will mirror God's justice and peace.
Christ, the King, we ask for ourselves, but especially for
    all young people
in their innocent, formative years, the gifts of openness
    and understanding,
of docility and creativity. May we help to build your
    kingdom in our world
as we await the coming of your eternal reign.
Give us courage and fortitude to live for you, to serve
    you, and, if necessary,

to die for you. May our life's motto be that of your holy priest,

"Viva Cristo Rey!" Amen.

About Blessed Miguel Agustín Pro

Born: January 13, 1891, in Guadalupe, Zacatecas, Mexico

Died: November 23, 1927, in Mexico City, Mexico

Feast Day: November 23

Beatified: September 25, 1988, by Pope John Paul II

Patron: Mexico, persecuted Christians

Notes on His Life

- Born José Ramón Miguel Agustín Pro Juarez, he was the third of eleven children of Miguel and Josefa.

- He was nicknamed "Cocol" (for a kind of sweet bread he craved as child).

- His father was a mining engineer.

- He entered the Jesuits at El Llano on August 15, 1911.

- The Mexican Revolution began in 1911, in 1914 the novitiate closed, and the Jesuits fled to Los Gatos, California.

- Pro studied in Granada, Spain, from 1915–1919, and taught in Nicaragua from 1919–1922.

- In 1922 he was sent to Enghien, Belgium, to study theology.

- After his ordination to the priesthood on August 31, 1925, his first assignment was with miners in Charleroi, Belgium.

- He spent time in a hospital undergoing ulcer treatment.

⚜ On July 8, 1926, he returned to Mexico through Veracruz, and performed his priestly ministry "underground."

⚜ After an initial arrest and release, in November 1927 he was arrested with his brothers, Humberto and Roberto, and accused of attempting to assassinate the president.

⚜ Although another man confessed, Pro was executed without a trial on November 23, 1927. His death from the firing squad was extensively photographed and published.

Lesser Known Facts

⚜ Fun-loving, outgoing, and proficient on guitar, he was a natural actor and mimic.

⚜ In 1926 he made a pilgrimage to Lourdes, France.

⚜ He often assumed disguises for his ministry, and often rode a bicycle.

⚜ Information on his clandestine ministry comes from his letters, signed "Cocol," the Miner, or other coded words.

⚜ 40,000 people witnessed his funeral procession, and 20,000 waited at his grave.

⚜ Miraculous cures were reportedly received at the funeral.

⚜ The Mexican Constitution was not amended until 1998, when some of the anti-religious laws were annulled.

In His Own Words

"May God have mercy on you! May God bless you! Lord, you know that I am innocent! With all my heart I forgive my enemies! Viva Cristo Rey!" ("Long live Christ the King!")

Saint Edith Stein

Her Science Was the Cross

"No one has greater love than this, to lay down one's life for one's friends" (Jh 15:13).

O n a warm morning in August 1933, a train pulled into the Breslau station and a small woman in her early forties stepped out onto the platform. Fraulein Edith Stein greeted her sister, Rosa, who was waiting for her. The two women gathered up Edith's few suitcases and started for home.

Rosa struggled to hold her tongue. It seemed strange that her sister wasn't saying a word about her new tutoring position—if such it was. Edith had only sent a few vague lines about finding a place with some nuns at Cologne. What a pity, Rosa thought, that the Nazi government had forced her sister—such a brilliant philosopher—to turn to private teaching!

After a few silent moments, Rosa ventured, "Edith, why are you going to Cologne?"

Edith looked intently at her sister and knew she could confide her most guarded secret. "I've been accepted into the Carmelite convent there."

"What?" gasped Rosa.

"Please, Rosa. I beg of you, don't breathe a word of it to Mama. I must tell her myself."

"I promise, Edith," Rosa answered softly. "It's going to be very hard on Mama, very hard. . . ."

"I know, Rosa. If my conversion caused her so much pain, I dread what will happen when I tell her what I'm going to do now."

Despite the sword that had pierced the hearts of both mother and daughter in the past, Frau Auguste Stein brightened when Edith arrived home. This daughter, her seventh and youngest child, had long been her favorite, and it was good to have her home for these few weeks.

At first, everything went well. Although Frau Stein was in her eighty-fifth year, she went daily to her office in the family lumberyard. She had built the business herself after being widowed when Edith was only two. But the business was struggling, due to the grave political situation. All that Frau Stein had worked so hard for in her long life was falling in a shambles around her. But the valiant matron would not allow herself to retire and "rust out," as she put it.

During the first weeks of Edith's visit, Frau Stein unburdened herself to her youngest daughter. Edith's calm attention and ready sympathy soothed the sorely tried old woman. In the evenings, after returning from the office, Auguste would sit contentedly next to Edith and pour out her troubles. As the weeks seemingly dragged by, Edith dreaded the day that she would again have to break her mother's heart. The fateful hour came on the first Sunday of September.

Mama Stein sat down in her armchair, pulled out her yarn and needles and began knitting. Without raising her eyes she asked, "Edith, what are you going to do with the Sisters at Cologne?"

"Live with them," Edith replied.

Frau Stein reacted immediately with a desperate outburst. Her hands began to tremble violently. And, while mother and daughter clung to their own sides of the issue, Edith bent over to untangle the yarn.

"You're going to cut yourself off from me!" Frau Stein cried pathetically. "You're unfaithful! You, my most beloved daughter! Don't my tears count for anything? How can you just brush my grief aside? Where is your compassion for your old mother? Why must you do this? Why? Why?"

And so it went. When Auguste had exhausted herself in outbursts, she fell into periods of despair and silence.

Edith was later to write: "I knew my mother had become more silent because she secretly hoped I would not do what she thought was the most dreadful thing imaginable. I often wondered which one of us would break first, my mother or me. But we both held out to the last. Mama was inconsolable, and I had to take the step in the utter darkness of faith." Edith was offering her life to God, in answer to his persistent call, and also for the sake of her beloved Jewish people, but her love was interpreted as an act of desertion in their hour of greatest need.

Finally, October 12 arrived. It was Edith's birthday and her last day at home. Early that morning, mother and daughter again pleaded desperately with each other to understand and give in. But it was useless. That night the poor old woman buried her head in her hands and wept. Edith stood behind her chair and pressed her mother's silver head against her heart. They remained like that for a long time. At last, Edith took Frau Stein by the arm and led her up the stairs. For the first time in their lives, Edith helped her mother undress. Then she sat on the edge of the bed until the exhausted woman urged Edith to go and get some sleep. After a sleepless night and tearful embraces, Edith boarded the train that would take her to Cologne.

During the past weeks she had engaged in many discussions, but they turned out to be futile. Her mother's despair, the opposition of her relatives, and the growing political dangers had thrown her into a whirlpool of doubt and confusion. She even began to wonder if she were doing right or wrong in taking this step. As the train pulled out of the station and the waving figures on the platform dissolved in the distance, Edith sank into her seat. She felt "no rapturous joy"; the anguish of the last week had been too dreadful. But she "was perfectly at peace in the harbor of the divine will."

On October 14, 1933, 42-year-old Doctor Edith Stein, brilliant lecturer and philosopher, ceased to exist. Postulant Edith Stein, of the cloistered Carmelites, began a new life. All the sisters liked her. Friendly and anxious to do her best, she took part in all the community duties and work. The Abbot of Beuron wrote of her during this period: "At Carmel she was the only intellectual and she soon became the least of the sisters there."

She even had to learn from a sister who was twenty years younger how to hold a broom.

During her postulancy, Edith never dreamt of asking permission to continue her philosophical work, nor did she allow any of her friends to influence her superior into giving permission to do so. But after having spent all her life in intellectual pursuits, Edith naturally found it very hard to adapt herself to manual tasks—including cleaning, cooking, and sewing. She was clumsy and slow—exasperatingly so. But she offered all this to God.

After two months, the former scholar pointed to her head and admitted to her prioress, "This machine finds a lot of difficulty trying to learn all those little rules."

The prioress smiled, reflecting that Edith seemed to have forgotten her past, all her knowledge and her abilities. and now only desired to become one of God's beloved children.

On April 15, 1934, Edith Stein received her habit and took the name Sister Teresa Benedicta of the Cross. The provincial superior told her it was time to continue her philosophical work and to write again. She should use her pen to make the Lord better known.

On April 21, 1935, Sister Teresa took her first vows, followed by final vows three years later.

At this time the storm clouds of war were quickly gathering. And this reminded Sister Teresa Benedicta of the purpose of her offering—she would be a victim of expiation for the world and for her people, upon whom the cross of Christ had fallen.

Deep in the night of December 31, 1938, Edith Stein left her beloved community at Cologne to find refuge from the Nazi threats in the Carmel of Echt, Holland. She found a new home with new sisters, and Sister Benedicta quickly adapted herself and showed remarkable cheerfulness. She set to work immediately, taking on new responsibilities. These included writing her study of Saint John of the Cross, which would later be published as *The Science of the Cross.*

In the spring 1939, Sister Teresa Benedicta obtained permission to offer herself to the Sacred Heart of Jesus in a formal way as a sacrifice of atonement for the peace of the world. "Jesus deserves this sacrifice, and he will doubtlessly request it of many other souls," she said.

In the summer of 1940, Edith was joined at Echt by her sister, Rosa, who had also embraced Catholicism. The persecutions of the Jews were getting worse, and someone suggested that Edith and Rosa attempt to escape to a more secure location, but Sister Benedicta would not hear of it. Such an action would bring serious consequences on her whole community. No, she would leave her hand in that of loving Providence.

However, efforts were begun to obtain passports to Switzerland.

On August 2, 1942, as the sisters gathered in chapel for evening prayers, the front doorbell rang repeatedly. Mother Prioress went to the parlor, where she found two policemen who asked to see Sister Stein immediately. Thinking they brought news of the passports to Switzerland, the prioress called Sister Teresa Benedicta, and then stepped out of the room.

"Sister Stein," one guard ordered, "you are to leave here in five minutes!"

"I can't do that," Edith answered calmly. "We have strict enclosure."

"Remove that grille and come out!" shouted the officer.

"You'd better show me how to do that," quipped Edith.

"Call the superior immediately!"

The prioress was called, and Sister Benedicta went to kneel before the Blessed Sacrament.

"Sister Stein must come with us," one of the men demanded.

"She can't do that. Besides, she's waiting for her passport to Switzerland."

"That can be taken care of later," retorted the guard. "Tell her and her sister to pack and bring food sufficient for three days."

Five minutes later, Sister Benedicta reappeared in the parlor, surrounded by her community. Rosa knelt at the feet of the prioress to obtain her last blessing.

The Stein sisters were loaded into a police van and taken to a prison camp. "Among the prisoners who arrived," one witness recalled, "Sister Benedicta made a strong impression on me by her calmness and composure. Everyone was crying or confused and excited. The misery of the camp was appalling. Sister Benedicta walked among the women and children, soothing and helping like an angel. Many mothers, who were almost mad from the strain, brooding and hysterical with weeping, had neglected their children. Sister Benedicta cared for the poor little ones, combed their hair, washed them and saw to it that they were fed and given attention. She amazed everyone."

Another eyewitness commented on Edith's serenity: "My personal impression is that she suffered deeply but without anxiety. She would look with indescribable sadness at her sister Rosa: She was thinking, not of her own sufferings, but of everyone else's. She continually prayed and filled her soul with peace."

Some Dutch authorities paid a last-minute visit to the prisoners and offered to intercede for the learned Carmelite. Horrified, she implored them to do nothing. "I cannot be an exception," she declared. "Everyone here is going. I cannot use my baptism for my advantage. If I am exempted, my life will be forever destroyed. I must go with my people."

On August 7, as a train carried the prisoners eastward, a former student standing on the station platform saw Edith and described her as a picture of complete peace and serenity. This was the last time anyone recorded seeing her. The train brought them to Auschwitz.

On August 9, 1942, Edith Stein—Sister Benedicta—was executed. Her self-offering was now total; she had nothing more to give to God or her people.

Prayer

Dear Saint, we know you as Edith Stein, doctor of
   philosophy,
who sought to honor Divine Truth through your own
   personal search
and to transmit the knowledge of that truth by your
   writing, teaching, and lecturing.
We also know you as Sister Teresa Benedicta of the
   Cross,
who lived and loved truth as a cloistered Carmelite
and as a glorious martyr in the Church.
Teach us to seek the truth in transparency and integrity.
Help us live our lives in prayer, humility, and service.
May we imitate you by learning in order to love and
   by loving in order to serve.
Lead us to understand, appreciate, and defend the rights
   of all people
to religious freedom, to social equality, and to peace.
   Amen.

About Saint Edith Stein

Born: October 12, 1891, in Breslau, Prussia
Died: August 9, 1942, at Auschwitz, Poland
Feast Day: August 9

Canonized: October 11, 1998, by Pope John Paul II
Patron: Jewish converts to Catholicism, martyrs, Europe, philosophers

Notes on Her Life

✿ Born on the Day of Atonement (Yom Kippur), October 12, 1891, Edith was the last of eleven children (four died young).

✿ Her parents, Siegfried and Auguste (Courant) Stein, were observant Jews.

✿ Edith became an atheist as a teenager.

✿ In 1915 she served as a Red Cross nurse in Moravia, now in the Czech Republic.

✿ In 1915 she also taught at Breslau, Poland.

✿ From 1916–1918 she was a research assistant to Edmund Husserl, founder of phenomenology.

✿ In 1917 she received a doctorate in philosophy from the University of Göttingen, Gremany, and presented her dissertation, "On the Problem of Empathy".

✿ In 1921 she discovered "truth" when reading the *Life* of Saint Teresa of Avila.

✿ Edith was baptized in the Catholic Church on January 1, 1922.

✿ From 1923–1931 she taught at a Dominican school in Speyer, Germany.

✿ In 1932 she lectured at the Institute for Scientific Pedagogy at Munster.

✿ The National Socialists (Nazi party) forced her to resign in 1933 because she was Jewish.

☙ In 1933 she asked Pope Pius XI to denounce the Nazi regime. (Later, in 1937, the pope issued the encyclical *Mit Brennender Sorge* condemning anti-Semitism.)

☙ She entered the Discalced Carmelite monastery in Cologne in 1833, and in 1934 she received her habit and the name Sister Teresa Benedicta of the Cross. She made perpetual vows on April 21, 1938.

☙ On December 31, 1938, she was transferred to the Carmelite Monastery in Echt, Netherlands.

☙ From 1934–1942 she wrote many works, including *Finite and Eternal Being* and *Science of the Cross.*

☙ She was arrested on August 2, 1942, and killed on August 9, in a gas chamber at Auschwitz, along with her sister, Rosa.

☙ In 1987 the miraculous cure of two-year-old Teresa Benedicta McCarthy from hepatic necrosis was accepted as a miracle for her beatification that year on May 1.

Lesser-Known Facts

☙ In 1933 she began writing her autobiographical *Life in a Jewish Family*, which she never completed.

☙ She always identified the search for the truth as her own passion.

☙ Her godmother at baptism was Hedwig Conrad-Martius, a Protestant.

☙ Besides many articles, poems, and letters, Edith also wrote *Essays on Woman*, and *World and Person*; she translated into German *Quaestiones Disputatae de Veritate* of Saint Thomas Aquinas and *Letters and Diary* of John Henry Newman.

❧ In July 1942 the Dutch bishops wrote a pastoral letter denouncing persecution of Jews; in retaliation the Gestapo transported all Jewish converts, including priests and religious, to death camps.

❧ Controversy surrounded her cause for canonization: was she killed because she was Jewish or because of the Church's condemnation of the Nazi regime's anti-Semitism? The pope declared her a martyr because she upheld the Church's moral position in defense of Jews.

❧ On October 1, 1999, Pope John Paul II declared her a co-patroness of Europe, with Saint Bridget of Sweden and Saint Catherine of Siena.

In Her Own Words

"When I entered (Carmel), I already knew the name I would choose, and I received it just as I had requested it. "Of the Cross" seemed to me to refer to the fate of God's people, which had actually started to reveal itself. I understood it this way: anyone who recognized the Cross of Christ had the obligation to accept and carry it in the name of all. I now know more about what it means to be betrothed to Christ in the sign of the Cross than I did back then. However, this is something that can never really be understood. It is a mystery."

— From a letter to Mother Petra Brüning, 1938

Blessed Manuel Lozano Garrido

Sacrament of Suffering

"Jesus said to them, 'They need not go away; you give them something to eat'" (Mt 14:16).

Λs Lucia Lozano Garrido entered the sunlit room, she heard her brother Lolo speaking.

"Your passing below in the street brought tears to my eyes. I wanted to leap down from this balcony just to walk at your side. Ah, my best friend, heart of my heart. . . . Ah, but you are my traveling companion even here."

Lucia and Lolo lived together in an apartment above one of the main squares of Linares, Spain. Hearing her brother speaking, but seeing no visitor, Lucia was alarmed. Perhaps his confinement was becoming too much: after all, it was 1951 and his paralysis had been progressing for the last decade or more.

"Lolo," she asked, "who are you speaking with?"

"Oh! Lucia, I am having one of my little conversations with Jesus over there in Saint Mary's. We were recalling the Eucharistic procession that passed through the streets the other day. You know how I love to chat with him face to face like this."

"I'm so sorry, Lolo. I didn't mean to interrupt your prayer."

"Lucia, come over. Sit down right here by me and join our conversation," her brother invited warmly.

"No, no, I'll . . ."

"Yes, yes, you must join us lest we begin to talk about you," Lolo teased.

Reassured that she wasn't troubling her brother, Lucia moved quickly to take a seat next to his wheelchair. For Manuel Lozano Garrido this chair was his chapel, his office, his living room, his study, and the place where he entertained his visitors . . . as he was doing at this moment.

Lolo smiled at Lucia and then gazed out the window. From this vantage point he had a direct view into the church— face to face with Jesus Host in the tabernacle.

"I was also reminiscing with Jesus about my previous career."

"You mean your time in the army?" Lucia prompted.

"No, we were remembering the days when we visited the prisoners together," said Lolo smiling.

"Did you remind him of my part in that story, my brother?"

Lolo glanced over at his much-loved sister and said, "He remembers. He remembers very well."

At this Lucia's cheeks reddened slightly. To cover for her momentary fluster, she began to recall those adventures. "You were quite a brave young man back then. . . ."

"And not so now?" Lolo teased.

"Oh, no, Lolo," Lucia corrected herself. "You are very brave now, but then it was a different kind of brave. Remember, you were just a boy of sixteen back then and our beautiful Spain was in the middle of a civil war."

"Sixteen, yes, but I *was* Catholic Action! We did what needed to be done. Persecution or not!"

"Thinking about it now though, Lolo, imagine . . . you had the courage to sneak the Eucharist into the prisons. And you also brought Communion to many people in their homes. It was a wonderful thing you did."

"Well, I had the best Companion! How could I be afraid?"

Lucia paused a moment and looked over at Manuel. "Lolo," she asked a bit cautiously, "do you remember the name of the person who put an end to your mission by reporting you to the police?"

"Honestly, I don't and I'm glad I have forgotten. I would rather just pray for that person, whoever it was. Don't you agree it's the best thing to do?" Then, moving slightly in his wheelchair, Lolo looked out toward the church and said, "Now we should remember what my brave sister did, don't you agree, Jesus? She, this sister of mine, did just as you commanded, Lord. She visited me in prison. And she brought with her a beautiful bouquet of flowers." Turning again toward his sister, he said, "By the way, Lucia, the guards thought that was such a sweet thing to do."

"I'm going into the kitchen to make us some lunch, Lolo," she announced as she got up and headed out of the room.

"We are going to keep on remembering, Lucia. We'll just reminisce louder so you can hear us. Okay?"

"I know what happened next, Lolo. You don't have to say it!" she called from the other room.

"Ha, ha, it's okay. We two out here enjoy retelling the story," retorted her brother.

Lolo cleared his throat and continued joyously. "That bouquet was the secret weapon, or rather it concealed the secret weapon. Do we agree?" he teased.

In the kitchen, his sister was smiling. She remembered so well.

"My brilliant sister had hidden you, my Lord, In that famous bouquet. Yes, the Host was well concealed among the blossoms. And we, the prisoners, spent a glorious Holy Thursday in adoration. It was perfect revenge on our captors."

Lucia came back into the room at that moment, slightly aglow at hearing the story again. "I'm sorry to interrupt everything," she said with a small bow toward the front window. "Here, let me move you over toward the table, Lolo. I made one of your favorites." She gently tucked the napkin in for him and sat down next to her beloved brother to feed him his lunch.

Manuel Lozano Garrido had by now lost most of his independence. He had needed a wheelchair since he was twenty-two years old. The illness seems to have begun around the time of his imprisonment. It attacked his back first, but with the passing years spondylitis had robbed him of the use of his hands. Even his head tended to loll to one side. And then, of course, he suffered constant pain from the progressive breakdown of his spine. Still, the disease had not affected his spirit. Despite the physical devastation, Lolo was a joyful man! And his mind was as clear and creative as ever. He was well-respected and sought after as an author. He had written nine books and hundreds of articles for magazines and newspapers. What did he write about, a man who was paralyzed and unable to leave his apartment? His reflections covered many subjects, but beyond question, the Eucharist and the Blessed Mother were his most frequent and favored topics.

Another obstacle could have impeded Lolo from his work, but he didn't allow it to stop him. By 1962 he was also totally blind. Initially he had been concerned about this, but a friend suggested using a tape recorder. He placed it on his knees and spoke his thoughts into the microphone. Lucia then transcribed them, and together they edited the copy.

"This is working out quite well, isn't it, Lolo?" Lucia asked. She felt privileged to work so closely with her brother.

"We do make a good team, Lucia," he replied. "Remember how hard we worked to get to this point?"

She did indeed. In the beginning, Lolo used a typewriter. And typical of him, he had it placed on the table used as an altar whenever Mass was celebrated in his room. Why? "Because," he explained, "the crucifix can stand on it. Then the machine will be full of the vision of Christ." In fact, the first thing he typed on the machine were the words, "My Lord, thank you."

"My first word?" he reflected. "Your name, Lord, which I pray may be the strength and soul of this machine."

After a time, Lolo lost the use of his right hand. Together, he and Lucia worked at getting him to write with his left hand. "If this doesn't work you can try tying the pencil to my fingers," he joked.

Eventually his left hand also became useless. That was when he began using the recorder. Nothing could deter his apostolic heart. "I make my living," he once quipped, "by the sweat of my brow." In a beautiful synthesis, he described his work in this way, "I believe in the positive power of solitude. As the marshes in the countryside collect the strength of water only to give it back later as light and energy, so I do with the power of suffering."

Having discovered this great powerhouse in his own solitude and suffering, he wanted to involve others in this
apostolate. As he announced one day to those around him, "I
want to provide a support group for journalists. It will be a
form of Catholic Action. Here is what I am thinking. We will
find twelve people who are very ill and couple their forces
with a convent of contemplatives. Together their mission will
be to pray for a particular newspaper. What do you think of
this idea?"

Everyone present liked his idea.

"That is brilliant! What name will you give it, Lolo?"

He sat there quietly for a few minutes reflecting, and then
said, "Its name will be 'Sinai.'"

"Why Sinai?" one friend asked.

Lifting his head slightly and flashing one of his signature
smiles, Lolo replied, "It will be Sinai because this group will
be like a new Moses as we see him in Exodus 17:11. Joshua
led Israel to victory as long as Moses kept his arms held high
in prayer. When he tired and lowered his arms, the Israelites
did badly. So his brother Aaron and Hur held his arms up.
That is what the members of Sinai will do. They will support
the work of the journalists with their constant offering of
prayer and suffering."

As the years progressed Sinai evolved into a full-fledged
apostolate with hundreds of members. Lolo even began a
magazine for the group, titling it *Sinai.*

No one could model better how to live with suffering
than Manuel Garrido. "My profession is 'disabled,'" he often
said.

Another person put it this way, "He was adept at imitating the suffering of his crucified Lord. However, because he
accepted his form of life wholeheartedly, he was also a man
who radiated joy. His mastery of suffering is his gift to the

Church. For himself he learned to find joy in sharing suffering with Christ. For other sufferers he showed how a life of pain could be placed at the disposal of others, as intercession for them."

Although Lolo couldn't attend daily Mass, each morning a priest brought him the Eucharist, which became the center of his day. His bishop had allowed the priests to take turns offering Mass once a month in Lolo's apartment, and, as one priest observed, "Lolo answered the prayers of Mass with the fervor of a young seminarian." In his chair he was riveted to the drama taking place before him. In one of his remarkable published reflections, "Prayer Before a Pierced Hand," he explained how he looked at life always through Christ—actually, through the hand of the Crucified. What the Lord accomplished by means of suffering inspired Lolo to embrace his own slow crucifixion with purpose and joy. He fervently believed that "God converts the suffering I give him into salvation for souls."

After receiving Christ in the Eucharist, Lolo's adoration and reverence never failed to inspire those present. He radiated not simply devotion to the Eucharist, but his own experience of the Eucharist. His final wish was that a Mass be celebrated at the moment of his death. That wish was faithfully fulfilled on November 3, 1971, when he passed into eternal life.

On the same date twelve years earlier, he had described the moment of anticipating death, comparing it to the experience of waiting for an arriving train. "When the train finally pulls into the station, and your long-awaited friend disembarks, you fall into an embrace that completely fulfills your desire, making your two hearts at last only one."

☙✦❧

Prayer

Blessed Manuel, we feel a closeness to you,
familiarity that allows us to call you "Lolo."
We thank you for giving us the example of a life
totally conformed to our Eucharistic Lord.
You have shown us the pure and heroic devotion
of a youth
and the total, lifelong acceptance of life as it unfolds
its mysteries.
In your case, life meant the intense labor of creative
journalism,
as well as selfless conformity to Christ's own crucified
body
for the sake of his life in us, the Church.
Jesus, we ask you to give us an understanding
and an attraction to your sacred presence in the
Blessed Sacrament.
Grant us a devotion to your will in our regard,
a devotion like that shown to us by Blessed Lolo.
We want to embrace our life with all of its circumstances
as a gift from you.
Help us to find grace and holiness in your holy will.
Amen.

About Blessed Manuel Lozano Garrido

Born: August 9, 1920, in Linares, Spain

Died: November 3, 1971, in Linares

Feast Day: November 3

Beatified: June 12, 2010, by Pope Benedict XVI

Patron: journalists, those suffering with spondylitis, devotees of the Eucharist

Notes on His Life

- One of eight children of a widowed mother, Manuel Lozano Garrido was nicknamed Lolo.

- As a teenager in the Spanish Civil War, he brought the Eucharist to villagers.

- He was arrested and imprisoned in 1937.

- In 1942 he joined the army, but was diagnosed with spondylitis and discharged.

- The disease deformed him and consigned him to a wheelchair.

- Monthly Mass was celebrated in his room.

- Besides being an active member of Catholic Action, he was a journalist for several publications, and he wrote nine books.

- He lost his sight in 1962.

Lesser-Known Facts

- He dictated much of his writing to his sister Lucia.

- When he lost use of his right hand, he learned to write with his left.

- He kept a typewriter under the table that served as the altar for home Masses.

- He received the prestigious Bravo award for his journalism from the Spanish Bishops' Committee.

- He started a prayer group and then a magazine for the sick, both called *Sinai.*

- One of his newspaper articles, "Prayer Before a Pierced Hand," is in the Office of Readings of the Liturgy in the Hours for the Diocese of Jaén, Spain (November 3).

In His Own Words

"Obviously, pain radically changed the course of my life. I had to leave the classrooms and hang up my title. I was confined to loneliness and silence. The journalist I dreamed of becoming was unable to enroll in school. The little apostle I thought I would be stopped traveling around the city streets. But, now I have my ideal and my vocation living within me more deeply than I ever thought possible before."

Blessed Mary Elizabeth Hesselblad

The Second Bridget

"But he said to them, 'Unless I see the mark of the nails in his hands, and put my finger in the mark of the nails and my hand in his side, I will not believe'" *(Jn 20:25).*

The young woman spoke with great enthusiasm, "Can you imagine, Father, what a grace was given to me at that moment? My friends, the Cisneros sisters, brought me to the Corpus Christi celebration at the cathedral in Brussels. When I saw the procession coming toward us, everyone suddenly knelt down. I ran to hide in a doorway. I said to the Lord, 'I will not be part of this. I only kneel before you, my God.' Just as I peeked out, I spotted the monstrance pass by and heard a voice in my heart say, 'I am the One whom you seek.' I sank to my knees. That was my first adoration, hiding behind a door."

"That is all certainly God's grace. But, Miss Hesselblad, you have had no instructions other than your discussions with your friends. How can you expect me to simply baptize you?" Father Hagen saw before him an enthusiastic young woman from a devout Swedish Lutheran family. She told him she had arrived in New York in 1888, when she was only eighteen. Then she spoke of her search of work, her training as a nurse at Roosevelt Hospital in Manhattan, her work as a nurse to the homebound, her struggle with Catholic teachings, but also her attraction to the sincerity of Catholic devotion. He was not sure she was ready, but he didn't want to discourage her.

"Father Hagen," Elizabeth protested, "that was two years ago. I have done a lot of praying, adoring the Blessed Sacrament in every church I pass. I've been reading, too. Test me. Ask me anything, I know the answers, Father. Please, just try me."

The Jesuit priest proceeded to ask Elizabeth Hesselblad many questions about the teachings of the Catholic faith, and to his astonishment, she answered each one precisely and with great conviction. "You have done very well indeed. I see no reason why I can't receive you into the Church. Come back for the next three days for further instruction and then I will gladly baptize you."

On August 15, 1902, in Washington, D.C., Elizabeth Hesselblad was conditionally baptized Catholic in the chapel of the Visitation Sisters. One of the Cisneros sisters, who was her godmother, had entered that convent. Two days later Elizabeth received her First Communion.

As a child Elizabeth had been troubled that there were so many different Christian churches. In the forest one day as she looked up through the tall trees at the sky, she begged Jesus to lead her to the church he spoke of when he prayed *that all may be one.* He called himself the Shepherd of *one* flock, she thought, but which one is it? As she prayed she heard Jesus promise that one day he would show her what he meant. *At last,* she thought on the day she was received into the Catholic Church, *what the Lord promised me many years ago in the pine forest has come to pass. Today was that very day.* Now she was a member of the one flock.

Some months after her baptism, Elizabeth sailed for Rome, where she received Confirmation and prayed to know the path God wanted her to follow. She sought out the house where Saint Bridget, the great fourteenth century Swedish saint, had lived. It was now the home of Carmelite nuns. The Lord again spoke to Elizabeth's heart, "This is where I want you to serve me." So she asked to be admitted as a postulant among the Carmelites. Despite a bout of serious illness, she eventually began her religious training. In this house Saint Bridget invaded Elizabeth's soul. Elizabeth longed to bring their native Sweden back to unity with the Church of Rome.

So in 1906 when it was time for her to make her profession, she petitioned Pope Saint Pius X for permission to wear the habit of Saint Bridget's community, the Order of the Most Holy Savior. The Holy Father gladly granted Elizabeth permission and allowed her also to take her religious vows as a Brigittine nun.

With the pope's blessing the newly professed Sister Mary Elizabeth set out on a pilgrimage. "I want to visit the four remaining convents of Brigittines. From them I will glean the pure spirit of our Mother Bridget's teachings and rule of life. Perhaps a few of the nuns will join me in establishing a convent in Rome." Although nothing concrete came from her years of pilgrimage, God rewarded her effort by inspiring three young women from England to apply on November 9, 1911.

"We heard of your plans to refound the ancient Brigittine Order and we want to join you," one of them said. Mother Mary Elizabeth gratefully embraced them as another sign that God willed new life for the Order of the Most Holy Savior, that he might be glorified and that Scandinavian Christians might be reunited with the Church of Rome. The foundation quickly grew under her guidance. New houses seemed to spring up like flowers. Papal approval came to her work in 1920, and as a crowning jewel in 1931, the Brigittines acquired the House of Saint Bridget in Rome in which Elizabeth had absorbed so much of the spirit of the great Swedish saint.

For all of her sisters, Mother Mary Elizabeth proposed the spiritual goals of contemplation, adoration, and reparation, by which they would strive toward unity, charity, and peace. However, their life of peaceful prayer was soon to be tested when World War II broke out in Europe.

Early one evening, as the community tried to chant Vespers, a great deal of commotion could be heard out on the street. A cacophony of shouts, cries, and blaring sirens shattered the silence. Fearing what it meant, the sisters intensified their fervor. Suddenly they heard a frenzied pounding on the convent door. Mother Mary Elizabeth directed one of the sisters to go see what was going on. "Just peek out the side window first, Sister," she whispered. "Be careful and come let us know what is happening."

A few minutes later a breathless Sister Riccarda dashed into chapel. "Mother," she gasped, "I think you should come to the parlor immediately."

Looking at the now mature face of one of her earliest English vocations, Mother Mary Elizabeth rose from her place and followed Sister Riccarda to the front entrance. As she was heading toward the door, Sister Riccarda stopped her, saying, "Not the door, Mother. Please come to the parlor." There, huddled together, she found a tall thin man, his distinguished features full of anguish, and two small boys shivering with fear, afraid to even raise their heads.

"My dear sir," Mother began as she placed a reassuring hand on his arm, "how can we assist you?"

"Sisters, thank you for opening your door to us. We are Jews from this city. Our biggest fear is beginning tonight. We are being hunted down. The police are out there searching for us. They have already taken away many people."

"Come. You must come away from the windows," Mother advised as she directed the family to an interior room.

"Thank you, Sisters, but my wife—their mother—is still outside with our two little daughters and my oldest son. They are hiding nearby." Suddenly the little boys jumped as police sirens wailed past the convent.

"My sons, you must trust God," he told the boys as he hugged them closer to his side. "We are in a good place, a holy place," he said, looking at the two nuns before him.

"All right," Mother continued, "for now you stay here. Sit still while Sister Riccarda and I go for a little walk. What is your wife's name?"

"Anna," he replied. "And my son, Samuel."

"So, Sister Riccarda," Mother announced, "let us go out to look for our two cats!"

"Father," a young voice piped up, "if they mention the 'kittens,' the girls will know the message is from you."

"You are right, my son," his father said. Then to the sisters, he added, "That is my pet name for the two little girls. They are my 'kittens.' Please find them, Sisters! They were right behind us."

Outside, the two nuns quietly called out for their cats. "Here, Anna! Here, Samuel! Come along into the house now.

Bring the kittens, too." To this they added in a whisper, "Their father is waiting for them. Come, come!" They heard someone stir behind a nearby stone wall. Up popped one head. It was Samuel. "Oh, thanks be to God!" declared Mother Mary Elizabeth. "Stay low, Samuel. Bring your mother and your sisters and follow me." And she whispered to her companion, "Sister Riccarda, keep calling the cats, but keep an eye on the street."

Once everyone was inside the convent and the family was reunited, the sisters ushered them all to an interior apartment reserved for visitors. "You will stay with us as long as you need to. Do not be afraid. We'll make some beds. And look, Sister is brining some warm tea and bread."

And so began the wartime refuge at the House of Saint Bridget in Rome. All through those frightening years Mother Mary Elizabeth encouraged her sisters to welcome as many Jewish refugees as possible. This welcome soon expanded to include many other people as well, all of whom the Nazi gestapo were pursuing.

Mother Mary Elizabeth Hesselblad's childhood musings about the identity of Christ's one flock led her to the idea of the Church's true catholicity. Her heart, like that of her Most Holy Savior, was able to embrace everyone: those who wished to join her in the life of Saint Bridget, the poor, the persecuted, the confused, those in any way afflicted. Her outer door was always open to anyone in need; her inner door, the one that led to her heart, was open to the call of the Shepherd who bid her to lie down in his pasture, to find rest for her soul (cf. Ps 23).

⋐✦⋑

Prayer

Blessed Elizabeth, you struggled with doubts,
yet you fervently prayed to know God's true Church.
Intercede for all who are confused or misled,
so that they may find the clarity and peace of heart
    to surrender before God's truth.
We ask your intercession also for those who dedicate
    their lives
to the health care profession, that they may see
    Jesus Christ
in those they serve, and that they may guard and defend
the lives of all those in their care.
Pray for us that each of us may know God's will,
honor his law, respect his image in everyone, share his
    gifts,
and serve after his example, that by our lives God may
    be glorified
and all will find a place in his fold. Amen.

About Blessed Mary Elizabeth Hesselblad

Born: June 4, 1870, in Faglavik, Sweden
Died: April 24, 1957, in Rome
Feast Day: June 4
Beatified: April 9, 2000, by Pope John Paul II
Patron: seekers of the true faith, ecumenism, nurses,
    home health care workers

Notes on Her Life

⚘ Elizabeth was one of thirteen children of August and
Cajsa (Dag) Hesselblad.

❧ She was baptized Lutheran several days after birth.

❧ In 1888 she emigrated to America. She studied nursing at Roosevelt Hospital in Manhattan, then worked in New York until 1904, also in home health care.

❧ In 1894 she spent a month in Sweden.

❧ She was befriended by the Catholic Cisneros family in New York.

❧ In 1900 she recognized Christ's True Presence at a Corpus Christi procession in Brussels.

❧ She was given conditional baptism as a Catholic on August 15, 1902, in Washington, D.C. She made a pilgrimage to Rome in the fall of that year, and was confirmed in Rome.

❧ From March 25, 1904, she lived with the Carmelites at the House of Saint Bridget of Sweden in Rome.

❧ In 1906 Pope Pius X gave her permission to wear the habit of the Order of the Most Holy Savior of Saint Bridget (the Brigittines).

❧ She traveled to four existing Brigittine foundations to learn the charism of their order.

❧ In 1911 the first postulants joined, and the first foundation of Brigittines was opened.

❧ Canonically approved in 1920, Mary Elizabeth was the first abbess of the community.

❧ In 1923 she opened Saint Bridget Rest Home in Stockholm.

❧ In 1929 the Brigittines reacquired the House of Saint Bridget of Sweden in Rome.

❧ In 1935 she reestablished the Brigittine presence in Vadstena (original foundation in 1343).

- In 1937 she opened a convent in India.

- Together with Sister Riccarda Hambrough, she hid sixty Jews in the motherhouse in Rome during World War II.

- She was instrumental in the conversion of the chief rabbi of Rome, Israel Eugenio Zolli, to the Catholic faith.

Lesser-Known Facts

- From childhood she prayed to be led to the one, true fold of Christ.

- As a nurse, when accidentally locked in a morgue, she revived a young man who was thought to have died.

- She cared for men injured during the construction of Saint Patrick's Cathedral in New York.

- At first she was scandalized by Catholic devotion to Mary and the saints.

- Currently her Brigittines are present in nineteen countries, including Sweden, India, the Philippines, Mexico, and the United States.

- The cause for canonization has been opened for two of her early Brigittine collaborators.

- She offered a home and collaboration to Father Charles Boyer, SJ, founder of the *Unitas Association* for ecumenism.

- She was known as "the second Bridget" and "the pilgrim of unity."

- She was honored in 2004 by Yad Vashem as one of the *Righteous Among the Nations* for her efforts to save Jews during World War II.

In Her Own Words

"We must nourish within ourselves a great love for God and for our neighbors; a love that is strong and ardent, that burns away imperfections, gently bears with acts of impatience or bitterness, that allows inadvertent acts of negligence to pass without comment, that gives itself quickly to acts of charity."

Saint Mark the Evangelist

Only a Boy

"Go into all the world and proclaim the good news to the whole creation. The one who believes and is baptized will be saved; but the one who does not believe will be condemned" (Mk 16:15–16).

M ark was not one of the Twelve whom Jesus appointed to be his companions, to go out preaching at his command. Mark was not even one of the disciples who followed the Master and listened to his teachings; nor did he witness the miracles Christ performed. When it all began he was too young, only a boy.

But, today, that unforgettable first day of the Feast of Unleavened Bread, Mark knew that something very special and important was happening. The Master, Jesus of Nazareth, sent his disciples to prepare the paschal meal in the upper room of Mark's home.

"Wow," thought Mark. "These are his companions. They've seen everything he's done and heard all his teaching, I wish Father didn't tell me to leave them be."

When it was evening, Jesus arrived with the twelve apostles. Just seeing him was enough to set Mark's heart ablaze. He had heard all the stories of this prophet, now here he was celebrating the holy day in his house.

"I'll do anything, go anywhere, give up everything, for him," Mark promised himself enthusiastically. If ever a boy longed to be a man, Mark was that boy.

"I wonder how old they are," he thought as he looked from one disciple to another. When he spotted John he did some quick math in his head. "Maybe five or six years and I can join them, but that's a long time."

Little did Mark realize as he dreamed of the future that this supper was to be the last supper for Jesus. That very night the betrayer, Judas Iscariot, one of those closest to the Master, would lead a great multitude with swords and clubs to find him as he was suffering and praying in the Garden of Gethsemane.

As soon as Mark heard of the betrayal, he ran to Gethsemane to help. He stood on the fringe of the shouting crowd and panic welled up inside of him. "Where are you going?" he called after one fleeing figure. "Somebody has to do something," his words trailed off. All the disciples had abandoned the Lord. All fled. Then Mark, too, turned like a frightened child and ran! He ran into the night, into the dark. Maybe the darkness would cover his shame, his cowardice. His thoughts tumbled one over the other. "Where are all my resolutions to do anything and everything for the Master? Where is my faith? Where is that love I thought was so great? I'm only a scared boy!"

During those terrible hours of waiting from Thursday night to Sunday morning, John Mark (as he is identified in the Acts of the Apostles), was hiding safely in his parents' house. There he mulled over the events in the garden. He was sick with shame when he realized just how badly he had failed the Master. He had been given one moment of time to prove his love . . . and he ran. . . .

"It will be different when I am a man," he promised himself.

Despite their panic, the Master did not fail his disciples. They had mournfully whispered to one another his promise to rise from death. But then the news of his unbelievable triumph spread like wildfire among them. Breathlessly Mark rejoiced with the others over the glorious resurrection of the Lord. New hope flowed in his heart. "Yes, things will be different now, I'm sure of it," he exclaimed.

With God's help, the infant Church grew steadily through the constant zeal of the apostles. It wasn't long, however, before Peter was thrown into prison in an attempt to stifle this new Way, as the young Church was called. A group of fervent Christians gathered in Mark's home to pray for Peter's safety. Mark prayed as he had never prayed before.

Suddenly Rhoda, the servant girl, dashed by to answer the heavy knocking at the front gate. As she got close to the door she recognized Peter's voice. "It's him! It's him! It's Peter! He's here at the gate," she announced as she ran inside.

"Wishing won't make it true, Rhoda," they said to her, but she insisted.

Outside, Peter was becoming impatient. He began to pound on the door, fearful that the sentries would hear the ruckus. Finally, the whole assembly ran to the door, flung it open and found that Peter really was there. When he had quieted them down, he explained just how the Lord had liberated him (cf. Acts 12:14–17). Mark was beside himself with joy and awe as he listened to the account.

"I was picked up during the Feast of Unleavened Bread and thrown into prison. Guarded, mind you, by not one, but four squads of soldiers. They intended to bring me to trial after the feast."

"We were all praying for you, Peter!" a young voice called out.

"Yes, yes, I felt your prayers. Even though I was securely chained with double chains between two guards with more of them at the door, God's angel got in. I thought I was seeing things, but he said, 'Hurry, get up!' I was so stunned, he had to keep prompting me to get dressed: 'Your belt! Your sandals, Peter! Now grab your cloak and follow me,' he said. I wasn't too sure what was happening. Maybe it was a dream! But, no, we went right past all those guards and out into the city where the angel left me. And so, by the grace of God, I'm here," Peter concluded.

"Amen, yes, amen," Mark cried out.

The grace of God was certainly with the little group in the days and years that followed. In time the Good News spread farther and farther. Paul the Apostle, who had had a miraculous encounter with the risen Lord, along with Mark's cousin, Barnabas, prepared to leave Judea to bring God's word to everyone they could find. John Mark watched and helped, dreaming of the day when his turn would come. Then, wonder of wonders, Barnabas actually invited the young man to accompany them in preaching the Good News.

Of course his good mother objected. "That kind of life is too hard," she insisted. Even Paul was not too enthusiastic about the idea.

"Come on, Paul," Barnabas said. "My nephew is still young, but he wants to do his part for the Good News."

His pleadings prevailed. Mark set out with the apostles, thrilled beyond words.

"Now is my chance," Mark thought. "This time I'll make good the test; I won't run. I'm older now, and my cousin asked for me! I am a man and an apostle. . . ."

The tiny caravan started on its way. Mark was exultant, triumphant, and bursting with what he thought was zeal. Soon the sight of Jerusalem sunk behind a hill, and Mark set his mind to the "business" of being a missionary. However, he learned quickly that it was not such a romantic "business" after all.

Tediously, they traveled over the hot, rugged miles to the city of Antioch. When they arrived the Holy Spirit promptly sent them off again to the port of Seleucia, and from there they set sail for Cyprus. The seemingly endless blue sea was new to Mark—so was the ship's constant pitching and rolling. . . .

"Will this never end," he moaned. "I'd give anything for steady ground again."

Finally they disembarked at Salamis in Cyprus, where the apostles proclaimed the word of God in the synagogues. John Mark accompanied them as an assistant. Soon enough, however, the three were trudging down the road again. *This certainly isn't Jerusalem, but at least it's solid ground,* Mark probably thought, as he forced one foot to follow the other, trying to keep up with the rhythmic gait of the older men. *I never knew there could be so many hills and rocks and unfamiliar people. . . .*

This time the road ended in Paphos, the far side of Cyprus. There the young apostle witnessed the conversion of the governor through an act of God. But soon the rocking of the ship and the swish of waves replaced the rocks and hills once more. On this longer voyage they were heading toward Perga in Pamphylia. Not even Mark was sure of what thoughts and emotions surged through his mind. But he was aware of a slowly tightening knot inside. By this time he, the man, the apostle, the one who had been so impatient to serve the Lord that he could scarcely wait to grow up—found that he couldn't take this missionary life any longer.

"I'm leaving," he announced. "I'm going back to Jerusalem to help there."

Despite the disgust of Paul and the disappointment of Barnabas, Mark left them and found his way back. Every mile of the trip, however, weighed heavier than the missionary sacrifices that he had allowed to break his spirit.

When he arrived, he turned to Peter. It was true, Peter had made his mistakes—but who hadn't, except the Divine Master himself?

"I really don't know what happened to me, Peter," he confided. "I just couldn't take it. I thought I was stronger, more mature, more ready, but. . . ."

Peter listened with the patience he himself had to learn. "I understand, John Mark. And you will, too, in time. Maturity can be a tricky thing and sometimes it only requires a little more reflection, a little humility and a lot of trust in what God wants of us. Pray and prepare. He will reveal his plan when you are ready."

And so Mark set about preparing himself in earnest. Before long he was again "on the road" for Christ. He and Barnabas journeyed, preached, and worked for the Lord. And Paul noticed the change and revealed his approval and encouragement. In writing to the Colossians, Paul refers to "Mark the cousin of Barnabas . . . welcome him . . . [he is] among my co-workers for the kingdom of God" (4:10-11). And again, in the letter to Philemon, he sends the greetings of "Mark . . . my fellow worker" (cf. v. 23).

Between journeys with Barnabas, Mark returned to Peter whenever he could, finally accompanying him to Rome. There

Mark became one of Peter's closest disciples and assistants. It was he, Mark, who set down in writing the preaching of Peter. Today it is known as "the Gospel according to Saint Mark." In all its vivid description it immortalized the life of the Master as seen by the "big Fisherman of Galilee."

Mark became so full of the Lord and so unshakably loyal that eventually Peter sent him to found the Church of Alexandria in Egypt. There he labored for the Master whom he had come to know and love so well. He faced far greater hardships than the rugged hills and rocky roads of his first missionary attempt. Through violent persecutions that ended in death, he was sustained by the inner force of which Saint Peter wrote:

> " . . . testify that this is the true grace of God" (1 Pt 5:12). "But rejoice insofar as you are sharing Christ's sufferings, ... And when the chief shepherd appears, you will win the crown of glory that never fades away" (1 Pt 4:13, 5:4).

Mark followed the Master. No longer depending on his own resources but with the strength that comes from God, he bore his share of the hardship that the Gospel entails. For the Spirit of God is no cowardly spirit, but one that strengthens us (cf. 2 Tm 1:7–8).

Mark was no longer only a boy. He followed the Master's will with a love that knew no bounds, obedient to death.

Prayer

Saint Mark, to me you are the perfect disciple of our
   Master, Jesus Christ.
You immediately perceived the truth of his Good News

and you longed to give all your youthful energy to his
   cause.
Even when your will faltered and your strength seemed
   to fail,
you sought guidance and took your place again with
   renewed fervor.
Help me, Saint Mark, to make the Gospel my life
   as you did.
Show me the way to pursue my Christian vocation
with a hunger and thirst for God's holiness. Amen.

About Saint Mark the Evangelist

Birth: unknown, probably early first century
Death: ca. 68 or 74 in Alexandria, Egypt
Feast Day: April 25
Canonized: universal acclaim
Patron: Venice, Italy, Egypt, Coptic Church, notaries,
   glass workers, opticians, cattle breeders, basket
   weavers

Notes on His Life

❀ Mark is often thought to be the young man who ran away
   naked when Jesus was arrested (cf. Mk 14:51–52).

❀ His mother's name was Mary (cf. Acts 12:12).

❀ Saint Barnabas was his uncle or cousin.

❀ He is best known as Saint Mark the Evangelist, author of
   the Gospel of Saint Mark, which is considered the first
   one written.

❀ His Gospel is addressed to the Gentiles of Rome.

✿ Mark is represented by a lion because of the vision in Revelation (4:6–7).

✿ The lion as symbol of courage also represents Jesus, "the Lion of the tribe of Judah" (Rv 5:5).

✿ Saint Mark was martyred in Alexandria, Egypt in ca. 68 or 74.

Lesser-Known Facts

✿ Mark is believed to be from the Levite tribe.

✿ Esteemed as the founder of the Coptic Church, he is also held in special esteem in Libya, Cyprus, Rome, and many countries of Asia.

✿ A famous Venetian legend has Saint Mark saving the city from evil spirits.

In His Own Words

"And all that had been commanded them they told briefly to those around Peter. And afterward Jesus himself sent out through them, from east to west, the sacred and imperishable proclamation of eternal salvation" (Mk 16:8).

Reader's Guides

Saint Marguerite Bourgeoys

Traveling from France to "New France" in the 1600s, Marguerite brings with her a desire to spread the kingdom of God in the New World. She becomes a religious and lays the foundation for Catholic schools in Montreal.

Personal Reflections

* The young Marguerite was totally changed from being self-absorbed to being generously concerned for others—and this from one look at a statue of Mary. Have you ever had a similar happening when an inspiration or insight comes suddenly through an encounter with something sacred?

* It is amazing that Marguerite would receive and accept an invitation to go teach in a small, new settlement amid constant danger. Think of the most difficult request ever made of you and what qualities you have that helped you succeed.

Group Discussion

❦ Marguerite was conflicted regarding her life plan. She did much soul-searching and praying, besides consulting many advisers. Consider when you or someone you know came to the choice of a direction in life. What was the most difficult thing about it? How was this overcome?

❦ At Ville-Marie, the new missionary won over those who had criticized her for traveling alone in the company of de Maisonneuve. She prayed, taught, counseled, nursed, and generally served all in need. And she showed wisdom in founding a community of religious who lived among the people. What needs exist in today's society, or right in your community, that a new religious or lay movement could serve?

Read ⋅➤⋅ Reflect ⋅➤⋅ Respond

In those days Mary set out and went with haste to a Judean town in the hill country, where she entered the house of Zechariah and greeted Elizabeth. . . . And [Elizabeth asked] "why has this happened to me, that the mother of my Lord comes to me?" (Lk 1:39–40, 43)

Luke 13:4

Mark 4:26–29

Matthew 9:35–38

Acts 10:34–43

Romans 3:21–26

Catechism of the Catholic Church 864, 871, 873, 900, 916, 931, 971

⟨❦⟩

Servant of God Satoko Kitahara

A young woman of good social standing, a college graduate and a recent convert, chooses to become a ragpicker in order to make Christ present to the poorest citizens of Tokyo.

Personal Reflection

❧ Just as the first apostles were drawn to Christ, so Satoko found herself impulsively following Brother Zeno. How magnetic is your example of Christian living?

❧ In time Satoko realized that volunteering time wasn't the same as "becoming" one of the ragpickers, so she went "to live among them." What does the Incarnation of Christ say to you about your life choices?

Group Discussion

❧ Satoko needed guidance from Brother Zeno to see the troubled face of poverty, but also to learn to engage the poor with respect. Is there an individual or an organization that you would turn to for such advice about poverty on a local level?

❧ Aware of her precarious health, Satoko went to live in Ant Town. She literally offered her life for the good of the community. Discuss if it is heroic to offer your life for a cause if your health is already compromised?

Read ⋆ Reflect ⋆ Respond

And she gave birth to her firstborn son and wrapped him in bands of cloth, and laid him in a manger, because there was no place for them in the inn (Lk 2:7).

Matthew 8:20
John 3:16–21
Ephesians 2:8–10
1 John 4:9–21
Catechism of the Catholic Church 520–521, 526, 1889

Saint Patrick

A teenager is kidnapped and brought to Ireland as a slave. Six years later he is safely home, yet listens to God's call to return as a missionary to his captors.

Personal Reflections

- Patrick admits he had not been practicing his faith before his capture. Only after the trials and sufferings of his exile did he turn to God. Reflect on this common scenario. What do you think is the blessing of suffering in this case?

- Patrick began to have visions and dreams, which eventually told him of his escape from Ireland and eventual return. Although you have probably had no supernatural intervention, think about any "direction" you have experienced.

Group Discussion

- The vision was over except "for the ache in his heart and his own terrible fears." Patrick was called to return to Ireland as a missionary. Discuss how "the ache" and "the terror" are integral parts of his prayer. Have you experienced anything like this?

❧ God doesn't usually work outside our human messiness. He invites some of us to come follow him and become fishers of others, but he expects us to use our natural human qualities and circumstances of life to accomplish this mission. Reflect and pray over this reality together.

Read ⤑ Reflect ⤑ Respond

"Follow me, and I will make you fish for people" (Mt 4:19).

Matthew 14:13–21, 28–31
John 21:22
1 Corinthians 1:18–2:5
Ephesians 3:1–13
Colossians 1:15–29
Catechism of the Catholic Church 849–852, 878, 2818, 2825

Saint Clare of Assisi

A young woman from a wealthy family decides to follow unreservedly the life she has seen lived by her contemporary, Francis. Her dramatic gift of self inspires and sustains the early "Poor Ladies," who become a great light in the Church.

Personal Reflections

❧ We find Clare clearing rubble from a doorway that will lead her to her destiny. What do you have to sort through or put aside so that Christ will find a way in?

❧ Clare did not pay attention to the rumors and reports about Francis and his odd lifestyle. When she observed how he treated the poor, she was struck by his gentle sincerity. Reflect on the dynamic between what we can hear about someone or something and what we observe firsthand.

Group Discussion

❦ Rarely does God himself witness to a person's vocational choice as he did for Clare's sister Catherine by making her immovable. But a religious vocation can be recognized by certain signs. Discuss what you think these might be.

❦ Clare and her companions embraced an austere life of prayer and poverty unfamiliar to religious of their time. Consider what the Franciscan charism has meant to the Church over the centuries. What impresses you most about it as a layperson?

Read ·→· Reflect ·→· Respond

"Is a lamp brought in to be put under the bushel basket, or under the bed, and not on the lampstand?" (Mk 4:21).

Matthew 7:7, 13–14
1 Thessalonians 5:16–25
Ephesians 5:19–20
1 Timothy 6:11–12
Catechism of the Catholic Church 2559, 2562–64, 2602, 2641, 2655, 2706

ᘒ☙❧ᘰ

Saint Benedict of Nursia

Born into privilege, Benedict desires only to spend his life in contemplation of God and in service to the Church. In pursuing his ideal, he gifts Christianity with the definitive form of Western monasticism.

Personal Reflection

❧ The Gospel says that "a city built on a hill cannot be hid." We see the same dynamic concerning Benedict's vocation: he cannot seem to put aside the idea of becoming a monk. What is the most burning desire of your life?

❧ The evil one insinuates that since Benedict deprives himself so much "a few minutes of enjoyment won't hurt." Ordinarily, that would be true for a balanced life, but the devil is misrepresenting these "pleasures." How do you balance purpose and pleasure in your life?

Group Discussion

❧ Benedict used solitude, deprivation, fasting, and violence against himself to gain self-mastery. If he were your son or brother, living in today's world, what would you suggest he do as personal discipline to gain self-control?

❧ Why do we say that baptism makes us "salt of the earth and light of the world"? Is it more than a poetic phrase?

Read ⇢ Reflect ⇢ Respond

"You are the salt of the earth. . . . You are the light of the world. A city built on a hill cannot be hid" (Mt 5:13–14).

Matthew 5:15–16
John 8:12; 9:5
James 4:7–10
Catechism of the Catholic Church 782, 918, 1243, 1253,
    2820–21, 2834

Venerable Pierre Toussaint

As a young man, Pierre moves to New York with his master's family to escape a revolution. Circumstances reverse his role, but not his status. Eventually he becomes a free man, but he continues to generously serve God's people.

Personal Reflections

- Although born a slave, Pierre lived a comfortable existence within the Bérard household. Some would think this was not a bad lot in life. How would you explain the inherent human right to freedom?

- For sixty-six years, Toussaint attended daily Mass, received Communion weekly (the custom of his time), and prayed the Rosary. This nourished and energized his life of charity. What place do Mass and prayer have in your life? Resolve to rely more on God.

Group Discussion

- Pierre was truly a philanthropist who gave generously to many causes. When he was dying and someone asked if he wanted anything, he replied, "nothing on this earth." How do you think those words characterized his entire life?

When the Bérard family fell into financial ruin, Pierre discreetly maintained a normality in their life even as he remained a dutiful slave. What does his example say about discretion as a key to happiness within human relations?

Read ⟶ Reflect ⟶ Respond

"Beware of practicing your piety before others in order to be seen by them; for then you have no reward from your Father in heaven" (Mt 6:1).

Matthew 6:1–4
Colossians 4:1
Galatians 5:13–14
Ephesians 6:5 91
1 Timothy 6:1–2
James 3:13–18
Catechism of the Catholic Church 1434–35, 1828–29, 1969–70, 2414, 2443–47

⟨€♥э⟩

Saint Teresa of Avila

Teresa of Avila is the great reformer of the Carmelites, a Doctor of the Church, and a teacher of prayer and contemplation. Because she suffered migraine headaches most of her life, she is patron of migraine sufferers, and yet a woman of constant joy.

Personal Reflections

 Teresa of Avila had some extraordinary prayer experiences, yet she was very practical in the advice she gave on prayer: "Be natural in your relationship with the Lord." How do you see your prayer life, as natural or forced? How can you progress in prayer?

☙ Although at first she did not feel called to monastic life, neither did she plan to marry, and she had turned down several marriage proposals. She became one of the greatest nuns in Church history. Reflect on how you came to your life choice and how grace has worked in you.

Group Discussion

☙ As a fifteen-year-old, Teresa was easily influenced, and she quickly assumed the habits of her peers. To assure her good formation, her widowed father sent her to a convent school. What have you learned from your experiences with peer pressure? Have you had an occasion to guide someone through such a situation?

☙ Saint Teresa was known for her wit, which brought her through many trials. The story says "she was a picture of constant joy." Discuss together the benefits of a joyful attitude and ways to maintain this quality in difficult times.

Read ⤙ Reflect ⤙ Respond

"But when you fast, put oil on your head and wash your face, so that your fasting may be seen not by others but by your Father who is in secret; and your Father who sees in secret will reward you" (Mt 6:17).

Matthew 6:21; 7:13
Ephesians 3:8–21
James 1:2–8; 4:13–16
1 John 3:18–24; 7:1–21
Catechism of the Catholic Church 227, 1821, 2709–10, 2729

⟨€✦9⟩

Saint Katharine Drexel

The Drexel heiress uses her vast fortune to support Catholic efforts among the Native American and African American population. In addition she gives her life and energy to found the congregation of the Sisters of the Blessed Sacrament.

Personal Reflections

✿ Today people buy lottery tickets, enter contests, and dream of making millions. In her day, Katharine dreamed instead of the day she could give her millions away and enter the convent. Think about how these priorities compare or differ.

✿ Kate received a letter essentially announcing that it was her duty to begin a religious congregation to serve Native Americans and African Americans. Reflect on her belief that it was God's will. How do you discern the will of God?

Group Discussion

✿ Together discuss Mother Drexel's view of America as not "a melting pot, but rather as a vivid mosaic in which every color, every hue of tradition and race, (brings) out the beauty of the whole."

✿ Katharine Drexel is considered a precursor of the civil rights movement for many reasons, including her stand in the controversy over what became Xavier University. Pick a present-day cause and as a group plan ways to show support.

Read ⬝⟶⬝ Reflect ⬝⟶⬝ Respond

"Do not store up for yourselves treasures on earth, where moth and rust consume and where thieves break in and steal; but store up for yourselves treasures in heaven . . . for where your treasure is, there your heart will be also" (Mt 6:19-21).

Matthew 19:16-30

John 10:10

1 Timothy 6:17-19

James 2:15-16

Catechism of the Catholic Church 919, 2052-53, 2402-04, 2443-49

Blessed Franz Jägerstätter

This young husband and father meets his death rather than violate his conscience, which told him that to serve Hitler's Third Reich would be sinful.

Personal Reflections

⚜ Franz asked that no one be bitter toward the bishop and priests who didn't protect him. "They are only human . . . and must be much more cautious than a single man for their responsibilities are much greater." Examine yourself on how you judge others. Are you lenient or stringent?

⚜ From the story we see that Franz was truly a blessed man. He started out as a "wild" youth, but everything changed when he met and married Franziska. What does this tell you about choosing your spouse well?

Group Discussion

🍀 The majority of Germans and Austrians found it possible to work with the Nazis. Do you consider Franz a fanatic for the extent of his opposition to the regime?

🍀 Franz declared that he would not serve and stood by his convictions despite threats, heartbreak, and imprisonment. Discuss whether or not this kind of moral discernment is something natural, or does it require training?

Read ⟿ Reflect ⟿ Respond

"No one can serve two masters; for a slave will either hate the one and love the other, or be devoted to the one and despise the other. You cannot serve God and wealth" (Mt 6:24),

Matthew 5:10–11
Acts 5:29
Galatians 5:18–25
Ephesians 6:10–20
Catechism of the Catholic Church 2113, 2237–38, 2242, 2304–05, 2311, 2313

Saint Thomas More

Chancellor of England and a good friend of King Henry VIII, Thomas More finds himself alone as he faces a crisis of conscience, one that means life or death.

Personal Reflection

🍀 As he encountered his daughter, More assured her that no matter what happened it would be God's will. "It would be for the best." Although he was unjustly condemned, he maintained that God was to be trusted. How would you defend his position?

🙊 Thomas More was married twice, to two very distinct women. He always said that his life was happy. What do you suspect was his secret?

Group Discussion

🙊 Thomas was a man known for his loyalty and integrity, so it is shocking that he stood alone among his peers. Why did they all condemn him? Was it fear, lack of reflection, fickleness? Does this mentality still surface today?

🙊 The saying of Jesus about entering by the narrow door reminds us of the role of conscience. Thomas More did not condemn others for their decision. How do you understand the working of conscience? How is a conscience formed?

Read ⤙ Reflect ⤙ Respond

"Enter through the narrow gate; for the gate is wide and the road is easy that leads to destruction, and there are many who take it. For the gate is narrow and the road is hard that leads to life, and there are few who find it" (Mt 7:13–14).

1 Kings 3:23–28
Matthew 5:31–37
Ephesians 3:14–19
1 Corinthians 4:1–5
Romans 8:31–39
1 Timothy 2:1–4
Catechism of the Catholic Church 313, 1730, 2471, 2476, 2484–85

✿

Saint Philip Neri

Commonly described as "the apostle of Christian joy," this priest breathed new life into the Church with his counsels and his spirituality.

Personal Reflection

✿ "If you wish to go to extremes, let it be in gentleness, patience, humility, and charity." How are these virtues practiced without fault?

✿ Philip made himself into a one-man renewal of the faith by discovering ways to attract people to friendly discussion of important truths. How can you see yourself becoming an apostle of amiability, an attractive model of Christianity?

Group Discussion

✿ "We are re-baptizing the Mardi Gras parades," Philip once said. Share ideas for breathing new life into some of your local celebrations or practices in order to make them more attractive, especially to the young.

✿ Misunderstanding and suspicion often accompany noticeable good works. Jealousy or fear can cause this discord. Examine any local initiatives that are under scrutiny. How can good be done and peace restored?

Read ⟶ Reflect ⟶ Respond

"To what then will I compare the people of this generation, and what are they like? They are like children sitting in the

*marketplace and calling to one another, 'We played the flute for
you, and you did not dance; we wailed, and you did not weep'"
(Luke 7:31-32).*

1 Chronicles 15:25-29
Matthew 11:28-30
1 Timothy 4:4-10
1 Thessalonians 5:12-25
Catechism of the Catholic Church 1156-57, 1818, 1828-29,
2702-03

Saint Peter Claver

Assigned to Colombia before his ordination, Jesuit Father
Peter Claver spends his entire priestly life serving the needs
of the slaves brought to the New World. His gentle goodness
wins many of these people for Christ.

Personal Reflections

⬤ Assigned to work with Father Claver, Brother Nicholas
looked for a way out. He considered Claver "superhuman" because he carried on his works of mercy day after
day. From your own experience in caring for the sick or
the poor, how would you explain Claver's dedication?

⬤ "He mustn't be punished on account of me!" With these
words Claver sought to protect an insensitive health care
worker from discipline. A saint can argue this way on his
own behalf, but explore ways you can intervene to ensure
that respectful and proper care is given to the elderly.

Group Discussion

It is hard to imagine the horror of a slave ship. However, too many people in our day and within our society are held as slaves. Discuss ways you can educate and legislate against this abuse of human freedom.

Today it would be prohibited to baptize people, even in these conditions, after only a few minutes of instruction. The missionaries, however, thought only of the sufferings endured and the dangers ahead. Baptism would give comfort and grace. Can you argue their case on the side of grace?

Read → Reflect → Respond

"... Whoever gives even a cup of cold water to one of these little ones in the name of a disciple—truly I tell you, none of these will lose their reward" (Mt 10:42).

Matthew 5:42; 10:8; 25:31–46
John 3:16
James 2:15–16; 5:1 6
Philemon 16
Catechism of the Catholic Church 2258, 2297–98, 2411, 2447–48

Saint John Vianney

After the French Revolution, faith was at low ebb in parts of France. An unlikely man is chosen to image God's love and longing for his people's return.

Personal Reflections

✿ John Vianney had his Father Balley who always believed in and supported him. Look over your life. Who has been the Father Balley figure for you? Perhaps there have been several. Send them a note of gratitude and remember them in your prayers. And do you know someone who could use your help and support?

✿ Vianney adopted what may seem a rather casual approach to the devil's attacks on him. He knew evil would not prevail, so he kept on working as he normally did. How do you try to resist the "wickedness and snares of the devil"?

Group Discussion

✿ What connection do you see between "an austere and prayerful life" and a successful ministry? What would such a life look like in our society today?

✿ John served as a saintly priest for forty-five years after an unpromising start. If you were asked to draw up criteria for accepting and forming men for the priesthood, what would you say? While you are at it, what criteria should be evident in parishioners?

Read •➤• Reflect •➤• Respond

[Jesus's] disciples asked him privately, "Why could we not cast it out?" He said to them, "This kind can come out only through prayer" (Mk 9:28–29).

Matthew 12:26–28
Romans 5:5
1 Corinthians 1:20–25
2 Corinthians 12:9–10

2 Thessalonians 3:3

Catechism of the Catholic Church 395, 550, 1551, 1589, 2656–58

Venerable Matt Talbot

Beginning from his youth, Matthew suffers a great thirst. His natural weakness is exploited, his dignity surrendered, his future compromised—but grace intervenes to transform his thirst into a burning desire for holiness.

Personal Reflections

❀ We see in Matt's struggles how one vice spawns another. He thought nothing of depriving his parents of financial help or of stealing in order to drink, ending enslaved to alcohol. From this we can also see how virtues are built on one another. Where would you begin?

❀ Matt's drinking buddies shunned him once he lost his income. People often use others for their own purposes. Examine your friendships to see if you are being used or if you are using another for personal advancement, profit, pleasure, or other things.

Group Discussion

❀ When Talbot was young he was introduced to liquor and goaded into trying it by someone at work. We have all known examples similar to this. Share ways you have had success in counseling another away from some dangerous behavior.

ᶻ Matt asked Our Lady for three things during his struggle for sobriety: "the grace of God, the presence of God, and the benediction of God." Discuss these requests. How do they encompass all he would need for success? Would they satisfy you?

Read ⋯• Reflect ⋯• Respond

Jesus said to his disciples, "Occasions for stumbling are bound to come, but woe to anyone by whom they come!" (Lk 17:1)

Matthew 18:6
Romans 6:8–11
1 Corinthians 8:10–13
Titus 2:12
1 Peter 4:1–8
Catechism of the Catholic Church 1809, 1848, 1852, 1889, 1989, 2287–90

Blessed Victoria Rasoamanarivo

As a convert this young royal stands firm despite trials in her marriage and persecution from the Church. She takes it on herself to guide and protect a priestless community.

Personal Reflections

ᶻ Victoria Rasoamanarivo took her duty as a believer seriously and held the Church together in creative ways. How do you respond to the challenges of today's society, where Christian values arc suspect and often legislated against?

🏵 When she was baptized, Rasoamanarivo received the name Victoria, which proved prophetic. Consider the meaning of your own name. Does it resonate with the path of your life so far?

Group Discussion

🏵 Marriage was arranged for Victoria with a very difficult man. Some recommended that she leave him, but she wanted to honor her commitment to him, as well as her duty within their society and the Church. Discuss the difficulties that could endanger marriage today, especially for newlyweds. Suggest practical advice you could offer.

🏵 Victoria was a strong woman, unafraid to put her life and reputation on the line for the faith. Share thoughts on how, as individuals or as a community of faith, you could emulate her courage and conviction.

Read ⤙ Reflect ⤙ Respond

"But as for what was sown on good soil, this is the one who hears the word and understands it, who indeed hears fruit and yields, in one case a hundredfold, in another sixty, and in another thirty" (Mt 13:23)

Matthew 18:20; 19:6
1 Peter 2:5
1 Corinthians 11:26
Catechism of the Catholic Church 76, 162, 863, 871–73, 910, 1605, 1616, 2156

Saint Joseph Mukasa,
Saint Charles Lwanga, and Companions

These two young men are chosen for their intelligence and integrity to lead the other men in the king's service. Because they serve the Eternal King first of all, they are martyred and continue to lead by their example and prayers.

Personal Reflections

❦ Of the two men, king Kabaka Mwanga and his major-domo, Joseph Mukasa, who was more of a true leader? Analyze their traits and actions to see if you can find a pattern.

❦ Charles had been baptized for less than six months when his final test came. He had pledged loyalty to the king, but stated that he could not deny what he knew to be true. You received the same baptism as he did. Do your convictions match his?

Group Discussion

❦ Mukasa Kiriwawanuvu, one of the young men listed at the end of the story, was never baptized. Could you explain to someone why he is considered a saint and a martyr?

❦ Joseph had to face his own fears of death, but as a good shepherd, he worried about the threat to those in his charge. Have you ever faced this dilemma: by standing up for the truth, others are put in a quandary?

Read ⋯ Reflect ⋯ Respond

So again Jesus said to them, "Very truly, I tell you, I am the gate for the sheep. All who came before me are thieves and bandits; but the sheep did not listen to them. I am the gate. Whoever enters by me will be saved, and will come in and go out and find pasture" (Jn 10:7–9).

John 10:1–18
2 Timothy 2:1–13
2 Corinthians 1:3–7
1 Peter 5:1–11
Isaiah 40:11
Ezekiel 34:15–16
Catechism of the Catholic Church 754, 764, 1691, 2471–74, 2520

⟨€✛❧⟩

Blessed Teresa of Calcutta

She is so poor in spirit—in her appreciation of self-giving—that she leaves everything to live with and minister to the poorest of the poor.

Personal Reflection

✎ Mother Teresa was called by God to leave teaching and go serve the poor in the streets. Reflecting on this radical change, have you ever felt a strong inclination to leave the familiar and comfortable to undertake a new challenge?

✎ At the Nirmal Hriday, the sisters were paid a beautiful compliment: they were called "living goddesses." Does this seem to be synonymous with the Christian vocation to be other Christs? How?

Group Discussion

- One of the first persons Mother Teresa found was refused admittance to the hospital. In response, she sat down and refused to leave the woman until she was admitted. Recall "drastic" steps you have taken to acquire justice for someone in need.

- Mother Teresa admitted that she lived in darkness since founding the Missionaries of Charity. She smiled at Jesus "to hide her pain and darkness even from him." This was her share in "the lot of the poor." How can we use the inevitable struggles, pains, and disappointments of life to serve God's poor?

Read ·•· Reflect ·•· Respond

"Truly I tell you, just as you did it to one of the least of these who are members of my family, you did it to me" (Mt 25:40).

Matthew 25:34–40

Psalm 103, 116

Galatians 6:9

Luke 4:40

Catechism of the Catholic Church 678, 1397, 1931–33,
2099–2100, 2731

Saint Rose of Lima

As the first Americas-born saint, Rose is one of the most popular. Despite her reputation for beauty, she desired only to live for God and to serve his people. She became a Dominican tertiary and lived her consecration through the tasks of ordinary life.

Personal Reflection

- The civil disturbance Rose witnessed on her Confirmation day led her to a deeper appreciation of the sufferings of the indigenous people. It also inspired her to offer prayers and sacrifices for their spiritual good. What connection do you see between your personal piety and your sense of social justice?

- Saint Rose was the contemporary of at least three other canonized saints. Together they were leaven for the life of Lima. Are there particular individuals you could join forces with to raise the level of life in your city?

Group Discussion

- Rose wanted to become a Dominican tertiary after the example of Saint Catherine of Siena. Today third-order members live very much in the world. How do you imagine they are able to make the spiritual/temporal balance work?

- Rose opened an "infirmary" in her parents' home. Within our communities today, what opportunities do you see to get involved in helping the sick and the poor, to be a leaven? Discuss local possibilities.

Read ⋯ Reflect ⋯ Respond

And again he said, "To what should I compare the kingdom of God? It is like yeast that a woman took and mixed in with three measures of flour until all of it was leavened" (Lk 13:20–21).

Deuteronomy 15:7–8, 11
Matthew 6:1–18; 8:14–17
Colossians 3:12–17
Catechism of the Catholic Church 929, 2449, 2659–60

Saint Hildegard of Bingen

This medieval nun, remarkable for the depth of her spiritual insight and her expansive realm of knowledge, was recently declared a Doctor of the Church.

Personal Reflection

⚜ Hildegard turned her permission to publicize her visions into an occasion not only to praise God, but also to involve her whole community. Her success reflected on them also as her support system. How do you react to success?

⚜ Although she is referred to as the Sybil of the Rhine, Hildegard was wary of her gifts as a seer. The ancient sybils were often fortune-tellers, and Hildegard wanted to know if her visions were from God or her own invention. She sought expert advice and also allowed time to test them. How would you go about seeking surety about your inspirations?

Group Discussion

⚜ Hildegard was a forward-thinking woman, as well as a woman expert in the feminine genius, the place of woman in the Church and in the world. What gifts of knowledge or grace do you see in the women on your life or parish community? How might their gifts be even better utilized?

⚜ This extraordinary woman offered many treasures old and new, and has been given the rare tribute of Doctor of the Church, yet her life was not free of serious controversy. In defying a diocesan order she brought a censure of excommunication on her monastery. How would you suggest dealing with disagreement or controversy today in matters of Church discipline, acknowledging the rights and duties involved?

Read ⤙ Reflect ⤙ Respond

"Therefore every scribe who has been trained for the kingdom of heaven is like the master of a household who brings out of his treasure what is new and what is old" (Mt 13:52).

Luke 8:16–18
1 Peter 4:10–11
2 Peter 1:19–21
Catechism of the Catholic Church 66–67, 1830–31, 2500

Saint Francis Xavier

One of the Church's greatest missionaries, Saint Francis Xavier lies dejected and discouraged on the island of Shangchuan, thinking only of his failure to reach China. Yet thousands owe their faith to his zealous and inventive preaching.

Personal Reflection

⚜ Francis railed against the merchant who failed to bring him into China. He then remembered that the situation must be God's will and should be left in his hands. Are you able to see God's will in some of your life's setbacks?

⚜ What does it profit a man to gain the whole world but lose his soul? (cf. Matthew 16:26) How does this question resonate with the desire for success, fame, or status?

Group Discussion

⚜ Francis wished to run through the corridors of the great universities calling the young educated class to service. Together, can you come up with ways to recruit future missionaries: priests, religious, and laity?

⚜ Xavier's zeal for the missions was like a wildfire racing across the East. While you are not necessarily called to be a missionary in foreign lands, what lights a fire in your heart?

Read ⤑ Reflect ⤑ Respond

"I came to bring fire to the earth, and how I wish it were already kindled" (Lk 12:49).

Matthew 9:36–38
Luke 8:4–8, 11–15
John 15:3–7
Acts 16:6–10
Romans 10:14–18
Catechism of the Catholic Church 678–679, 696, 84–854, 856, 1127

Blessed James Alberione

A priest of northern Italy, James Alberione listens to the concerns of the Church and the voice of Christ guiding him "to do something for the new century." He founds the Pauline Family, giving the Church a way to evangelize in an age of ever-changing communication.

Personal Reflection

* James had been dismissed from his diocesan seminary because of an attitude he acquired from certain reading. Fortunately, he was guided to reenter the seminary in Alba. Think of your own reading (and viewing) habits. In what ways can you be critical and discerning in your choices?

* Alberione is quoted as saying that the holiness of each person is a reflection of God's perfection seen from an angle that matches the mission entrusted to them. Reflect and pray about the "angle" of your holiness.

Group Discussion

* In reading the incidents of Alberione's childhood, how would you say they molded his future life? Share from

your own experience something that influenced your present faith.

✒ Blessed Alberione began reading encyclicals in the seminary. He said that his inspiration for the Pauline Family was born of *Tametsi futura.* Have you, individually or in a group, done a serious and prayerful reading of an encyclical in order to enter into the mind and heart of the Church? How has that inspired you?

Read ⟶ Reflect ⟶ Respond

"Therefore whatever you have said in the dark will be heard in the light, and what you have whispered behind closed doors will be proclaimed from the housetops" (Lk 12:3).

Mark 4:13–20, 26–32

Acts 17:16–34

Galatians 5:7–10

Romans 8:26–30

Colossians 2:6–8

Catechism of the Catholic Church 571, 849, 852, 917–918, 927, 2493–97

⟨⟨✿⟩⟩

Saint Joan of Arc

The Maid of Orleans is a simple country girl called to fulfill an extraordinary mission. This soldier-saint is the symbol of youthful heroism. Supernatural "voices" lead her to victory, but her real triumph comes through martyrdom.

Personal Reflection

  Betrayal is one of the hardest things to forgive. For Joan it wasn't merely that friendship was betrayed, but that her king used and disregarded her sacrifice of talent and devotion. Pray for the ability to value and honor the gifts of friendship and service.

  Joan's trial was a farce, a predetermined setup. Think of judgments you have made, whether important or insignificant. Were they made justly and with sincerity? Are you capable of retracting and apologizing, if necessary?

Group Discussion

  This young, unlettered woman trusted God implicitly to give her the wisdom and courage needed during her trial. How strong is your faith in the promise of Jesus: "Do not worry . . . for the Holy Spirit will teach you . . . what you ought to say"?

  Under duress Joan recanted her testimony and then retracted that denial of the truth. For this she was condemned as a heretic. Do you think God holds a sincere believer culpable for weakness due to torture and threats? How merciful are you toward human weakness?

Read ·►· Reflect ·►· Respond

"When they bring you before the synagogues, the rulers, and the authorities, do not worry about how you are to defend yourselves or what you are to say; for the Holy Spirit will teach you at that very hour what you ought to say" (Lk 12:11–12).

Matthew 26:69–75
Luke 13:31–35
Ephesians 6:10
Romans 2:1–16
2 Corinthians 4:16–5:10
Catechism of the Catholic Church 1287, 2005,
    2297–98, 2308–10

Saint Anthony of Padua

A young follower of Saint Francis of Assisi, Anthony throws himself completely into a life of poverty and mortification. Relying on obedience, he becomes the most sought-after preacher of his time.

Personal Reflection

- Comparisons are almost never helpful. Anthony became discouraged by comparing himself with other friars. In the end, he became the most popular Franciscan after Saint Francis himself. Look at the workings of grace in your own life. How are they guiding you toward true success?

- Anthony preached spontaneously at the ordination reception after only a short prayer for guidance. However, thinking of his life to that point, would you consider him unprepared? How have you prepared yourself to be successful in your chosen state in life?

Group Discussion

As a new Franciscan, Anthony set out to be a missionary/martyr to Morocco, but was felled by illness. Although he lived only thirty-six years, the Church would have lost a lot had he been martyred. Have you ever been reversed by God only to discover something positive and unexpected?

Educated and ordained by the Augustinians, this young nobleman chose the destitute Friars of Saint Francis. He even gave up intellectual pursuits because of the Franciscan stress on simplicity. Discuss your thoughts on whether or not this was a waste of his talent and preparation.

Read ·→· Reflect ·→· Respond

"On the last day of the festival, the great day, while Jesus was standing there, he cried out, 'Let anyone who is thirsty come to me, and let the one who believes in me drink'" (Jn 7:37-38).

Isaiah 41:17–18
Matthew 10:19–20
John 4:10; 7:37–41
Acts 13:15–16
2 Timothy 1:6
Romans 12:3–8
Catechism of the Catholic Church 728, 1287, 1587, 2562-63

Saint Zita

Placed in domestic service with a wealthy family, this thirteenth century Italian girl finds holiness amid a life of work well done, generosity to the poor, and familiarity with God in prayer.

Personal Reflection

⚜ The young Zita received life-altering news from her parents and pastor that she was to become a servant in another town. We are used to having a say in such decisions. Imagine how you would react in her place, then reflect on why you would have that reaction.

⚜ The citation from Luke used below speaks of being humbled and being exalted. How did this teaching play out in Zita's daily life, not just in her canonization? Study this same citation in relation to your life.

Group Discussion

⚜ Zita "saw work as her way to God." Take a look at your own attitudes toward work. Discuss the positives and negatives of work, perhaps referring to Pope John Paul II's encyclical *On the Dignity of Human Work* (1981).

⚜ Acts of Christian charity do not normally produce such extraordinary results as seen in Zita's life. However, we understand the obligation of doing charity and often practice it at significant personal sacrifice. How would you encourage your family and friends to participate in charitable works?

Read ⟶ Reflect ⟶ Respond

"For all who exalt themselves will be humbled, and those who humble themselves will be exalted" (Lk 14:11).

Psalm 27:4–5
Matthew 6:25–34
John 6:32–34
2 Corinthians 9:1–15
James 2:14–17
Catechism of Catholic Church 1734, 2544–46, 2559–61

⟨⟨✠⟩⟩

Saint Pio of Pietrelcina

Marked by the stigmata, this Capuchin friar, living in an obscure mountaintop monastery in Italy, becomes a sought-out confessor and adviser to people of every class and nation.

Personal Reflections

※ The stigmata are a rare spiritual gift, a true participation in the Passion of Christ, as Padre Pio illustrated. In your spiritual life, do you embrace hidden sufferings and misunderstandings more readily than acclaim?

※ Padre Pio declared that the hospital he founded "was the gift of Divine Providence, but [the doctors'] mission was to bring God to the sick." How were they to do this? How do you bring God to the sick?

Group Discussion

🕮 In addition to the trials and accusations he had to endure, Padre Pio was deprived several times of his public ministry. The Church did this as a caution while investigating the presence of supernatural phenomena. How does this wisdom of the Church reflect on your discernment in difficult cases?

🕮 Padre Pio was unsuccessfully called up several times for military service. He might not have seen active combat; however, there is always a lack of military chaplains for the armed services. Do you have any suggestions for how to better meet the spiritual needs of our military personnel?

Read ᐧ᠊ᐧ Reflect ᐧ᠊ᐧ Respond

"You do not know what you are asking. Are you able to drink the cup that I am about to drink?" They said to him, "We are able" (Mt 20:22).

1 John 4:1–6
Philippians 2:8
1 Timothy 2:5
Romans 5:19
Isaiah 53:10–12
Catechism of the Catholic Church 618, 1368, 1464, 2100

✿

Blessed Miguel Agustín Pro

During the early twentieth century, some persons make violent efforts to rid Mexico of all traces of Catholicism. Of the many martyrs, Padre Pro is the most popular and remains the most famous protagonist of the Mexican struggle.

Personal Reflections

✿ Padre Pro endured constant stomach pain in his formative years and his years of active ministry. It seems all saints endure some physical affliction. Think of your own physical afflictions, significant or not; what purpose do they fulfill in your life as a Christian?

✿ Pro referred to himself as "a pretty good sin-sifter." Do you give much thought to the sacrifice priests make in their ministry as confessors? Resolve to make better use of their loving service.

Group Discussion

✿ Miguel Pro had always been a good actor. As an underground pastor he often used this talent to dodge his pursuers. We, too, are called to use our talents. Share ways you put your gifts to work for the Gospel.

✿ By publicizing Padre Pro's death, President Calles inadvertently gave Catholics a lasting platform for the cause. "Viva Cristo Rey!" became the anthem of resistance. Together, make a plan to publically acknowledge all the Christians who today undergo persecution.

Read ⋯ Reflect ⋯ Respond

"But he passed through the midst of them and went on his way"
(Luke 4:30).

Matthew 5:44–45
John 18:37
Ephesians 2:14–18
Colossians 1:20–22
2 Timothy 1:17
Catechism of the Catholic Church 933, 992, 1009–10, 2126,
    2305–06, 2473

Saint Edith Stein

A brilliant Jewish philosopher who discovered "truth" in reading Teresa of Avila, Edith enters the Carmelite monastery in Cologne. World War II soon breaks out, leading her to Auschwitz and martyrdom.

Personal Reflections

⁂ Even though she had endured a painful parting from her family, Edith "was perfectly at peace in the harbor of the divine will." Explore the presence of peace in tense and troubling situations.

⁂ This saint is known to us as Saint Edith Stein and as Saint Teresa Benedicta of the Cross. How do you understand the statement that upon entering the Carmelite cloister "Doctor Edith Stein, brilliant lecturer and philosopher, ceased to exist"?

Group Discussion

🕸 Consider together the constant appearance of the cross in her life: in her profession name; in the title of her last book, *Science of the Cross;* and in the way she embraced her personal offering in death. What does the cross of Christ mean to you personally and to us as a believing community?

🕸 "I cannot be an exception." With these words Sister Benedicta's fate was sealed. Realizing what she could have offered the Church with her intelligence, would you have counseled her to escape to safety in Switzerland? Why or why not?

Read ⤙ Reflect ⤚ Respond

"No one has greater love than this, to lay down one's life for one's friends" (Jh 15:13).

Psalm 13
Romans 12:9–21
1 Corinthians 13:1 7
2 Timothy 1:8–11
1 John 4:16–21
Catechism of the Catholic Church 1823, 1846, 1971–72, 2471–73

Blessed Manuel Lozano Garrido

With his double vocation as a journalist and as a disabled person, this modern apostle gives an example of living and active devotion to the Blessed Sacrament.

Personal Reflections

⁂ In the quote from Matthew, Jesus says that it is not enough to feel the needs of others, but that we should do something to satisfy them. Lolo spent himself to present the Good News to his contemporaries, especially to youth, in an appealing way. How do you serve the needs of those around you?

⁂ Manuel identified his profession as "disabled." By this he meant that he employed his sufferings in union with Christ for the good of others. How do you understand the power of intercession through prayer and suffering?

Group Discussion

⁂ As teenagers during the Spanish Revolution, Lolo and Lucia both did remarkable things to express their devotion to the Eucharist. Reflect on your personal Eucharistic devotion, as well as the devotion within your parish. Is there anything you can do as a group to assist others to understand and participate better?

⁂ Because of his sickness Lolo spent most of his life in a wheelchair. Despite becoming ever more incapacitated, his spirit and creativity stayed alive and active. Consider the needs of the disabled in your town or parish. How can more assistance be organized for their spiritual and physical needs?

Read ·→· Reflect ·→· Respond

Jesus said to them, "They need not go away; you give them something to eat" (Mt 14:16).

Exodus 17:10–12
John 6:60–65

Acts 2:42
2 Corinthians 12:9–10
Colossians 1:24–29
Catechism of the Catholic Church 898–901, 905–907, 1335,
   1500–01, 2015, 2276, 2497

Blessed Mary Elizabeth Hesselblad

This Lutheran convert aspires to reinvigorate the faith in her native Sweden by re-establishing the ancient Brigittine Order. She is also an apostle of Christian unity.

Personal Reflection

- Mary Elizabeth admired Catholics but felt their practices were misguided. Her prayers to know the true Church were answered during a Eucharistic procession. Think of an occasion when your prayer was answered in an indisputable way.

- She was inspired to reestablish the Order of the Most Holy Savior, but could muster little enthusiasm among existing communities. How do you fare when you must "go it alone" when you have a good initiative in mind?

Group Discussion

- "That all may be one." Mother Mary Elizabeth felt these words in her heart. She acted on them with open dialogue and shared prayer. Consider efforts done locally, both personal and parochial, toward "oneness in Christ." What have been the results?

⚒ Mother Mary Elizabeth and her sisters were among many religious in Rome who risked retaliation by hiding Jews and other persons fleeing the Nazi regime. How do you envision such courage and conviction playing out in the situations of modern persecution?

Read ⋅⋅ Reflect ⋅⋅ Respond

But he said to them, "Unless I see the mark of the nails in his hands, and put my finger in the mark of the nails and my hand in his side, I will not believe" (Jn 20:25).

Hosea 2:19–20
Matthew 28:18
John 17:14–17; 21:17
1 Timothy 3:15
Catechism of the Catholic Church 820ff., 847–48

Saint Mark the Evangelist

As a young man, Mark presumed his performance would equal his desires. With experience and prayer he finds his place as a follower of Christ, preeminently as one of the four evangelists.

Personal Reflection

⚒ The young Mark had such an intense desire to accompany Christ that he could almost taste the adventure. However, when danger came, his resolve failed. Can you identify his mistake of judgment? How would you have advised him?

⚜ Take to heart Peter's advice to Mark: "Maturity can be a tricky thing and sometimes it only requires a little more reflection, a little humility, and a lot of trust in what God wants of us. Pray and prepare. He will reveal his plan when you are ready." What does this advice say to me about my life's journey?

Group Discussion

⚜ Mark's mother objected to her son's desire to be a missionary. "That kind of life is too hard," she said. How can you individually or as a group encourage and foster vocations to the priesthood and religious life, especially missionary vocations?

⚜ Mark finally caught up with the trust placed in him. He became a great evangelizer and wrote the gospel that bears his name. Discuss what a great motivator simple trust can be. Is there anyone or any group with unchallenged potential that you could empower to do something good?

Read ⟶ Reflect ⟶ Respond

"Go into all the world and proclaim the good news to the whole creation. The one who believes and is baptized will be saved; but the one who does not believe will be condemned" (Mk 16:19–20).

2 Timothy 4:11
Hebrews 10:23
1 Peter 3:15
Catechism of the Catholic Church 125–26, 849–50

Alphabetical Listing of Saints

About the Authors

SISTER MARIE PAUL CURLEY, as a child, found her imagination captured by the stories of the saints. Her early fascination continues today as a Daughter of St. Paul: in addition to co-authoring this book, she has produced children's storybooks for Catholic cable TV, as well as an English adaptation of an animated series on the saints. Sister Marie Paul continues to write for print and screen, including her recent book, *See Yourself Through God's Eyes: 52 Meditations to Grow in Self-Esteem* (Pauline Books & Media). For more resources on the saints in this book, or to contact Sister Marie Paul, visit: www.pauline.org/mariepaulcurley.

SISTER MARY LEA HILL, a member of the Daughters of St. Paul since 1964, has enjoyed communicating the faith through a variety of apostolic assignments. Her skills as a storyteller were honed as director of audiovisual productions when Pauline Books & Media first produced animated features in the early 1980s. An editor and author for many years, Sister Mary Lea has written several books, including the best-selling *Basic Catechism* (co-authored with Sister Susan Helen Wallace). Sister Mary Lea can be found on Twitter as @crabbimystic.

BOOKS & MEDIA

The Daughters of St. Paul operate book and media centers at the following addresses. Visit, call, or write the one nearest you today, or find us at www.pauline.org

CALIFORNIA
    3908 Sepulveda Blvd, Culver City, CA 90230   310-397-8676
    935 Brewster Avenue, Redwood City, CA 94063   650-369-4230
    5945 Balboa Avenue, San Diego, CA 92111   858-565-9181

FLORIDA
    145 S.W. 107th Avenue, Miami, FL 33174   305-559-6715

HAWAII
    1143 Bishop Street, Honolulu, HI 96813   808-521-2731
    Neighbor Islands call: 866-521-2731

ILLINOIS
    172 North Michigan Avenue, Chicago, IL 60601   312-346-4228

LOUISIANA
    4403 Veterans Memorial Blvd, Metairie, LA 70006   504-887-7631

MASSACHUSETTS
    885 Providence Hwy, Dedham, MA 02026   781-326-5385

MISSOURI
    9804 Watson Road, St. Louis, MO 63126   314-965-3512

NEW YORK
    64 W. 38th Street, New York, NY 10018   212-754-1110

PENNSYLVANIA
    Philadelphia—relocating   215-676-9494

SOUTH CAROLINA
    243 King Street, Charleston, SC 29401   843-577-0175

VIRGINIA
    1025 King Street, Alexandria, VA 22314   703-549-3806

CANADA
    3022 Dufferin Street, Toronto, ON M6B 3T5   416-781-9131

¡También somos su fuente para libros,
videos y música en español!